89-0967

Law and Economics

Recent Economic Thought Series

Warren J. Samuels, Editor
Michigan State University
East Lansing, Michigan, U.S.A.

Other titles in this series:

This series is devoted to works that present divergent views on the
development, prospects, and tensions within some important research
areas of international economic thought. Among the fields covered are
macromonetary policy, public finance, labor and political economy. The
emphasis of the series is on providing a critical, constructive view of
each of these fields, as well as a forum through which leading scholars of
international reputation may voice their perspectives on important related
issues. Each volume in the series will be self-contained; together these
volumes will provide dramatic evidence of the variety of economic
thought within the scholarly community.

Law and Economics

edited by
Nicholas Mercuro
Professor of Economics
University of New Orleans

WITHDRAWN

Kluwer Academic Publishers
Boston/Dordrecht/London

Distributors

for the United States and Canada: Kluwer Academic Publishers, 101
Philip Drive, Assinippi Park, Norwell, MA 02061, USA

for the UK and Ireland: Kluwer Academic Publishers, Falcon House,
Queen Square, Lancaster LA1 1RN, UK

for all other countries: Kluwer Academic Publishers Group, Distribution
Centre, P.O. Box 322, 3300 AH Dordrecht, The Netherlands

Library of Congress Cataloging-in-Publication Data
  Law and economics.

  (Recent economic thought series)
  Includes index.
  1. Law.   2. Economics.   I. Mercuro,
Nicholas.   II. Series: Recent economic thought.
K487.E3L378 1988   340   88-12979
ISBN 0–89838–282–3

Printed in the United States of America

Contents

Contributing Authors

Professor Louis De Alessi
Law and Economics Center
University of Miami
P. O. Box 248000
Coral Gables, FL 33124

Professor Lewis A. Kornhauser
New York University
School of Law
40 Washington Square South,
Room 321
NY, NY 10012

Professor Nicholas Mercuro
Director, Institute for the Comparative Study of Public Policy
University of New Orleans
New Orleans, LA 70148

Professor Gary Minda
Brooklyn Law School
250 Joralemon St.
Brooklyn, NY 11201

Professor Susan Rose-Ackerman
Law School
Yale University
Box 401, Yale Station
New Haven, CT 06520

Professor Charles K. Rowley
Dean, Graduate School
George Mason University
4400 University Dr.
Fairfax, VA 22030-4444

Professor A. Allan Schmid
Department of Agricultural Economics
Michigan State University
E. Lansing, MI 48824

Professor Robert J. Staaf
248 Sirrine Hall
School of Business
Clemson University
Clemson, SC 29631

Professor Thomas Ulen
Department of Economics
University of Illinois
Box 64, David Kinley Hall
1407 W. Gregory Dr.
Urbana, IL 61801

1 TOWARD A COMPARATIVE INSTITUTIONAL APPROACH TO THE STUDY OF LAW AND ECONOMICS

Nicholas Mercuro

The purpose of this chapter is twofold. First, it attempts to describe one perception—broad in scope and inclusive in nature—of the fundamental interrelations between law and economics. It is argued that this characterization can serve as a basis for building what may be termed "a comparative institutional approach" to the study of law and economics [1]. It is hoped that this characterization of law and economics will provide an unbrella framework within which the several perspectives comprising the law-and-economics movement can be better understood. Second, from the vantage point of this characterization, selective works from the literature of comparative economic systems are introduced in order to provide what appears to be a logical extension to the comparative institutional approach as one potential avenue of development in the emerging field of law and economics. Perhaps the characterization of law and economics presented here can serve as a prism to disentangle the conventional so-called "isms of standard political economy" [2].

I wish to thank Gerald Whitney and Walter Lane for helpful comments on an earlier draft of this chapter.

1

1. Introduction

The character of economic life[1] in a society is dependent upon, among other things, its political-legal-economic institutional setting.[2] Within that institutional structure, the individuals who comprise that society attempt to cooperate with one another to their mutual advantage so as to accommodate their joint utility-maximizing endeavors. In addition, these same individuals call upon certain societal institutions to adjust the conflicting claims of different individuals and groups. In this regard, a society is perceived as both a cooperative venture for mutual advantage where there are an identity of interests and, as well, an arena of conflict where there exists a mutual interdependence of conflicting claims or interests. The manner in which a society structures its political-legal-economic institutions 1) to enhance the scope of its cooperative endeavors and 2) to channel internal political-legal-economic conflicts toward resolution, shapes the character of economic life in that society.

In contemplating the structure of its institutions intended to promote cooperation and channel conflict, a society confronts several issues. At the most general level an enduring issue is how a society both perceives and then ideologically transmits (perhaps teaches or rationalizes), internally and/or externally, its perceptions of so-called "cooperative endeavors" and "arenas of conflict." There can be no doubt that the resultant structure of a society's institutions will reflect that society's perception as to what cooperation entails and what conflict constitutes. Second, and directly related to the former, are the issues of what the nature will be of the underlying constitution and what the *initial* structure will be of the institutions that will go toward shaping the character of economic life. And finally, there is the recognition that the institutions can be changed in response to economic needs of the society. The issue here then is one of how a society allows for orderly (incremental or "radical") change of its political, legal, and economic institutions.

These are the background questions underlying much of law and economics. Whether one or another political-legal-economic system (i.e., one ism or another) is seen to emerge in a society, its emergence can be interpreted, in part, as a response to this set of issues confronting it.

2. Stages of Choice

The selection or establishment of a specific set of institutions, and thus the character of economic life in a society, is the product of choice. With respect to law and economics, the literature has focused attention on three different stages of choice. First, it becomes necessary to describe and understand the emergence of the most basic social contract that binds its people together. This can be termed the *constitutional stage of choice*. Second, it is necessary to describe and understand both the structuring and the revising or restructuring of the political-legal-economic institutional decision-making processes—the so-called *institutional stage of choice*. Finally, the consequent economic impacts of the prevailing or potentially revised legal relations governing society must be analyzed and understood—the *economic impact stage of choice*. In attempting to address these concerns, most of those contributing to the literature of law and economics have divided their labors to describe these three different levels of choice.

2.1. *Constitutional Stage of Choice*

In order to understand the nature of the choices necessary at the constitutional stage, it is useful to start in a conceptual state of anarchy. Individuals will then contemplate the opportunity costs associated with the protective-defensive resource diversions that are necessary and essential for life under a system of anarchy. Once they recognize the potential prospects for improvement in the character of their economic life brought on by establishing a social contract or constitution, they will enter into some form of social contract or formally adopt a constitution. In establishing the constitution, the individuals will seek to spell out the behavioral limits of what is and what is not mutually acceptable conduct and lay out the so-called "rules for making rules." It must be noted that while the established constitution is typically thought to have only a subtle effect on the allocation and distribution of resources, that subtle impact cannot go ignored.

Among the decisions made at the constitutional stage of choice that ultimately affect the character of economic life is the following: the structure of the law-making institutions (e.g., one or two house legislature) will be established together with whether a majority or perhaps two-thirds vote will determine a legislative choice. In addition, since constitutions are not immutable, the methods by which constitutional rules can be revised are developed at this level of choice. Further, it should be noted that the relationships among emergent institutions are also partially resolved at the constitutional stage of choice. For instance, the choices that govern which institutions will prevail over others in making choices (to provide a system of checks and balances) must be decided.

The essential point to be understood here is that whatever institutions come to characterize a society, they owe their development, existence, and legitimacy to the initial choices made at the constitutional stage of choice. Once the constitution is framed, it will then provide the basis for the emergence of a broad assemblage of legal-economic institutions— institutions that will more directly affect the allocation and distribution of resources in society. The structuring of these legal-economic institutions constitutes the *institutional stage of choice*.

2.2.   The Institutional Stage of Choice

The institutional stage of choice focuses directly on the structure of the political-legal institutions (commonly referred to as *the state*) as well as the revision of those institutional structures. It is the specific *working rules* comprising the institutional decision-making processes that are at center stage. More often than not the decision-making processes of an institution are formally worked out by the institution itself in developing its own working rules. Examples of this might include: judiciary—rules of evidence; legislature—committee structures and procedures; government agencies—determining the procedures by which standards are arrived at (EPA, OSHA, FDA, etc.); regulatory commissions—rules governing intervenors at rate hearings for a regulated utility.

In addition, not only are the decision-making processes of a legal institution partially established by the rules worked out at the constitutional stage of choice but they are also a partial function of the decisions of other institutions often under complex procedures. An example of this would be a court decision that imposes certain restrictions or obligations upon a legislative body or government agency. As in the case of constitions, legal institutions are not set in stone, but rather are themselves a response to economic needs and, as such, can and do undergo structural revisions. Changes in the working rules of a legal institution will revise the decision-making processes of that institution and, as a result, may alter the institutional choices that directly impact the legal relations governing a society, that is, the extant structure of property rights. It is these choices as to the structure of property rights to which I now turn by exploring the economic impact stage of choice inasmuch as it is this stage of choice that comprises the most prominent interface between law and economics.

2.3. The Economic Impact Stage of Choice

Conceptually, it is useful to begin with the notion of three distinct property right systems for organizing and controlling the allocation and distribution of resources: the market sector, the public sector, and the communal sector. Initially each sector is treated as if it exists separate and apart from the other sectors. As will be seen, typically, all three systems operate contemporaneously to allocate and distribute resources.

2.3.1. The Market Sector. In the pure market sector, all property rights are held privately as bundles of fee simple absolute rights. According to the conventional legal-economic definition of property rights, what individuals own are not goods or resources but the rights to use goods and resources. Armen A. Alchian and Harold Demsetz stated, "What are owned are socially recognized rights of action" [3]. Thus, as outlined by Alan Randall, in the pure market sector, property rights must have four characteristics. They must be:

1. Completely specified, so that it can serve as a perfect system of information about the rights that accompany ownership, the restrictions upon those rights, and the penalties for their violation.
2. Exclusive, so that all rewards, and penalties resulting from an action accrue directly to the individual empowered to take action (i.e., the owner).
3. Transferable, so that rights may gravitate to their highest-value use.
4. Enforceable and completely enforced. An unenforced right is no right at all [4].

With this structure of private property rights established by the individuals of a society acting through their institutions, and with a market as the system of social control, it is then possible for the individuals to further enhance their welfare by specializing and engaging in exchange through trade. This process of trade in conventionally viewed as a purely voluntary endeavor and characterizes that which takes place in the market sector. The voluntary nature of this market process is such that no individual will engage in a trade that leaves him/her worse off. The final allocational and distributional outcome will be arrived at once all the gains from trade have been exhausted. Thus, given a set of private property rights so structured and given some initial distribution of rights, barring externalities and the problem of public goods, the market outcome can be shown to be efficient (more specifically, Pareto efficient).[3]

2.3.2. The Public Sector. The public sector is yet another arena for organizing and controlling the allocation and distribution of resources in a society. In this idealized sector the allocation and distribution of all resources wil be determined through the public sector. That is, in response to the individuals who comprise the society, the institutions will define and assign status rights which are, in effect, eligibility requirements for individuals to gain access to goods and resources. Status rights are rights to goods or resources which are exclusive, nontransferable, and provided to individuals via the state [5]. Thus, the provision of status rights may be conceived of as "government regulation" in its broadest sense. As such, political-legal institutions are understood to make a broad spectrum of decisions that give rise to status rights. For example, status rights emerge through judge and jury verdicts, in the drafting of legislative statutes, through government agency or commission pronouncements, and through a host of other public sector actions. With a public sector as the system of social control, the emergent structure of status rights has a direct impact on the allocation and distribution of resources.

2.3.3. The Communal Sector. In a similar manner, individuals of a society, acting through institutions, may decide that commodities or resources will be communally owned and hence equally available to all (i.e., nonexclusive) and nontransferable. In this case, rights would be assigned equally to each individual, resulting in a communal allocation and distribution.

3. The Complex Legal-Economic Arena

Typically, a society is structured so that the character of economic life is determined by all three systems of social control: the market sector, the public sector, and the communal sector. The relative scope and content of each of the systems of social control is the result of a collective determination of those who prevailed in choice-making processes in the political-legal-economic arena (see figure 1–1).

Members of society, acting both individually and collectively, will endeavor to revise the constitution, to structure and restructure the institutional working rules, and to alter the property rights (be they private, status, or communal) in the market, public, and communal sectors in order to achieve an allocation and distribution of resources that enhance their individual welfare. This is accomplished under the recognition that neither 1) the constituton, 2) the decision-making processes of

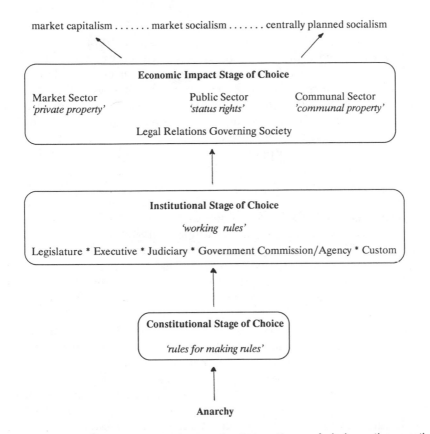

market capitalism . . . . market socialism . . . . centrally planned socialism

Economic Impact Stage of Choice

Market Sector　　　　　　Public Sector　　　　　Communal Sector
'private property'　　　　　*'status rights'*　　　　　*'communal property'*

Legal Relations Governing Society

Institutional Stage of Choice

'working rules'

Legislature * Executive * Judiciary * Government Commission/Agency * Custom

Constitutional Stage of Choice

'rules for making rules'

Anarchy

FIGURE 1–1.　This diagram integrates the three stages of choice—the constitutional, institutional, and economic impact stage together with the market, public, and communal sectors. The participants in the political-legal-economic arena will (from the bottom up) establish a constitution; they will set in place working rules in structuring their legal-economic institutions; and they will structure the legal relations governing society—private property rights, status rights, and communal rights, respectively giving rise to the private, public, and communal sectors.

the legal institutions (i.e., the working rules), nor 3) the legal relations governing the size and scope of the market, public, and communal sectors are given immutably by nature but are themselves a response to economic needs and flexible in response to changes in those needs.

It should be noted that the particular construction set forth in this section parallels that which Walter Ullmann has described as "the ascending theme of government and law" [6]. He traces the origins of this conception to the late thirteenth century. It is a conception of government and law where the individual is perceived as sovereign—not as a mere subject but as a citizen—and where the government and law owe their legitimacy to the *consent* of the sovereign individuals. With greater robustness, Thomas Hobbes and John Locke, latter in the seventeenth century, developed a parallel conception of government and law wherein the principal function of the government was seen to be, among other things, to protect the purported "well-settled" sovereign natural rights held by individuals.

While the characterization of law and economics described in this section more or less follows the general contours of the ascending theme of government and law, it is not the only theme that can describe the origin and thus legitimacy of the prevailing constitution and government institutions. Ullmann also presented what he termed the "descending theme of government and law." His characterization purports to describe much of pre-late thirteenth century Europe. As elaborated upon by James S. Coleman [7], this conception is not unlike the ideas of rights and sovereignty latter developed by Jean-Jacques Rousseau and Karl Marx. The descending theme of government and law suggests that sovereignty is located in the state with government there as the collective instrument to implement the will of society. If founded in this manner, then the constitution and government institutions gain their recognition and legitimacy accordingly. It should be noted that while the argument throughout the first section implies some form of democratic government, perhaps more consistent with Ullman's "ascending theme," the essential point—that the institutions have a direct impact on the allocation and distribution of resources—is equally valid with respect to choices made by institutions of nondemocratic, coercive governments.

It is important to understand the nature of the choices made at the constitutional, institutional, and economic impact stages of choice. Specifically, at the constitutional stage of choice, it is the "rules for making rules" that will undergo revisions. Further, working through the insititutions, at the institutional stage of choice individuals restructure institutions by altering working rules, whereas at the economic impact stage of choice, they work to revise property rights. In one capacity or the other, they ultimately alter the legal relations among members of society and thereby redetermine (perhaps only incrementally) the relative scopes of the market, public, and communal sectors in the society.

Some specific examples may help to understand further what is at issue here. While at the constitutional stage of choice the basic elements of the social contract may be altered, at the institutional stage of choice, individuals may try to 1) revise rules for determining legislative committee structures; 2) determine the criteria as to who may have standing in a court of law or raise or lower the maximum limits for litigation in a small claims court; 3) expand or limit the role of the intervenor at rate hearings; 4) alter the criteria and/or the process by which pollution permits are obtained; and 5) broaden or curtail actions that come under the notion of executive privilege.

The nature of the choices are different at the economic impact stage of choice. Here individuals may work to: 1) determine which goods, services, and resources will be directly under the state's supervision (e.g., more or less public or private education); 2) determine status rights by defining specific eligibility requirements for individuals to gain access to certain goods or resources (e.g., healthcare, welfare, foodstamps, etc.); 3) enhance or diminish the scope of (a) residential, commercial, and industrial zoning restrictions, (b) blue laws, or (c) price supports and price ceilings; 4) have specific rate structures adopted at public utility hearings; 5) have a parcel of land made readily available for private development or have the same parcel declared communal property for conservation or wilderness purposes; 6) either assign the right to an upstream chemical firm which allows it to dump its residuals into the stream or assign the right to the downstream farmer who uses the water for crop irrigation to have unpolluted water available; and 7) have environmental commissions either closely monitor and strictly enforce standing environmental laws or rarely monitor and thus loosely enforce the same laws.

These examples are intended only to illustrate that individual participants in the political-legal-economic arena can restructure their constitution, their institutions, and work to revise property right structures through the prevailing institutions and thereby reshape the ultimate character of economic life. As will be seen in the comparative economic systems literature (in a latter section), taken together, the emergent private, status, and communal structures of rights—the property rights—will comprise one of the four fundamental characteristics—the power structure, mechanisms for coordinating information, property rights, and incentives—of the three stylized *political-economic systems*—market capitalism, market socialism, and centrally planned socialism (top of figure 1–1).

4. Necessity of Choice

Whether at the constitutional, institutional, or economic impact stage of choice, the emphasis here is on the continuing necessity of choice—the fact that there are no neutral principles to which society can turn in making political-legal-economic choices. Making choices means the introduction of values. One may observe in a society that *the* dominant system of social control to allocate and distribute that society's scarce resources is the market sector, or the public sector, or the communal sector. The essential point to be understood is that whichever one is chosen (or, more realistically, whatever relative mix obtains), the outcome is to be seen as an expression of the values of those who have participated and prevailed at each stage of choice in the political-legal-economic arena.[4] The necessity of choice has been recognized by many. In writing on the institutional level of choice James M. Buchanan states:

> Man must look to all institutions as potentially improvable. Man must adopt the attitude that he can control his fate; he must accept the necessity of choosing. He must look on himself as a man, not another animal, and upon "civilization" as if it is of his own making [9].

Warren J. Samuels, in writing on the interrelations between legal and economic processes, also states:

> There is, first of all, an existential necessity of choice over relative rights, relative capacity to visit injury or costs, and mutual coercive power (or claims to income). The economy, in which the legal process is so obviously involved, is a system of relative rights, of exposure to costs shifted by others, and of coercive impact of others....
>
> If the issue is one as to which interest government will be used to support, part of the character of the legal process is clarified. The legal system (government, law) is not something given and external to the economic decision-making process. Rather, since goverment is a mode though which relative rights and therefore relative market (income securing) status is given effect, the critical question is *who* uses government for *what* ends....
>
> Simply put, the question of whose interests the state will be used to effectuate reduces in part to the question of which specific interests or values will dominate in a particular case. This ultimate specificity of choice is the existential burden of man, which no reference to general or neutral principles or choices will avoid [10].

Perhaps Kendall P. Cochran expresses it best. In writing on the necessity of moral assumptions in shaping the future character of economic life, he states:

> In sum, man, as a social being, has a degree of control over his future destiny. Today and yesterday are *irretrievably* gone. But the future can be of his own making. If one were to take a purposeful, a moral look at the future and ask himself, ask his generation, "What do we want to do with it?" he would find

that meaningful alternatives were available. But only if we make a clearly defined choice regarding the moral assumption we choose to use. And that is the moral imperative for members of the economics profession. The only alternative is one of laissez-faire indifference. And the consequence of that moral position, for laissez-faire indifference is equally a moral position, will be that meaningful alternatives are not made available and known to society [11].

5. Toward a Comparative Institutional Approach

Given the necessity of choice, the problem then becomes one of choosing the "appropriate" institutional arrangements or rearrangements for shaping the character of economic life. That there exist competing theories (economic as well as noneconomic) to prescribe the "appropriate" institutional arrangements is incontrovertible [12]. Utilizing the characterization of the interrelations of law and economics as summarized in figure 1–1, one approach—what be termed *a comparative institutional approach*— emerges. It is based on the belief that systematic relationships exist between legal institutions and the character of economic life. The scope of the comparative institutional approach is then to describe and analyze the systematic relationship between 1) the structure of political-legal-economic institutions, focusing on the rights and rules by which they operate; 2) the conduct or observed behavior in light of the incentives (penalties and rewards) created by the structure of the institutions; and 3) the consequent economic performance, i.e., the allocation *and* distribution of resources that determine the character of economic life under those institutions.[5]

This is not unlike what has been proffered by some of the contributors to the law and economics literature. In one of the least celebrated passages of one of the most celebrated law and economics articles, Ronald A. Coase suggested that, notwithstanding his predisposition to the market sector:

> The discussion of the problem of harmful effects...has made clear that the problem is one of choosing the appropriate social arrangement for dealing with the harmful effects. All solutions have costs and there is no reason to suppose that government regulation is called for simply because the problem is not well handled by the market or the firm. Satisfactory views on policy can only come from a patient study of how, in practice, the market, firms and government handle the problem of harmful effects.... It is my belief that economists, and policy-makers generally, have tended to over-estimate the advantages which come from governmental regulation. But this belief, even if justified, does not

do more than suggest that government regulation should be curtailed. It does not tell us where the boundary line should be drawn. This, it seems to me, has come from a detailed investigation of the actual results of handling the problem in different ways [14].[6]

With a comparative institutional approach, an attempt is made to avoid prescription and to try to describe rigorously, in a more positive sense, the systematic relationships between the structure of the political-legal-economic institutions and the conduct in the market, public, and communal sectors—sectors, that are, a priori, equally viable as systems of social control. Pure logical positivist, descriptive analysis cannot advocate any one system of social control; nor can it advocate any one particular legal-institutional arrangement; and finally, neither can it promote one decisional-criteria (e.g., efficiency) over another under the guise of objectivity or purported positivism. A viable approach to the study of interrelations between law and economics should be content with describing the full array of economic impacts (including both the allocation and distribution of resources) of alternative institutions and legal arrangements together with an articulation of whose interests will be served and at whose expense. In addition, the approach suggests that there be a sensitivity to other values (in addition to those ensconced in microeconomics) that a society may deem appropriate. While the manner in which such values may be brought into the analysis remains problematic, so too does continuing to ignore such values. So structured, a comparative institutional approach may help unmask the options open to individuals in a society. There remains a continuing necessity of choice as to which institutions should prevail in society including the structure of those institutions and thus the rights structure of the private, public, and communal sectors. But once the options are made known through something akin to the comparative institutional approach, the participants in the political-legal-economic arena may be able to make a more informed choice based on those values deemed appropriate.

6. Comparative Economic Systems

Regardless of whether those political-legal-economic institutions that actually emerge, emerge via the route of "ascendancy" or "descendancy," they are the product of choices made in that society. The conventional comparative economic systems literature suggests three different stylized structures that represent the spectrum of what will be termed here *political-economic systems*—1) capitalist market economy, 2) market socialism, and 3) centrally planned socialism [16]. Each of these systems can be defined within a multidimensional framework—a framework that in many ways represents a logical extension of the comparative institutional approach outlined earlier. In comments equally apropos to the comparative institutional approach, Morris Bornstein, commenting on the approach of comparative economic systems, stated:

> The field accommodates- indeed requires -a variety of research methods and analytical approaches, disciplinary and interdisciplinary....Comparative economic studies make a unique contribution to economics as a whole, by providing the perspective to overcome the parochialism inherent in economic thinking- on both theoretical and policy questions -based on the experience of a single economic system. The comparison of systems enriches the analyst's understanding of his own system, sharpening his appreciation of its merits and demerits and suggesting organizational and operational changes to improve its performance [17].

7. Classification Criteria and Political Economic Systems

The three stylized political-economic systems are characterized in the comparative economic systems literature by the following four basic criteria [18].

1. The power structure: the structure of power (i.e., who prevails in the decision-making process) in the complex organizations that comprise society's institutions. While it remains clear that the degree of centralization or decentralizaion of power will impact the character of economic life, there is, as yet, no general theory of organizational power to incorporate into the analysis.[7]

2. Mechanisms for information flow and coordination of the economy: there are three basic mechanisms to provide information with which to coordinate the political-economic decisions. They are the market economy, indicative planning, and the planned economy.[8] Paul R. Gregory and Robert C. Stuart summarize each as follows:

> the market—or, broadly speaking, the impact of the interaction of supply and demand on prices provides signals that trigger subunits in the system to make resource utilization decisions. The market thereby coordinates the activities of different decision-making units.
>
> indicative planning—the market serves as the principal instrument for resource allocation, but a plan is prepared to guide decision making. An indicative plan is one in which planners seek to indicate projected aggregate or sectorial trends and provide additional informatin beyond that normally sup-

plied by the market. An indicative plan is not broken down into directives or instructions for individual production units; enterprises are free to make use of the information contained in the indicative plan as they see fit, though indirect means are used to influence economic activity.

a planned economy—one where subunits (for example, firms) are coordinated largely by specific instructions or directives formulated by a superior agency (a central planning board) and disseminated through a document called a plan. The participants are induced to carry out the directive by appropriate incentives, which are designed by the planning authoritises. Obviously the specifics differ from one case to another. The basic point, however, is that in a planned economy economic activity is guided explicitly and implicitly by instructions or directives devised by higher units and subsequently transmitted to lower units, with rewards to the latter depending on the achievement of the directives [21].

3. Property rights structure: the relative mix of private, public (status rights), and communal property rights. These rights are the same as those described in section 5. Not only is the mix of these rights significant for impacting the allocation of scarce resources but equally important is the distribution of these rights. The manner in which these rights are distributed, and to whom, will have an important economic impact inasmuch as their assignment gives rise to claims to income. Different regimes of property right structures lead to different penalty/reward structures and, therefore, individually held goals/motivations, thus resulting in different economic outcomes.

4. Incentives: there are two types of incentives—material and moral.

material incentives—a reward system that promotes desirable behavior by giving the recipient a greater claim over material goods than one who has performed less well.

moral incentives—a system that rewards desirable behavior by appealing to the recipient's responsibility to society (or the company) and accordingly raising the recipient's social stature within the community. Moral incentives do not give the recipients greater command over material goods. In simpler terms, the difference between material and moral incentives is the difference between a cash bonus and a medal for an outstanding job [22].

The relationship between these four criteria and the three stylized political-economic systems is now evident. Real-world political-economic systems make choices (perhaps in a manner that conforms to either the theme of ascendancy or descendancy) at the constitutional, institutional and economic impact stages of choice. These societal choices will together determine the characteristics—especially the power structure of organizations; the information flows/coordination; the property rights structure;

and the associated incentives—of the political-economic system. These four characteristics (or variations thereof) can be combined in almost an infinite number of ways. Once selected, the particular combination chosen will give rise to the legal relations governing that society in the form of the capitalism, market socialism, or planned socialism described by Gregory and Stuart as follows:

> Capitalism is an economic system characterized by the private ownership of the factors of production. Decision making is decentralized and rests with the owners of the factors of production. Their decision making is coordinated by the market mechanism, which provides the necessary information. Material incentives are used to motivate participants toward goal achievement.

> Market Socialism is an economic system characterized by the state ownership of the factors of production. Decision making is decentralized and is coordinated by the market mechanism. Both material and moral incentives are used to motivate participants toward goal achievement.

> Planned Socialism is an economic system characterized by state ownership of the factors of production. Decision making is centralized and is coordinated by a central plan, which issues binding directives to the system's participants. Both material and moral incentives are used to motivate participants toward goal achievement [23].

8. Performance Criteria

Given the spectrum of possible political-economic systems, the next obvious question becomes, what are the relevant criteria by which to evaluate the alternative systems? The literature is quite consistent here and typically suggests the following performance criteria that can be applied to assess various systems [24].

The level and composition of output is one of the criteria used to evaluate a political-economic system. Ordinarily, the objective is to sustain as high a level of output as possible. As to the composition of output, this will vary depending upon whether resources are channeled through the market, public and/or communal sectors generating private consumption, business investment, public expenditures, and/or collective consumption. A second criterion is the annual aggregate and per capita rate of growth of GNP or GDP. Typically, most political-economic systems aspire to attain as high rates as possible, inasmuch as higher rates of economic growth are thought of as tantamount to the enhancement of welfare and progress of society. Efficiency, either static (single period) or dynamic (through time), is one of the most fundamental criteria used to evaluate the economic status of a political-economic system. In measuring static efficiency, productivity calculations are measured by the ratio of the output of an economic system to available inputs. Dynamic efficiency is measured by changes in this ratio over time [25].

The income distribution generated by a political economy is the fourth criterion for assessing economic performance. While a society may aspire to attain a so-called "equitable" distribution of income, what a society thinks is equitable is ultimately a value judgment as to what is deemed fair. The criterion of macroeconomic stability includes three components—providing for stable growth rates, maintaining an acceptable level of unemployment, and avoiding excessive rates of inflation. Finally, the paramount goal of any society is the provision of individual and national security. A political-economic system devotes economic resources to provide the political, military, and social power to ensure national security. It is within the realm of national security that individuals can then enjoy their individual security.

As presented here, the literature on comparative economic systems can be viewed as an extension of the comparative institutional approach set forth in the whole first section and summarized in figure 1–1. The fundamental link between the two is the legal relations governing society—that is, the extant structure of property rights. The private property rights, the status rights, and the communal property rights that emerge in the context of the comparative institutional approach not only give rise to a combined market, public, and communal sector allocation and distribution of resources but also comprise one of the four fundamental components and thus an integral part of the more widely conceived notion of the political-economic system.

As described earlier, a particular political-economic system is ultimately the product of choices made at the constitutional, institutional, and economic impact stages. Not only is there a necessity of choice involved in structuring rights but so too does that same necessity of choice prevail in the societal structuring of power, of information flows, and in establishing incentives. Further, there remains a necessity of choice in providing weights to the various performance criteria to evaluate and assess prevailing political-economic systems. Through a collective determination, a political-economic system will emerge somewhere along the continuum between market capitalism and planned socialism (top of figure 1–1). The modest hope here is that understanding political-economic systems from this perspective may serve to inform choice and avoid the often acrimonious debates over isms of standard political economy.

9. Issues and Prospects

The extension of the comparative institutional approach into the field of comparative economic systems presented here raises many of the same issues that are prevalent in the current debates regarding the role of economics in law. Perhaps this extension may provide a different vantage point from which to frame and analyze some of the ongoing debates.

In extending the comparative institutional approach to incorporate the basic elements of the comparative economic systems literature, one comes to appreciate better some of the continuing criticisms of the Chicago-Virginia blends of new law and economics, the economics of property rights, and public choice theory. One prevalent criticism concerns the general phenomena known as "economic imperialism into law"; the second relates to the Chicago-Virginia adherence to a strict economic efficiency analysis, while the third raises questions regarding the role of economic efficiency within jurisprudence.

10. Economic Imperialism and Law

There exists a broad-based skepticism on behalf of many in the law profession of what has come to be known as "economic imperialism"— with law seen as the victim, not necessarily a willing participant [26]. While the inherent "imperialistic" nature of economics provided the *supply* of economics into the law-and-economics movement, the *demand* was provided by the unfilled agenda left by the legal realists in law. Proponents of the legal realist movement had counseled legal scholars to incorporate the social sciences (especially economics) into the law curriculum in an attempt to provide more unifying themes in and of the law. Once the legal realist movement sputtered in the mid-twentieth century, the continuing work of the institutional economists and the rapid emergence of the Chicago-Virginia contributors to the law-and-economics movement quickly filled the void left by the legal realist movement.

It is clear that economic analysis, with its focus on "rationale" utility-maximizing behavior, has improved both the clarity and the logic of legal thought and argumentation by providing a consistent framework to analyze legal policy. However, while providing a more powerful syntax, the increasing formalization of many legal-economic models has systematically diminished their heuristic value.

The result has been a demonstrated reluctance by many of those in law to embrace economics in any wholesale manner. Their preference is to stay within the more familiar confines of "reasonable behavior" and well-accepted legal doctrine and avoid the "rational behavior" ensconced within the microeconomic models. Further, as mentioned earlier, regarding the work on comparative economic systems, those interested in truly understanding political-economic systems call for an interdisciplinary approach to avoid the parochialism inherent in economic thinking.[9] The nature of microeconomic models is such that the models require a host of assumptions, many of which do not comport to the broad spectrum of political-economic systems that presently exist. The call here is not for less assumptions but for altering existing assumptions to better reflect the political and legal institutions evident in alternative political-economic systems.

11. Efficiency as the Cornerstone of Law and Economics

A second line of criticism stems from the Chicago-Virginia strict reliance on economic efficiency as the primary (typically, the only) criterion to analyze political-legal-economic issues and to be used as a basis to formulate legal-economic policy. Indeed, it has been observed that the emergence of law and economics (particularly the Chicago-Virginia reliance on private and market institutions) evolved contemporaneously with an intellectual climate that was increasingly receptive to the view that markets are an effective form of social organization. In this climate, it was not surprising to witness the legal-academic community's enhanced interest in private-law structures, market-oriented policies, and hence, necessarily, the efficiency concepts imbued in microeconomic theory [27].

The dominant theme in the Chicago-Virginia blend of the new law and economics, the economics of property rights literature, and public choice theory is that *efficiency* can be used to describe the development of law and legal institutions and ought to be used as a (perhaps *the*) dominant decisional criterion to (re)structure society's political and legal institutions and/or to guide legal outcomes, especially legislative and court decisions. The attempt is to set forth theories and methods of analysis that rely heavily on the Pareto efficiency concept borrowed from welfare economics. Utilizing this principle or one of its variants, these practitioners attempt to determine the "correct" structure and hence "appropriate" conduct of political and legal institutions from which would emerge the "proper" character of economic life. Such attempts are extremely useful in describing the efficiency of resource allocations generated through Pareto-structured institutions, in the sense of logical positivism. However, there is no basis to claim that such institutions are "appropriate." Logical positivist analysis does not allow for conclusive statements as to the appropriateness of alternative institutional arrangements.

From the vantage point suggested in extending the comparative institutional approach into comparative economic systems, much of the Chicago-Virginia literature appears purposely narrow (some might say conservative[10]) both in scope and substance. To take one performance criteria—efficiency—and to build an entire edifice of law and economics from which both to 1) analyze legal-economic institutions and 2) promote legal-economic institutional (re)arrangements, is but a small part of a scholarly legal-economic research agenda needed to inform choice. The point here is not to denigrate the contributions of those in the Chicago-Virginia school but rather to underscore the attenuated significance of their work for legal-economic policy. Juxtaposed to the comparative institutional approach as extended and other schools of thought within the law-and-economics movement, much of the Chicago-Virginia approach is less open, less realistic, and consequently less informative. This observation is becoming more and more common among legal-economic scholars; it continues to be embraced by institutional economists, and it lies at the heart of many of the criticisms of law-and-economics movement by those in critical legal studies and those in the reformist school.

Michael J. Trebilcock, providing a Canadian perspective (not exactly a political-economic system significantly different from that of the United States along the political-economic spectrum) commented on the thrust of much of the Chicago-Virginia blend of law and economics. He stated:

> All of this is to say that many Canadian legal academics and law students are likely to be less sensitive or sympathetic to a framework of analysis that stresses the importance of individual preference, the virtues of voluntary exchanges in freely functioning markets, and the alleged inefficiencies induced by many collective interventions in those markets. Allocative efficiency, as a single-value policy touchstone, is clearly far too narrow to capture central forces at play in Canadian policy making [29].

Commenting on the prerequisites for understanding other cultures, Frank I. Michelman stated:

> If all you think to search for in other cultures in correlation between variations in "cost conditions" and "the structure of legal institutions," you foreclose the possibility of recognizing a culture in which one of the controlling "conditions" is that crucial promptings and motivations do not take the "commodity" form of marginally interchangeable "costs" at all. And so you may fail to see that one of the distinguishing and contingent features of our own thought process is its relentless urge to reduce every motivation to a cost [30].

In the light of these prevailing attitudes, one wonders what the Chicago-Virginia blend of law and economics is contributing to the understanding of issues of legal-economic policy for countries along the political-economic spectrum significantly different from the United States and Canada.

12. The Jurisprudential Niche for Efficiency

There is an additional tension that exists within the law-and-economics movement. The tension emanates directly from the above-described exclusive reliance on economic efficiency as the touchstone or guide to legal-economic policy making. Due to the perceived narrowness of the efficiency concept, the legal-academic community continues to demonstrate a reluctance to provide "economic efficiency" a well-settled jurisprudential niche. Both economists and lawyers have been and will continue to be intensely involved in legal-economic policy issues—issues that inherently involve value judgments. Neither is apt to step aside in deference to the fact that the disputes involve basic value choices that transcend both law and economics.

Be that as it may, most legal as well as political scholars prefer to rely on the more familiar political and legal decisional criteria based on long-standing notions of justice and fairness or the public interest. Economists, on the other hand, particularly those inclined toward the Chicago-Virginia approach to law and economics, advocate the adoption of efficiency-based legal rules and Pareto-efficient structured political institutions resulting in efficient judicial and legislative outcomes.

That the legal community remains adverse to much of this type of thinking (for better or worse?) is incontrovertible. Some specific examples of the type of efficiency-based policy that have lead to a reluctance of legal scholars to provide efficiency a secure jurisprudential niche include: 1) contractarian theories of public choice that advance the use of Pareto-optimal rules to derive an efficient constitution and, subsequently, efficient legislative outcomes [31]; 2) judicious use of "wealth maximization" normatively employed to resolve property disputes or tautologically to discern the efficiency of the common law [32]; 3) the adoption of least-cost avoider rules in lieu of justice of fairness to guide the placement of liability in tort law [33]; and 4) the promotion of nonattenuated rights structures [34], to mention only a few. Considering the extent to which the law-and-economics movement continues to adhere to these Chicago-Virginia precepts, there is little reason to think that this particular tension will diminish.

13. Tentative Forecasts

Within the marketplace of ideas pertaining to law and economics, it
is inevitable that various schools of thought emerged and, with them,
the above-mentioned tensions. For the future, I believe political-legal-
economic policy will increasingly be influenced by the various schools of
thought comprising the law-and-economics movement (perhaps not as
deeply as some in the field may wish). One of the more interesting future
developments will be to see which direction the movement takes and if
and how these tensions are resolved.

At this time one could anticipate a slow, gradual decline in the emphasis placed on the Chicago-Virginia school of law and economics. If
this occurs, one may attribute it to the aforementioned growing reluctance of legal-economic academic scholars to embrace a mode of analysis
that offers so narrow an insight into legal-economic policy. The anticipation here of the Chicago-Virginia school's decline is directed at its rate of
growth, not its existence—which is to say, its diminished position will not
produce a void along the lines of the earlier void left by the legal
realists. Much work remains to be done within the efficiency of law, and
there is little reason to forecast its sudden demise.

With the continuing but diminished role played by the Chicago-
Virginia school, one can also anticipate the development of the other
schools of thought currently contributing to the law-and-economics movement. These approaches are less ideological in character, more inclusive
in analytical framework, and more eclectic in their approach toward
public policy. I have in mind the contributions of the institutional
economics-based law and economics, the so-called reformist tradition
(most often attributed to New Haven), the law and economics component
of the critical legal studies movement, as well as the more moderate
elements of the new law and economics, economics of property rights,
and public choice theory.

Whether or not there will be a convergence of any of these various
schools of thought or whether they will evolve in relative isolation from
one another remains to be seen. However, at this time these various
approaches represent an emerging trend in law and economics that promises to be more robust than the Chicago-Virginia approach and thus
more viable in helping to describe and ultimately understand the realities
of the political, legal, and economic systems. That a necessity of choice
remains is incontrovertible. However, here the necessity of choice centers
on the selection of which of the various schools of thought relevant to the
study of the interrelations between law and economics will emerge as *the*

conventional wisdom (however ephemeral). Like other societal choices, that choice will reflect the collective will of those who prevailed in the choice-making political-legal-economic arena. To that extent, we must work to ensure that it is an informed choice.

Notes

1.   The "character of economic life" is meant to convey the allocation and distribution of resources that emerge through a society's private, public, and communal sectors. These sectors are described in section 5.

2.   Hereafter, throughout this chapter, I sometimes use the word "institutions" as the short form of "political-legal-economic institutions." For the United States they refer to an eclectic assemblage of the following:

The Judiciary—including federal, state, and local judicial bodies as well as accompanying support or associated services.

The Executive Offices—including the office of President, governors of the several states, and local executives.

Government Commissions and Bureaucratic Agencies—including federal, state, and local regulatory commissions (e.g., ICC, local zoning commissions, etc.) and government agencies (e.g., EPA, welfare agencies, natural resource departments in state governments, etc.).

Custom—an eclectic assemblage of traditional or informal decision-making units (e.g., religious organizations, grassroot issue groups, etc.).

For forms of government different from that of the United States a similar political taxonomy of their institutions would suffice.

3.   If the existing property rights were randomly redistributed among all households in society, a new state of general equilibrium incorporating the new distribution of resources in the economy would also satisfy the necessary conditions for Pareto efficiency. Because there are an infinite number of random redistributions of property in any society, it follows that there is also, literally, an infinite number of Pareto-optimal outcomes, each corresponding to a different initial distribution of property rights. Thus, any assignment of property rights will yield an efficient solution. However, the distribution of goods and services will vary with alternative assignments of rights.

4.   Morris Bornstein describes three mechanisms for expressing the community's aggregate preferences:

The social preference (or utility or welfare) function expresses the community's effective aggregate preferences regarding the ends and means of economic activity. In analyzing and comparing systems, we wish to consider both how the community's decisions are reached and what these decisions are.

In regard to the first aspect, three mechanisms may be distinguished: (1) individual preferences expressed through individual choice in markets (consumer sovereignty); (2) individual preferences expressed through the political process, either by direct voting on certain issues or by indirect voting through the selection of legislators and government officials; and (3) the preferences of a ruling group not selected through the electoral process [8].

5.   The fact that the study of law and economics encompasses analysis of both allocation *and* distribution is generally accepted but often neglected, resulting with a major focus on allocation. Werner Z. Hirsch, in his introductory text entitled *Law and Economics*, stated the following:

> Our task would be so much easier if efficiency could be rigorously defended as the only and ultimate objective. Instead we face two all-too-often opposing objectives-efficiency and equity. It must be remembered that the ultimate goal is what economists like to call social efficiency, which requires trading off resource-allocation efficiency against distribution of income. Unfortunately, as all will agree, what is the most desirable distribution of income is a highly subjective decision. Nevertheless, legal rules must be concerned about both efficiency and income distribution. . . . Guidelines given by economic theory require two successive steps—first, income should be redistributed in the most desirable manner; second, resources should be allocated in the most efficient manner, preferably in response to competitive forces. An effort must thus be made to agree on a subjectively preferred income distribution and it must be followed by an effort to attain allocative efficiency. The formulation of prudent legal rules would have to proceed by considering both goals, not just allocative efficiency—a formidable task [13].

6.   Coase reiterated this point several years later:

> It is obvious that if you are comparing the performance of an industry under regulation with what it would be without regulation, there is no reason to assume (indeed there is good reason not to assume) that either of these situations will correspond to anything an economist would call optimal. The same is true if one is thinking of modifications in the system. None is likely to be optimal since it is quite certain that, whatever may be the characteristics of the ideal world, we have not yet discovered how to get to it from where we are. Contemplation of an optimal system may suggest ways of improving the system. . . But in general its influence has been pernicious. It has directed economists' attention away from the main question, which is how alternative arrangements will actually work in practice. . . . Until we realize that we are choosing between social arrangements which are all more or less failures, we are not likely to make much headway. . . . The kind of question which usually has to be decided is, for example, whether the administrative structure of an agency should be changed or a certain provision in a statute amended. That is to say, what we are normally concerned with are social arrangements and what is economically relevant is how the allocation and use of factors of production will change with a change in social arrangements [15].

7.   Egon Neuberger offers a classification of economic systems that includes four criteria. One of the four focuses on "power" in the context of the locus of decision-making power [19]. In his discussion of power he describes four basic types of decision-making structures:

1.   *Complete centralization*—an abstract notion defined as a central monolithic authority with an information, technology, and level of automation consistent with total and complete cybernetic control of all economic decisions;

2.   *Administration decentralization*—a central authority would make a broad array of basic decisions and then delegate the responsibility to implement the decisions and the right to make necessary subordinate decisions to lower-level authorities;

3. *Manipulative decentralization*—central authorities do not place explicit limitations of the freedom of action or discretion of the lower-level authorities, but instead alter the economic environment (e.g., changing taxes, subsidies...etc.) within which the decisions are made;

4. *Complete decentralization*—an abstract notion with the numerous independent decision-making centers completely free to make decisions of their choice.

See also "Samuels' General Paradigm of Choice and Power," in Cento G. Veljanovski's *Research Review* [20].

8. Some economists are inclined to identify "centralization" with planned economies and "decentralization" with market economies. The suggestion here is that the real-world political-economic systems are significantly more complex.

9. See quote in text at reference [17].

10. Indeed, George Stigler, a leading proponent of the Chicago school, set forth the hypothesis that the professional study of economics makes one politically conservative. Some years ago he argued that economists have been trained to believe in the superiority of individual choice over collective choice and to prefer market-like solutions to social problems over political solutions [28].

References

1. A more detailed version of this characterization of law and economics is provided in Mercuro, Nicholas, and Ryan, Timothy P., *Law, Economics and Public Policy* (Greenwich: JAI Press, 1984). Much of section 1 of this chapter borrows generously and directly from portions of chapters 1, 2, and 6.

2. The connection between law and economics and comparative economic systems has been touched on by several scholars. For example, see Gay, David, "Towards a Theory of Entitlements in Comparative Economics," *Revista Internazionale di Scienze Economiche e Commerciali*, Vol. 28, No. 3 (1981), pp. 216–225. See also Pryor, Frederic L., *Property and Industrial Organization in Communist and Capitalist Nations* (Bloomington: Indiana University Press, 1973).

3. Alchian, Armen A., and Demsetz, Harold, "The Property Rights Paradigm," *Journal of Economic History*, Vol. 33, No. 1 (March 1973), pp. 16–27 at 17.

4. Randall, Alan, *Resource Economics* (Columbus: Grid Publishing, Inc., 1981), p. 148.

5. The concept of status rights is more fully developed by Dales, John H., "Rights in Economics," in Wunderlich, Gene, and Gibson, W.L. (eds.), *Perspectives of Property* (University Park: Institute for Research on Land and Water Resources, Pennsylvania State University, 1972), pp. 149–155.

6. Ullmann, Walter, *The Individual and Society in the Middle Ages* (Baltimore: The Johns Hopkins Press, 1966).

7. Coleman, James S., *Power and the Structure of Society* (New York: W.W. Norton and Company, 1974), pp. 72–76.
8. Bornstein, Morris (ed.), *Comparative Economic Systems* (Homewood: Richard D. Irwin, Inc. 1985), p. 8.
9. Buchanan, James M., "Law and the Invisible Hand," in Bernard, Siegan H. (ed.), *Interaction of Economics and the Law* (Lexington: Lexington Books, 1977), pp. 127–138 at 136.
10. Samuels, Warren J., "Interrelations Between Legal and Economic Processes," *Journal of Law and Economics*, Vol. 14, No. 2 (October 1971), pp. 435–450 at 442, 445.
11. Cochran, Kendall P., "Economics as a Moral Science," *Review of Social Economy*, Vol. 37, No. 2 (October 1974), pp. 186–195 at 194.
12. For a discussion of these competing theories, see Leff, Arthur A., "Economic Analysis of Law: Some Realism About Nominalism," *Virginia Law Review*, Vol. 60, No. 3 (March 1974), pp. 451–482 at 469–477.
13. Hirsch, Werner Z., *Law and Economics: An Introductory Analysis* (New York: Academic Press, 1979), pp. 4–5.
14. Coase, Ronald H., "The Problem of Social Cost," *Journal of Law and Economics*, Vol. 3 (October 1960) pp. 1–44 at 18–19.
15. Coase, Ronald H., "The Regulated Industry—Discussion," *American Economic Review*, Vol. 54, No. 3 (May 1964), pp. 194–197 at 194–195.
16. A similar taxonomy is provided by Bornstein, *supra* note 8, Introductions to Parts II, III, and IV. See also Gregory, Paul R., and Stuart, Robert C., *Comparative Economic Systems* (Boston: Houghton Mifflin Company, 1985), chapters 1 and 2, especially p. 21.
17. Bornstein, *supra* note 8, p. 17.
18. Gregory and Stuart, *supra* note 17, pp. 13–21.
19. Neuberger, Egon, "Classifying Economic Systems," in Bornstein, *supra* note 8, pp. 18–26 at 19–21.
20. Veljanovski, Cento G., *The New Law-and-Economics: A Research Review* (Oxford: Centre for Socio-Legal Studies, 1982), pp. 58–60.
21. Gregory and Stuart, *supra* note 16, pp. 16–17.
22. *Ibid.*, p. 20.
23. *Ibid.*, p. 21.
24. *Ibid.*, pp. 33–42. See also Bornstein, *supra* note 8, pp. 11–13.
25. *Ibid.*, p. 36.
26. Becker, Gary S., *The Economic Approach to Human Behavior* (Chicago: University of Chicago Press, 1976) is the classic work on the so-called "imperialism of economics."
27. Kitch, Edmund W., "The Intellectual Foundations of 'Law and Economics,'" *Journal of Legal Education*, Vol. 33, No. 2 (June 1983), pp. 184–196.
28. Stigler, George, J., "The Politics of Political Economics," *Quarterly Journal of Economics*, Vol. 73, No. 4 (November, 1959), pp. 522–532 at 522, 524.

29. Trebilcock, Michael, J., "The Prospects of 'Law and Economics': A Canadian Perspective," *Journal of Legal Education*, Vol. 33, No. 2 (June 1983), pp. 299–293 at 289–290.
30. Michelman, Frank I., "Reflections on Professional Education, Legal Scholarship and the Law-and-Economics Movement," *Journal of Legal Education*, Vol. 33, No. 2 (June 1983), pp. 197–209 at 202.
31. Buchanan, James M., and Tullock, Gordon, *The Calculus of Consent* (Ann Arbor: The University of Michigan Press, 1965).
32. Posner, Richard A. "Utilitarianism, Economics and Legal Theory," *Journal of Legal Studies*, Vol. 8, No. 1 (January 1979), pp. 103–140.
33. Brown, John P., "Toward an Economic Theory of Liability," *Journal of Legal Studies*, Vol. 2, No. 2 (June 1973), pp. 323–349. For a review of a variety of approaches see Veljanovski, Cento G., "The Economic Theory of Tort Liability—Toward a Corrective Justice Approach," in Burrows, Paul, and Veljanovski, Cento G. (eds.), *The Economic Approach to Law* (London: Butterworths, 1981), pp. 125–150.
34. Furubotn, Eirik, and Pejovich, Svetozar, *The Economics of Property Rights* (Cambridge: Ballinger Publishing Co., 1974), pp. 1–9. See also, Randall, Alan, "Growth, Resources and Environment: Some Conceptual Issues," *American Journal of Agricultural Economics*, Vol. 57, No. 5 (December 1975), pp. 803–809.

2 THE NEW ECONOMIC ANALYSIS OF LAW: LEGAL RULES AS INCENTIVES

Lewis A. Kornhauser

By general agreement, the new economic analysis of law began with the near-simultaneous publication roughly 25 years ago of "The Problem of Social Cost" [1] and "Some Thoughts on Risk Distribution and the Law of Torts" [2]. Though no one doubts the subsequent flourishing of the endeavor, many question its significance, and most cannot articulate its fundamental challenge to more traditional understandings and analyses of law. Frequently, critics have considered fundamental to economic analysis of law the claim either that the law *ought* to be or *was in fact* efficient. Occasionally, critics have dismissed the endeavor as obfuscation through the introduction of a new technical jargon and formal mathematical techniques into the verbal tangle of the law.

Lucian Bebchuck, Robert Ellickson, Jeffrey Gordon, David Leebron, Richard Revesz, Roberta Romano, Lawrence Sager, and Katherine Stone commented on earlier drafts. I also benefited from discussions of an earlier draft at the Harvard Workshop on Law and Economics, the University of Pennsylvania workshop on law and economics and the Vermont Law School workshop. The financial support of the Filomen d'Agostino and Max E. Greenberg Research Fund of the New York University School of Law is gratefully acknowledged.

This essay offers a different interpretation of the challenge and contribution of the new economic analysis of law to legal studies. This new
analysis elaborates an *economic* theory of how individuals (or "agents")
behave in response to legal rules. Sometimes this theory is developed
explicitly; often, articles urging that some doctrine is or ought to be
efficient rely implicitly on this economic theory of behavior. In every
instance, this attention to the behavior of primary actors (as opposed to
judges, legislators, or lawyers) constitutes a radical development in legal
studies. While that development has matured, it promises further, dramatic changes in traditional legal understanding.

Prior to the emergence of the new economic analysis of law, assumptions concerning the effects of legal rules on behavior were generally
implicit rather than explicit, oftern ad hoc, occasionally inconsistent, and
almost always "naive." According to the tacit, naive theory that under-
lay, and continues to underlie, much discussion and debate of law,
individuals conform their behavior to that required by the legal rule.
Thus, under the naive theory, evaluation of a legal rule reduces to an
inquiry of what society wants or requires.

Economic analysis of law offers a more complex understanding of the
effects of legal rules on behavior under which every agent will only rarely
conform his/her conduct to that required by the legal rules. Thus, if one
believes that the appraisal of legal rules requires evaluation of their
consequences, this shift from the naive to the economic behavioral theory
implies that our appraisal and understanding of legal rules must extend
beyond a discussion of what is socially desirable or necessary to an effort
to "see through" the legal rules to the behavior that they induce.

An assumption of relentless and calculated pursuit of self-interest
characterizes a theory of legally induced behavior as an *economic* theory.
Economic analysis of law currently offers at least three distinct paradigms
of the influence of legal rules on behavior. According to the economic
analysis of legal duties, agents consider the consequences of violation of a
legal rule in choosing their actions. The economic analysis of property
rights argues that different distributions and bundling of entitlements will
induce different behaviors. The public choice perspective focuses on the
agents' attempts to determine the legal rules they face.[1] In section 1, after
outlining in somewhat more detail the contours of each of these three
paradigms, I suggest that their varying emphases derive from different
conceptions of law as directive or as nondirective.

In section 2, the economic analysis of legal duties are considered in
more detail. This section does not provide a comprehensive, or even
haphazard, survey of the numerous analyses of legal rules and doctrine

that the analysts have studied. Rather, it attempts to identify key features of the economic structure of analysis.

The naive theory that agents will (generally) conform their behavior to that required by the legal rule rests on the idea that the legal rule itself provides a compelling reason for action. Despite the elaboration of the economic analyses of property rights and legal duties, legal scholars still resist the idea that these economic motivations can replace (or exhaust) the concept of law's normative force. Section 3 attempts both to make more precise the concept of normative force and to suggest how economic analysis of law might model those aspects of it that escape the current formulation of the economic theory. Section 4 offers some concluding remarks.

1. Economic Theories of Behavior Under Law

The concept of rationality that informs economic analysis of law has two aspects. First, it imposes a minimal substantive constraint on the ends that the agent may pursue. Heuristically, an agent's ends must provide a thorough and noncircular ranking of any set of options presented to him/her. More technically, economic rationality requires that each agent have well-defined, complete, and transitive preferences over the relevant alternatives. Second, economic rationality postulates that, in any choice situation, an agent has sufficient persistence, foresight, and analytic ability always to chooses the best, feasible alternative.

The various strands of the new economic analysis of law differ in either of two ways. First, a legal rule may have at least three different influences on the decisions of agents: 1) the sanction against infringement of the legal rule may serve as a price that a *dutyholder* (or *potential infringer*) faces; 2) the assignment of the entitlement may alter the distribution of wealth between entitlement holders and dutyholders (and hence the pattern of demand of the agents); and 3) the distribution and (Hohfeldian) structure of entitlements may offer *entitlement holders* different incentives. The economic analysis of legal duties studies primarily emphasizes effects of type 1; the economic analysis of property rights emphasizes effects of type 3.

Second, the various strands define differently the set of decisions subject to influence by a legal rule. The economic analysis of legal duties analyses the effects of "fixed" legal rules on various decisions of agents. In accident law, for example, the relevant decisions are the choice of activity and care levels. The public choice perspective, in contrast, allows agents not only to alter their activity and care levels but also to attempt to alter the legal rule itself. Put differently, economic analysis of legal duties draws a sharp distinction between the legal policymaker who makes law and the agents who as *law-takers* are subject to it, while, in the public choice perspective, agents are not only subject to law but also participate, as *law-makers*, in its formulation.

1.1   The Structure of Legal Rules and its Influences on Behavior

The new economic analysis of law (see reference [3]) divides each legal rule into two components: an entitlement and its protection. The entitlement delineates the permitted and prohibited "uses" or "actions" of the entitlement holder. The protection determines the consequences either of unauthorized actions of the entitlement holder or of impermissible incursions into the holder's permitted activities.

In its study of entitlements, the new economic analysis of law has rarely discriminated among the various possible forms and structures of entitlements that Wesley N. Hohfeld elaborated in his four-way classification of entitlements into rights, privileges, powers, and immunities [4]. The economic analysis of legal duties has concentrated exclusively on the effects of a legal duty on the various choices of the dutyholder. In contrast, the economic analysis of property rights has concentrated on the effects of legal regimes on the decisions of rights-holders.

One may crudely distinguish two decisions facing a dutyholder: 1) the intensity with which he/she engages in the duty-bearing activity and 2) given that he/she engages in the activity at all, whether he/she should breach his/her duty (and thereby infringe the correlative Hohfeldian claim right) or meet it.[2] In this context the protection of the entitlement sets a price on the agent's decisions. The decision to breach a duty depends on the relative costs of breach to those of compliance; the activity-level decision depends in turn on the costs incurred from breach or compliance. The analysis of accident law, for example, considers an injurer's duty not to impose the adverse effects of certain activities on victims. The legal rule defines the injurer's duty in terms of the level of care he/she adopts, but the costs of compliance with (or violation of) this legal duty also influence the level of activity the injurer adopts. Similarly, the economic analyses of contract have dealt almost exclusively with the promisor's duty to perform (and the promisee's correlative right to performance) once a contract has been formed. The sanction for breach of contract, of course, may also influence the willingness of parties to enter contracts at all.

In the economic analysis of legal duties, two protections of entitlements (or Hohfeldian rights) are distinguished. Each determines the consequence of a third party's invasion of the entitlement-holder's right. Property rules protect entitlements by enjoining the infringement. The owner of the entitlement can thus "unilaterally" set the price at which the entitlement will transfer. A liability rule protects entitlements by awarding the owner damages. In this case, a court sets the price at which the entitlement transfers.

In its focus on the behavior of potential infringers, the economic analysis of legal duties has distinguished two effects a legal rule may have on behavior. First, ex ante, in choosing an action, the agent will consider the price set on any entitlement that the action may infringe. In accident law, for example, "victims" have an entitlement not to suffer economic loss from the negligence of others; that entitlement is protected by a liability rule. Injurers, in adopting a level of care (or an activity level), take into account the "price" that the liability rule sets on their choice of that care level. Similarly, the promisor, in contemplating breach, considers the cost he/she would incur from infringing the promisee's right to performance. Second, ex post, after an infringement, the legal rule determines the bargaining game that the infringer and the infringed play. That is, the legal rule determines the endowments in any settlement negotiations between the parties.

The economics of property rights, by contrast, has primarily examined the behavior of the entitlement holders rather than the behavior of the potential infringers. This attention to a different decision maker has occasioned two shifts in perspective on the legal rules. First, in the economics of property rights, rights and their correlative duties no longer hold center stage. Powers, privileges, and immunities play an equal if not greater role in the analysis. The privileges of an entitlement holder are those acts he/she may undertake without fear of state sanction. A holder of a power may transfer, abrogate, or destroy the specific entitlement over which he/she has power (whether he/she "holds" the entitlement or not). To hold an immunity (with respect to a specific entitlement X) implies that no other person has the power to alter that entitlement.

Second, in contrast to the economic analysis of legal duties which often analyzes the behavioral effects of a *single* legal duty, the economics of property rights compares the incentive effects of differing bundles (and distributions) of rights, powers, privileges, and immunities. The concern is thus less often with the correct formulation of a specific legal rule, such as the determination of the optimal standard of care in a negligence rule governing a particular class of accidents; instead, the economics of property rights compares legal regimes: private property as opposed to "communal" property or "capital cooperatives" (corporations) as opposed to workers' cooperatives. In particular, they attend to conditions in which transactions are costly or information asymmetrically distributed; in these circumstances, different structures of property rights yield different incentives to their owners.

For example, under the property rights analysis, common pool problems such as overgrazing or overfishing arise because of the distribution of both the privilege to use the property and the power to transfer those privileges. The wide distribution of the privilege implies that each holder of the entitlement chooses to overexploit the jointly held resource. In contrast, the jointly held power to transfer the privilege raises transaction costs and makes it difficult for a single agent to acquire an exclusive privilege. In this property rights analysis, the protection of the entitlement, so central to the analysis under the economic analysis of legal duties, plays no role.

In principle, the economic analyses of legal duties and of property rights complement each other; the first examines the effects of a legal rule on the duty holder and the second of that same rule on the rights holder. In practice, analyses rarely offer such a complete picture. this failure to integrate the two perpsectives arises from their different foci of single rule and legal regime.

1.2. Agents' Options and Conceptions of Law

The public choice perspective generally examines, as legal duties' analysis does, the behavior of dutyholders rather than of rightsholders. In the economic analysis of legal duties, however, the citizen has a limited repertoire of actions he/she may adopt in response to a legal rule: he/she may obey the rule or breach it (perhaps in a number of different ways).[3] But, as a *law-taker*, she may not strive to alter the legal rule. To these two options, public choice theory has added a third: attempt to alter the legal rule so that it promotes rather than hinders the *agent's* interest. Agents may thus influence the legal rules they face as well as be influenced by them.

The view of agents as lawmakers dramatically alters the tone and thrust of the economic analysis of law. A typical analysis of accident law in the economic analysis of legal duties, for example, sharply distinguishes between the goals of the legal policymaker and those of the agents. The policymaker, it is often assumed, pursues some "economic" goal such as maximization of social welfare or minimization of social costs. As section 2 elaborates, the policymaker then chooses a legal regime that directs agents' self-interested behavior into the policymaker's desired effect.

In the public choice perspective, the agents' self-interest determines both the agents' response to given legal rules and the laws to which the agents respond. The analysis often emphasizes the agents' rent-seeking behavior, a behavior which not only prevents the maximization of social welfare or the minimization of social costs but also implies that the legal corpus does not promote any coherent set of goals.

The economic analysis of legal duties thus adopts, at least implicitly, a directive conception of law, while the public choice perspective more consciously espouses a nondirective conception.[1] A directive conception of law maintains that society chooses legal rules in order to promote social goals, as when, for example, a policymaker selects the negligence rule to minimize the sum of accident costs and accident prevention costs.

Directive conceptions of law may differ in various ways. Policymakers (or societies) may differ in their objective functions. Both an economic analyst of law who believes that the law ought to be efficient and a natural lawyer who believes that judges should do justice between the parties may have directive conceptions of law. They differ in the goals they ascribe to society on the policymaker. Alternatively, two.individuals may agree on the societal goal the law should consciously pursue but differ in their views of how individual citizens respond to legal rules. Thus, despite the identical social aims, the differing theories of behavior might dictate the announcement of different legal rules.

As already noted, not every conception of law need be directive. Directive conceptions are distinguished by the intentionality of the legal system *as a whole*. A nondirective theory may assert that individual agents—judges, legislators, citizens—act purposively without maintaining that the legal system as a whole may be viewed as pursuing some consistent set of goals.[5] Posner's work on statutory interpretation [7,8], for example, holds a nondirective view of law. By contrast, Dworkin's concept of integrity, in reference [9], implicates a directive conception of law.

In the directive conception of law implicit in the economic analysis of legal duties, analysts generally impute an economic content to the social goal of the legal policymaker. In the nondirective conception of law of the public choice perspective, the self-interest of the agents influences the decisions of policymakers who also act self-interestedly. An interest in reelection is generally assumed to move legislators, while regulators are often assumed to be motivated by future employment activities. The public choice perspective has not offered a clear of convincing assumption of judicial motivation.

Though the central ideas of directive (and nondirective) institutions and of an economic theory of behavior under law lie at the center of economics, they mark a radical departure from both the old law and economics and more traditional legal scholarship.[6] Microeconomic theory, after all, offers models of consumer and firm behavior, and then aggregates these individual behaviors into the paradigm of nondirective institutions, the market. Traditional legal scholarship, on the other hand, has been concerned largely with texts. Indeed, all too often the study of law is identified with the study of legal texts: statutes, administrative regulations, and judicial opinions. The analyst scrutinizes these texts to determine what behavior they command, or argues that a text ought to announce some right or duty. In either instance, words, not actions, are the focus of concern. This concentration on texts has had two consequences. As textual analysis often turns on the intention of the author (or of the reader), the legal analyst often implicitly adopts a directive view of law. Second, from doctrinal analysis that seeks to rationalize case law to the current concerns of legal theorists with interpretation, lawyers, judges, and legal scholars have long focused on the announcement of rights and rules of law rather than the realization of these rights in social practice. This emphasis on texts again leads, often implicitly, to the adoption of the naive theory of behavior.

The new economic analysis of law has not been the sole movement to recognize the significance of legal behaviors as opposed to legal texts. The law and society movement also desires to look beyond texts and to locate the law in behavior. Though many of those laboring in law and society adopt a constitutive, nondirective conception of law, few, if any, adopt an economic theory of behavior under law. Indeed, in reaction to traditional legal scholarship, some in the law and society movement seem to ignore texts altogether. One of the strengths of the economic analysis of legal duties is its attempt, however crude, to elucidate the link between legal texts and social behavior.[7]

2. Economic Models in the Economic Analysis of Legal Duties

Of the three strands of the new economic analysis of law considered here, the models of the economics of legal duties exhibit the most uniform structure. This uniformity has two sources. First, the emphasis on the analysis of the protection of a right implies that legal rules may be modelled as "prices." Second, the implicit assumption of a directive conception of law permits modeling the legal policymaker's choice of legal rule as a problem of mechanism design. Though the economic models are in general quite simple in terms of information structure and other features, the formal models do present a few common threads and novelties that bear closer examination.

2.1. The Structure of Economic Models of "Directive" Law

The structure of a generic model in the economic analysis of legal duties may be simply stated. The analyst distinguishes the legal policymaker from the citizen/agents. The citizen/agents engage in some (primary) activity that the policymaker desires to control, redirect, or otherwise regulate. The policymaker cannot *command* particular behaviors; rather he/she must choose among some class of legal rules. Each legal rule determines the "rules" of a game played by the agents. Generally, the legal rule alters the costs and benefits associated with an agent's various courses of action. The policymaker adopts the legal rule that induces the game with the "best" equilibrium outcome.

An example may illuminate this curt, abstract characterization. Consider John Brown's model of accident law [14] which underlies much of the subsequent economic analysis of rules of negligence, a clear and coherent presentation of which appears in reference [15]. In Brown's model, there are three decisionmakers: the legal policymaker and two agents, generally labeled Injurer and Victim. Injurer and Victim are each independently engaged in an activity, the levels of which I shall, for ease of exposition, assume are exogenously given. The Injurer chooses a level of care x (at a cost of s per unit) with which to pursue an exogenously fixed level of his activity. Simultaneously, Victim chooses a level of care y (at a cost of r per unit) with which to pursue an exogenously fixed level of her activity. Given the choices of care levels x and y of Injurer and Victim (and the exogenously fixed levels of the two activities), a loss A may occur with probability $p(x, y)$. The legal policymaker seeks to regulate the agents' choices of care levels.[8]

The legal policymaker selects a legal rule from some family of permissible rules. The legal rule determines who bears, as a function of the agent's choices x and y and of the legal policymaker's adoption of the standards of care X and Y, the loss A. Brown focuses on the class of negligence with contributory negligence rules which he characterizes as a two-parameter family of legal rules $L(x, y; X, Y)$ that assign the entire loss to one of the two parties according to a particular pattern of liability;

the parameters $X \geq 0$ and $Y \geq 0$ are interpreted as the injurer's and victim's standard of care, respectively, and $L(x, y; X, Y)$ is the proportion of the loss A born by the injurer:

$$L(x, y; X, Y) = \begin{cases} 1 & x < X \text{ and } y \geq Y \\ 0 & \text{otherwise.}^9 \end{cases}$$

For any given rule $L(x, y; X, Y)$, each agent who selects a *level* of care seeks to minimize his/her (expected) personal costs $Ap(x, y)L(x, y; X, Y) + sx$ for the injurer and $Ap(x, y)[1 - L(x, y; X, Y)] + ry$ for the victim (where s and r are the injurer's and victim's costs per unit care, respectively). Since the personal costs of each of these agents depends not only on his/her own choice of care level but also on the level of care chosen by the other party, for any given legal rule $L(x, y; X, Y)$, injurer and victim find themselves in a two-person, nonzero-sum game which Brown analyzes.

In the economic literature on accident law, the legal policymaker seeks to minimize the expected social costs of accidents: $sx + ry + Ap(x, y)$ by choosing $L(x, y; X, Y)$ from the family described above. To choose, the policymaker compares the equilibria of the games induced by various members of the family $L(x, y; X, Y)$ and chooses from among all possible pairs (X, Y), some pair (X^*, Y^*) which induces an equilibrium with the lowest costs.[10]

This description makes evident that the economic analysis of legal duties is an exercise in mechanism design in which a legal policymaker determines the game that economic agents play. The theory clearly rests on a directive conception of law because every model requires imputing some objective function to the policymaker. Similarly it clearly rests on an economic theory of behavior under law as the game induced by the policymaker is analyzed with the usual game theoretic assumptions and tools.

As exercises in mechanism design, these legal problems, at least as formulated thus far, are apparently quite simple. The models either explicitly assume that all agents are alike or do not attend to difficulties arising from a multiplicity of agent types.[11] The policymaker generally faces no incentive-compatibility constraints[12] or the need, as in reference [16], to conceal his/her own desires from the agents. Moreover, the information structure of the game played by the citizens is generally quite straightforward. The economic interest, if any, of these models of response to legal duty derives from "enforcement" features of the legal system that they attempt to capture.

In these models, two sorts of outcomes may be distinguished. Generally, the agents' payoffs are unmediated by any third party; they result "directly" from the agents' choice of actions and the realization of random variables. Occasionally, however, the mechanism contemplates that payoffs are mediated by a third party, often, though probably erroneously, assimilated to, the legal policymaker.[13] In the accident situation each party chooses a care level, and when no accident results, the payoff to each consists solely of his/her incurred costs of care. In the event of an accident, the payoff to the parties may require a (forced) transfer of income from the injurer to the victim. Even in the event that no forced transfer occurs, the models implicitly suggest both that a third party verifies the strategies chosen by the agents and that the agents may circumvent such vertification. The literature of the economic analysis of legal duties has focused on two aspects of this third party intervention. Some of the literature has considered the *timing* of the intervention, while other segments have examined the *triggering* of the intervention.

2.2. The Timing of Legal Intervention

Economic analysts of law have confronted two distinct issues of timing; unfortunately they have used the same terminological distinction between ex ante and ex post to describe each issue. In one context, ex ante and ex post refer to times before and after some relevant decision; the analysis examines the varying effects of the legal rule on behavior both before (and including) and after this decision point. Often, the crossover point has been identified with the initiation of legal proceedings; ex post analysis considered the effects of the legal rule on the negotiations of the parties before the court, while the ex ante analysis considered how the legal rule affected future parties' choices of the variable that determined liability. For example, in the accident context, ex ante effects refer to the impact of the legal rule on choices of activity and care levels, while ex post effects refer to the endowments set by the legal rule in the bargaining game of settlement/litigation. At least one commentator has identified (in reference [18]) this timing issue, formulated as the distinction between the legal rule's effects on the parties before the court and its effects on other parties' future behavior, as the core contribution of economic analysis to legal study.

The onset of legal proceedings does identify a crucial point in the analysis, but a more detailed breakdown of the sequence of events often proves useful. Thus, the decision node, the point in time at which the individual makes a particular decision, rather than the onset of legal proceedings is the relevant time point because, in many instances, the legal rule may influence various sequential decisions and the analyst may wish to distinguish among them. In contracts, for example, one might distinguish, among others, decisions to search, to form, to draft, and to perform.

In the second context, ex ante and ex post refer to times before and after the realization of some random variable. Often the distribution of the relevant random variable is determined by some decision of the agent and that decision is governed by some legal rule. Enforcement of the legal rule thus requires monitoring of the decision actually taken. As any such monitoring must occur subsequent to the decision itself, its timing as ex ante or ex post the realization of the random variable cannot directly influence the decisions agents actually take. In the accident context, the agent's choice of care level determines the distribution from which the dichotomous random variable accident/no-accident will be drawn. A driver's speed, for example, determines the likelihood of an accident; the state may choose to monitor that speed either before or after the realization of the accident/no-accident "variable." Most models of the common law study rules with ex post rather than ex ante monitoring. As in the example of accident law, the agents resort to the courts only in the contingent event that a loss occurs. The court then determines the levels of care that the agents had adopted and allocates the loss accordingly. Many legal rules, however, monitor the care levels ex ante, before it is known whether the agents' actions have had any adverse effects. The "rules of the road," for example, permit ex ante (i.e., prior to accident) monitoring of the care levels of the agents. Many health and safety regulations require monitoring of the safety provisions adopted regardless of whether an accident or ill health has resulted.

As has been suggested in reference [19], the choice between ex ante and ex post monitoring depends in part upon the relative costs of the two enforcement patterns. The costs of ex ante monitoring may differ from those of ex post monitoring in two ways. The costs of *policing* or the costs of *verification* may differ. Policing entails the observation of the event; thus, to police ex ante drivers' care levels requires one to observe the speed with which all (or some random sample of all) agents drive and the degree of attention they give to the task. To police ex post requires simply that one observe the accident. Ex ante policing thus seems more costly than ex post policing. Conversely, verification of ex ante violation of the rules follows almost immediately from their detection. Precisely those observations that permit detection serve to verify an infraction. Ex post, however, verification requires significant additional expenditures.

One must determine the causes of the event detected, and observing these events after they occurred presents complex problems of proof. Thus ex post verification costs exceed ex ante verification costs. The choice of regime turns on such complex issues.[14]

2.3   Triggering Legal Intervention or "Seeing Through" the Law

Within an interpretation of an economic model of the law, the "invocation" of the law may have two different senses. First, an agent might consider his/her options and decide that breaching his/her legal duty, with its concomitant costs, maximizes his/her personal welfare. Second, once a party has breached a duty, an entitlement holder who believes his/her right has been infringed might invoke the legal process to resolve the dispute.

Initially, the economic analysis of legal duties concentrated on this first sense of invoking the law. The analyses assumed that once an agent chose to breach his/her legal duty, he/she unquestionably bore the costs the law imposed. Thus, in the models of breach of contract [21, 22], an agent chooses to bear the costs of breach when and only when the legal sanction for breach is less than the benefit of nonperformance. With the appropriate choice of remedy the legal policymaker can then use contract law efficiently to complete otherwise incomplete contingent claims contracts.[15] Similarly, Brown's and subsequent models of accident law assume that, once an accident occurs, the party liable to bear the cost under the legal rule cannot avoid the burden.

Invocation of the legal system in the second sense raises a set of problems that has generally been investigated separately from the analysis of specific legal rules. Once an agent has breached a legal duty and a dispute has arisen, the parties face a bargaining game in which their endowments are fixed by the legal rule. This game need not be zero-sum for several reasons. Invocation of the legal system may be costly, and an aggrieved plaintiff may avoid these costs either by not filing suit or by settling outside of court (as, e.g., in reference [23]). Second, as in references [24, 25], a party may be unsure of his/her prospect of prevailing at trial because he/she is uncertain if the defendant has indeed violated his/her entitlement. Or, the parties may value different outcomes differently and the court-imposed outcome need not be, from the perspective of the agents, a Pareto-optimal one. The parties would benefit from bargaining in the shadow of the law. The legal rules then do not impose an outcome; rather they determine the bargaining game faced by the parties. For example, consider, as in reference [26], the disputes concerning the allocation of financial assets and custodial responsibilities that may arise upon the dissolution of a marriage. Suppose the legal rules governing the division of responsibility and property as "solomonic" in that they divide equally between the spouses both financial assets and child care. If the parties' preferences over these two "commodities" differ, there are bargains that each would prefer to the legally required outcome.

Such a bargaining game may arise under any legal rule policed with an ex post monitoring system. Often, models of doctrine ignore the bargaining problem in part by formulating the model to remove incentives for the agents to circumvent the courts. For example, in the accident law situation, one might, in the event of an accident, impose the cost A on both injurer and victim. Under this rule, or any rule in which the legal rule imposes costs of more than A on the two parties, injurer and victim have an incentive to evade the legal system, to settle out of court. By restricting attention to legal rules that impose costs of no more than A, the economic analysis excludes these problems.

The incentives to settle, however, greatly alter the incentive effects of the legal rules. If the injurer knows that, after an accident in which he/she has acted negligently, he/she need only pay $A/2$ in settlement, the injurer will choose ex ante a lower standard of care than if he/she has to pay A as required by law. In principle, then, the policymaker, in choosing a mechanism, must take into account the way in which the bargaining game created by the legal rule discounts the incentives.[16] Recent developments in bargaining theory [28, 29] should now permit this extension of economic analysis of law.

For example, consider the standard economic model of contract law. In the typical analysis, either the value v to the buyer of the contract is unknown at the time of formation or the cost c to the seller is unknown. After formation, the uncertainty is resolved and one party, contingent on the rule of law, may have an incentive to breach. Efficiency requires that breach occur when and only when $c > v$. For convenience assume that the cost c is uncertain at the time of formation, that both c and v are common knowledge at the time the seller decides whether to perform, and that the contract sets a price p. Then the standard analysis argues that, in this simple world, the rule of expectation damages, under which the buyer receives $v-p$ in the event that the seller fails to perform,[17] induces efficient breach. For the seller will perform as long as the benefits of performance $(p-c)$ exceed the costs of breach $(p-v)$; that is, he/she will perform precisely when and only when $v \geq c$. Two-sided uncertainty at the time of formation, i.e., ignorance of both c and v, should not disrupt this result as long as ex post, the realized values of c and v are common knowledge. Ex post negotiations play no role in this analysis of expectation damages. Indeed, the assumption of common knowledge of v and c assures that any damage measure will, if post-breach negotiations are possible, yield efficient performance.

Under asymmetric information, the possibility of ex post negotiations may affect the performance of expectation damages and other measures.[18] Suppose that, at the time of formation, buyer and seller know only the distributions of costs of production c and value of the ouput v to the buyer. After contract formation, which establishes a price p, the seller learns c and the buyer learns v. The seller, however, knows only the expected value Ev that the buyer realized, and the buyer knows only the expected cost Ec that the seller realized. Each must now decide, given the legal rule, whether to breach or not. In the event of breach, the parties may renegotiate their contract, but now they face a bargaining game of incomplete information. Consider the seller's decision whether to announce breach. He/she must compare the benefits of performance $p - c$ to the expected costs of nonperformance. If no renegotiation were possible, these expected costs of nonperformance would be $p - Ev$ and, since Ev is less than the largest possible buyer's value, the seller would sometimes announce breach when performance was desirable and we know, from reference [30], that some desirable contracts will not be performed.

The possibility or renegotiation, however, complicates this calculation of the expected costs of nonperformance. Successful renegotiation may yield an increased price to the seller; this prospect offers an incentive to overstate his realized cost c (or to announce breach when his costs are less than Ev) in an effort to increase his profits at the risk of paying damages more frequently. Moreover, each party might agree to perform even when nonperformance was desirable. Decreasing the measure of damages makes inefficient performance less likely, while increasing the damage measure makes inefficient nonperformance less likely. Expectation damages may not be the damage measure that most efficiently balances these various complications.

In all these economic models of legal phenomena the legal policy-maker is assumed to act only once, at the outset, when he/she chooses the game form that the agents will play. As applied to common law courts, this assumption may seem strikingly inapt as, in the process of case-by-case adjudication, the courts "make law." This perspective suggests that adjudication might present problems of consistency similar to those investigated in the planning literature [31]. Judicial practices, such as *stare decisis* in particular, and the rules of precedent more generally, might be conceived as aimed at binding the discretion of future policymakers and hence permitting the achievement of optimal plans. This mode of explication of precedent has not, to my knowledge, been pursued in the literature.

The introduction of renegotiation under asymmetric information promises to alter the standard conclusions concerning the efficiency of various rules of law. Analysis of these more elaborate models that admit noisy courts [32], asymmetric information [15], and costly courts offer a rich territory for further research.

3.   Law, Preference, and Motivation to Action

As elaborated thus far, the naive and economic theories of behavior under law apparently offer antithetical resolutions to one of the central dilemmas of legal philosophy: to what extent do legal rules provide reasons or motives for action? According to the naive theory, the embodiment of a directive in a legal rule offers an insurmountable reason and motive for action. One does as the law directs because the law authoritatively demands the specified act. In contrast, the economic theory denies that the mere embodiment of a directive in law offers *any* motive for action.[19] A legal rule may alter an agent's self-interested calculation, but this effect on the decision process no more constitutes a motive for action than the price of a product constitutes a motive for its purchase.

Despite these differences, at least two reasons suggest that the contrast between the two theories may be less extreme. First, because discussions of the law generally have relied only implicitly on the naive theory, its causal mechanisms have rarely been explicated. What I have termed the "naive" theory of behavior hence describes a class of different theories that might explain why agents conform their behavior to legal requirements. Second, the economic influences of legal rules on behavior currently modelled in economic analyses of law do not necessarily exhaust the range of actual phenomena that an economic model might capture.

This section has several goals. First, I seek to identify arguments for agents generally conforming their behavior to legal rules. Second, I suggest why the law, in both the economic analysis of legal duties and the property rights perspective, fails to serve as a motivation for action. This discussion is less explicit than I would desire because intuitions of "normative force" are inchoate and vague. The third portion of this section, offers three examples (or thought experiments) as tests of these intuitions. The section closes with a brief discussion of how some simple modifications of current economic models might attempt to capture the phenomena suggested by the examples.

3.1. Normative Force in the Naive Theory of Behavior

One may usefully distinguish two types of argument inherent in the naive theory. In one the legal rule serves as an informational *signal* to the agent who thus learns which action will best further his/her aims. In the second type of argument, the legal rule influences action not through altering the informational base on which the agent makes his/her decision but somehow through altering his/her desires or preferences.

Traffic laws exemplify the signaling aspects of legal rules. As a driver approaches a curve on a mountain road in an unfamiliar country, a sign posting the speed limit on that curve may inform him about safety conditions. If he takes the speed limit very seriously as an indicator, he will conform his conduct to that announced by the sign. More usually, a driver will consider the information in light of his knowledge of similar roads and own driving skill, and then adopt a speed that may or may not conform to the speed limit. This argument, then, does not fully support the naive theory as it is consistent as well with an economic theory under which some actors do and others do not obey the law. Further, posted speed limits might perform this informative role whether they were legal norms or not.[20] Any reliable agent, perhaps akin to consumer reports or underwriters laboratories, that posted safety information might work as well.

Occasionally, the signal serves a slightly different function. The traffic regulation that, in the United States, requires traffic on two-way streets to drive on the right *coordinates* the actions of all drivers. Here agents wish to follow one of possibly many feasible conventions, and the legal rule serves to identify the prevailing convention. This argument does in general imply that agents will conform their conduct to the rule.

In the above the legal rule serves as a signal to the agent that behavior conforming to the legal rule most furthers the direct purposes of his/her activity. In other contexts, an agent's nonconformity to the legal rule serves as a signal to *others* that he/she should be stigmatized or chastised.

This deviance theory of law supports the naive theory only if the costs of chastisement or stigmatization are sufficiently high to deter all potential violators of the law. Otherwise, the social and personal costs of stigmatization operate similarly to a judgment, fine, or other penalty, yielding a deterrence theory similar to that discussed in section 3.2 below.

Legal rules might also induce conforming behavior through preference "manipulation" in at least two ways. First, agents may have, among their preferences for wine, wealth, and song, a preference for conforming to norms. For example, even though not actively enforced, the New York City ordinance mandating that dog owners clean up after their dogs had a dramatic effect on dog-owners' behavior. The ordinance, through its clear articulation of the social norm, perhaps relied for its effect on the meta-desires of individuals to conform to norms. This assumption suggests a "natural" modification of the economic theory of behavior; the assumption is discussed further in section 3.4 below.

Second, the legal rule may influence directly the preferences that an individual has. When a legal rule requires X, individuals come to desire X itself and not simply to desire to do X because the law requires. Consider how a speed limit induces conforming behavior under this "hegemonic" view (discussed in reference [6]) of law's normative force. A driver adheres to a 55 mph limit not because he/she considers it a signal of safe driving or because he/she wants to be a law-abiding citizen but because he/she *wants* to drive 55 mph.

Each of these arguments for the naive theory of behavior fits easily into the fundamental decision-theoretic framework of economic theory in general and of an economic theory of legally induced behavior. If none of these arguments captures all of our intuitions of how legal rules provide reasons for action, abandonment or extension of that framework may be called for.

3.2.   *Normative Force in the Current Economic Theory of Behavior*

In the new economic analysis of law, agents act rationally in their own self-interest. Legal rules influence an agent's rational calculation but such influence can hardly be characterized as motivating his/her choices. A review of the ways in which legal rules influence choice in the various economic theories of behavior may clarify the somewhat obscure notions of motivation and reasons for action.

In the economic analysis of legal duties, an assignment of entitlement has, in the absence of transaction costs, no effect on behavior. It could thus hardly constitute a motive to act. Even in the presence of transaction costs the assignment of entitlement offers neither a reason to act nor a motivation. Behavior differs under the differing assignments of the entitlement not because of the law's directive but because, given the excessive costs incurred in contracting around the assignment, the agent considers the price placed by the entitlement protection on violation of the entitlement. A property rule differs from a liability rule *only* in that the price under the property rule should on average exceed the price under the liability rule (and perhaps in that negotiation may sometimes fail inefficiently under the property rule). On this account, the law carries no normative force; the manner in which a legal rule influences behavior does not differ from the manner in which a price or a threat influences behavior.

In the property rights perspective, the manner in which legal rules are bundled may affect behavior. The bundling, however, does not *direct* a specific action, and hence provides neither a direct *reason* nor direct *motive* for one action over another. Consider, for example, the exploitation of some communally held property such as a commons. Nothing in the formulation of the property right directs its holders to exploit the property in one manner in another. The property rights perspective contends that, nonetheless, the formulation of the right will induce inefficient exploitation.

The property rights perspective thus attributes an enabling rather than a motivating force to law in part because it generally focuses on secondary rules of empowerment rather than primary rules of behavior. The law of testamentary succession, for example, does not require any particular disposition of property. It thus has no normative force in the sense of the text.

3.3. Paradigms of Normative Force

Determining whether economic models can, with their "bare" conception of human psychology, capture the idea of law's normative force requires a clearer articulation of that concept. Unfortunately, legal discussions do not provide much guidance beyond H.L.A. Hart's distinction (in reference [27]) between the gunman's threat and the noncoercive force of the law. Several examples, however, may illuminate the lawyer's intuition about the normativity of law.

These examples rely upon a distinction among three aspects of a legal rule: its content which identifies the behavior required of the law-subjects; its protection (or sanction) which, in the examples, will be identified with the level of fine incurred for noncompliance; and its form or its legal classification as a civil or criminal statute, and, in the civil case, whether the payment goes to a private party or to the government as a tax or a civil fine.

The first example holds the legal sanction and the legal form constant while varying the content of the legal rule. If the law has normative force, this should yield different behaviors. Thus, compare 1) a legal regime in which the speed limit is set at 55 mph but all drivers know that no one driving less than 70 mph will be cited to 2) a legal regime in which the speed limit is 65 mph, but again all drivers know that no citations occur for speeds less than 70 mph. The fines and likelihoods of detection are identical under the two regimes. The economic theory of behavior under law predicts that we would observe, for a given population, the same distribution of driving speeds under the two legal regimes. Intuition suggests that the distribution under the 65 mph regime would stochastically dominate the distribution under the 55 mph regime; people would drive more slowly when the speed limit is lower.[21]

In the second example, the legal form varies while both the content and the sanction are held constant. Consider a typical nuisance case such as Coase's cow in the corn or flax by the tracks hypotheticals. Coase compares the behaviors induced by different assignments of the entitlement implicitly to those induced by a tax.[22] He might equally have compared them to those induced by criminal penalties or civil fines in which the amount paid were keyed, as in the liability rules, to actual damages done. Again the economic theory of behavior under law predicts no differences among the rules other than those attributable to differences in the mechanism of enforcement of these rules. The proof requirements for a criminal penalty, for example, may be more rigorous than for civil fines or for a civil damage suit. Civil damage suits are policed by those injured and hence may yield a higher probability of detection of violations than criminal or civil fines which are policed by the state. For inquiry into the normative force of law, one holds these proof requirements and enforcement patterns constant across legal forms. Under these ceteris paribus conditions, most people would probably infer that the criminal rules would induce more compliance than civil rules.

The third example responds to a peculiarly legal intuition. It compares changes in two legal regimes in which the costs imposed by the change is identical in each regime though the legal nature of the change differs. In regime A, the content of the rules is constant while the fine varies; in regime B, the fine remains constant and the content varies. Consider the following two histories of legal regimes.[23] In each the agent must adopt a technology at time 0 which would be extremely costly to alter at time 1. In each case, at time 1, though the costs of operation have risen, it is still more profitable for the agent to operate than to close down.

In regime A, at time 0, the EPA announces an emission standard X. The agent meets the standard. At time 1, EPA reduces the permissible level of emissions to X − 10. The agent is now in violation of the standard and hence subject to a fine of c. In regime B, EPA announces at time 0 an emission standard of X − 10 and a schedule of civil penalties of c/10 dollars per unit emitted above X − 10. The agent emits at a level X. At time 1, EPA raises the penalty to c/5 dollars per unit of emission above the standard X − 10. The agent maintains his emission levels at X; his total expenses increase, as under the alternative regime, by c.

Most lawyers, I think, regard these two histories slightly differently. Enforcement of the standard X − 10 in the first case has a tinge of unfairness. The agent conscientiously chose his technology at time 0 to meet the standard X. Alteration of the standard at time 1 unfairly imposes costs on him. In the second case, initial noncompliance makes the retroactive increase in penalties appear less onerous.

If, at both time 0 and time 1, the agent faced identical costs under each regime, then the choice of emission level X at time 0 was optimal regardless of regime. It is difficult to see in what way the two changes in regime differ. Perhaps the difference lies in the normative content we ascribe to the enunciation of the standard versus the less significant content attributed to the level at which penalties are set. On this account, the normative force of the negligence rules lies not in the measure of damages a tortfeasor would be required to pay but in the compliance or noncompliance with the enunciated standard.

3.4. Two Potential Economic Models of Normative Force

One might attempt to model the phenomena suggested by these examples with either of two simple modifications of conventional models of legal duties. In a "types-model," one might introduce two types of agents: law-abiding agents (proportion r of the population) who always conform to the law and Justice Holmes' "bad men" (proportion 1 − r of the population) who always act economically. Alternatively, one might, in a "preference-model," impute to each agent a preference for compliance with norms in addition to substantive preferences over acts (or consequences).[24]

Both models identify the source of the legal intuitions evoked by the EPA example. Under the types-model, regarding regime A as formally equivalent to regime B implies indifference to the labels of the agents as law-abiding or as bad men. In fact, we think the labels matter. The preference-model yields the same intuition in a somewhat muddier way. Those agents with sufficiently strong preferences to conform to the norm are treated identically to those with little or no preference for conformity. While this may seem unfair, the preference-model suggests that our intuitions might treat individuals on the border between obedience and disobedience radically differently even though their preferences for compliance differed only marginally.

In the Coase examples, the types-model yields the same result as the standard models of legal duties. After all, law-abiding citizens conform to the law regardless of its form while bad men attend only to the sanction. The types-model does alter the prediction of the speed limit example but not in a particularly plausible way. The bad men, of course, behave identically under the two legal regimes; when the law shifts, the law-abiding agents, however, may find it desirable to increase their speed from 55 to 65 mph (or any speed in between). If every agent would prefer driving at 65 to 55 mph, the two distributions would be the same, except for a shift in the mass point induced by the presence of the law-abiding. Intuition suggests a "smoother" shift. In both cases, the all-or-nothing quality of compliance of law-abiding limits the normative effects that the law might have.

The preference-model performs better than the types-model in the speed limit example. Different agents may have stronger or weaker preferences for compliance to norms, and hence they may respond to the lower speed limit with varying degrees of disobedience. Analogously, if one allows the preferences for compliance to have subtle shadings induced by the legal form, the preference-model might replicate the legal intuitions underlying the Coase example. In both cases, however, the introduction of preferences for norm-compliance is ad hoc.

More fundamentally, the preference-model does not capture our sense of the way in which legal norms influence underlying preferences or publicize the preferences agents *should* have. Consider some act X that the law wishes an individual to undertake. Suppose that, prior to the announcement of the legal rule, some individual considers the act X undersirable and would not voluntarily undertake it. One may distinguish two ways in which the announcement of a legal rule might induce this individual to undertake X. First, she might continue to regard X as undesirable but do it nonetheless because performance also meets the law's requirements. Alternatively, she might perform X because the announcement of the legal rule has induced a change in her underyling (substantive) preferences and she now finds X desirable. The latter explanation of altered substantive preferences suggests that a given legal rule may alter choices beyond those within the narrow ambit of the legal rule. One might attempt to model this educative aspect of legal rules by introducing second-order preferences, or preferences over substantive preference relations. One must then explain not only the relation between second- and first-order preferences but how legal rules influence the "choice" of first-order preferences.

4. Concluding Remarks

Much of the literature of economic analysis of law offers analyses of particular legal rules of doctrines. These have enriched and enlivened virtually every legal discipline, and the massive literature, which resists summary, certainly merits the attention of all serious legal scholars. Concentration on specific studies and particular legal doctrines, however, may obscure the major way in which economic analysis of law has altered our understanding of legal phenomena in general.

This essay has argued that the major innovation and contribution of economic analysis of law derives from its explicit attention to how legal rules influence behavior. In the economics of property rights, law influences the behavior of entitlement holders through the manner of bundling rights, privileges, and powers. By contrast, both the economic analyis of legal duties and the public choice perspective elaborate an economic theory of behavior in which the protection of entitlements act as prices faced by potential infringers of Hohfeldian rights. In the public choice perspective, however, agents may not only decide, as in the economics of legal duties, to conform or not to the legal rule but also may decide to attempt to alter the prevailing legal rule.

Close attention to the question of how legal rules influence behavior has illuminated traditional legal studies in a variety of ways. First, the differences between the analysis of legal duties and the public choice perspective calls into question an often-made assumption of the directive nature of law. The assumption of directiveness appears most blatantly in the structure of models of legal duty; they have the form of a policymaker choosing the legal rule that induces the games among agents that has, on the policymaker's view, the most desirable equilibrium. Second, attention to legally induced behavior redirects attention away from texts and the announcement of norms to the actual behaviors that agents adopt in the world. The gap between the behavior required by a legal rule and the behavior induced among agents presents problems, more alluded to than discussed, of evaluation of legal rules.

Finally, the last section of this essay attempts to extend the range of economic analysis of law to an important, traditional aspect of legal phenomena that the current economic models capture poorly if at all. The naive theory of behavior rests on some concept of law's normative force. Section 3 attempted to show how economic formulations might assist in making more precise the inchoate ideas about the normativity of law currently implicit in more traditional legal studies. In addition to clarifying ideas, this section suggests how the current economic models of property rights and legal duties might be extended to capture other ways in which the law influences behavior.

Notes

1.   A welter of terms describes various portions of the vast literature of economic analysis of law. The three strands of economic analysis of law discussed in the text may not exhaustively describe the endeavor, but I believe most of the literature can be sorted into these three categories. Some brief remarks on the relation of other descriptions of the literature to my terminology may be useful.

Occasionally, the term "the new law and economics" appears. Often it substitutes for the generic "economic analysis of law." Occasionally, it refers more specifically to the economic analysis of legal duties. Studies of transaction costs economics are significant for the economic analysis of both property rights and legal duties. Institutional law and economics may also cut across this classification. Finally, empirical studies may address the issues raised by any of these three paradigms.

2.   The distinction is crude because the set of decisions influenced by a legal rule varies with the legal rule and the conduct it seeks to regulate. Much of the insight provided by the economic analysis of legal duties derives from the illunination it offers of the decisions indirectly influenced by the legal rule.

3.   As noted earlier, in the economic analysis of legal duties, the legal rule may also influence various "primary" decisions such as the intensity with which a dutyholder engages in an activity or the level of reliance of a promisee.

4.   In references [5] and [6], I have used "instrumental" in lieu of "directive," but this prior terminology proved misleading because of the various different ways in which the term instrumental has been used.

5.   The text thus implicitly assumes that nondirective conceptions of law have no normative aspirations. Such a conception may explain how a society's law has arisen and where it may develop, but it offers no criteria against which to evaluate the legal system.

As some practitioners of the public choice perspective demonstrate, one may employ a nondirective conception of law normatively if one distinguishes between constitutional and nonconstitutional aspects of a legal system. That is, one may offer a nondirective conception of law to argue for the basic political and legal institutions in which individual self-interest will play out. To do this, the analyst must, of course, attribute some social goals or other normative views to the constitution drafter who chooses among nondirective legal regimes in much the same way that the legal policymaker chooses among legal rules.

6.   These two ideas, of directive vereus nondirective conceptions of Law and of a theory of behavior under law, clarify the relation of the "old" and "new" economic analysis of law. Prior to the 1960s, of course, various legal scholars used economics. These uses, however, were restricted to areas of law, such as antitrust and regulated industries, in which economics seemed somehow central. The centrality of economics lay in the dual assumptions of a directive conception of law and that the social goal of the legal area was the promotion of efficiency. Moreover, the legal scholar generally adopted a naive theory of behavior under law in which one assumes that those subject to the laws follow them.

7.   The link between texts and action postulated by law and economics is, in fact, rather weak. The empirical literature in economic analysis of law is slight but growing. More problematic, at least for a directive conception of law, adjudication rarely provides the judge with sufficient information with which to make an informed choice about the consequences of different legal rules. Nor are judges trained to make such choices well.

These observations have led some to conclude that economic analysis of law, as traditional legal scholarship is, is concerned with texts only and that the "language of economics" provides a useful medium in which to express doctrinal coherence that would not otherwise be apparent. Cento Veljanovski [10–12, citing 13 as origin of the claim] has offered the fullest and most compelling expression of this understanding of the new economic analysis of law.

I have some difficulty understanding this enterprise. Veljanovski contends that an economic theory of doctrine need bear no relation either to the effects the legal rule actually has or to the (conscious) reasons judges have in reaching their decisions. As I interpret Veljanovski, an economic theory of doctrine should thus be understood as a reconstruction of the world view implicit in the case law. Veljanovski offers the interesting example of the nineteenth century law of employer liability. Veljanovski offers an economic theory of how labor markets function that renders this body of law choerent, though he admits that this underlying theory was demonstrably false at the time.

What does this exercise of rationalizing doctrine with economic theories, possibly (or probably) false, explain? It may be an exercise in sociology of law; if we impute this false theory to judges and understand this theory to motivate their decisions, then it would explain how the beliefs of judges influenced outcomes. Alternatively, one might view the exercise as a critical one; one identifies the economic theory underlying the decisions and, if that theory is false, one argues that the doctrine should be changed. This latter understanding of the endeavor relies, of course, on both the directive conception of law and the economic theory of behavior under law.

8.   In a more complex model, the policymaker might seek to regulate the agents' choices of both care and activity levels. Though this complexity presents the policymaker with a more difficult set of comparisons to make, the form of the analysis does not change in principle.

9.   This formulation of the class of negligence with contributory negligence rules encompasses both "pure" negligence and strict liability. For pure negligence set $Y = 0$, for strict liability set $Y = 0$ and $X = $ infinity. Strict liability with contributory negligence sets $X = $ infinity and $Y > 0$. Strict liability with dual contributory negligence, also considered by Brown, has a different pattern of liability defined by:

$$L(x, y; X, Y) = \begin{cases} 1 & x < X \ or \ y \geqslant Y \\ 0 & \text{otherwise.} \end{cases}$$

The formulation in the text also excludes comparative negligence and precaution rules which permit dividing the loss between injurer and victim.

10.   In fact, for $p(x, y)$ strictly convex, there are an infinite number of pairs of standards of care (X, Y) that will induce the parties to choose the social cost-minimizing levels of care of (x^*, y^*). For example, if $X = x^*$, then any Y in $[0, y^*]$ will induce the parties to adopt levels of care x^* and y^*. Discussion, however, has generally focused on $(X^*, Y^*) = (x^*, y^*)$.

11.   The analyses of accident law almost universally assume that agents are identical. In the analyses of measures of contract damages, complications in evaluating the performance of various rules are eliminated by focusing on the decision to breach of risk-neutral agents. Agents may differ in terms of the distribution of possible production costs (or arrivals of higher valuing buyers) and in terms of the benefits of reliance. Characterizing agents by degree of risk-aversion or analyzing the effects of the rules on decisions to form would enrich the design problem.

12.   This problem disappears because the liability rule allocates A between the parties such that each party bears no more than A and the total loss allocated is A. If, in the event of an accident, injurer and victim each bore a cost A, then they would have an incentive not to report the accident.

13.   Reference [17] illustrates the inslights to be gained from separation of the interests and actions of the third-party enforcer from the legal policymaker.

14.   The analysis of the choice between ex ante and ex post monitoring includes the investigation of enforcement practices that have focused on the tradeoffs between the size of the fine and the probability of detection. The initial models followed Becker [20] in analysing enforcement problems basically as single-agent decision problems in which a rational actor chooses to commit a crime or not given the probability of detection and the penalty if caught. More recent formulations conform more closely to the choice of game analysis of common law rules. Graetz, Reiganum, and Wilde [17] analyze a game between the IRS (the enforcement agency) and the potential criminal (the taxpayer). They take the penalty level and the enforcement agency budget as given by Congress and solve the game for the equilibrium probability of detection. A legal policymaker, of course, would then choose penalties and budgets to maximize its objective function given the equilibrium outcomes.

In investigating the choice between ex ante and ex post monitoring, one seeks to determine the optimal ex ante levels of fine and detection and the optimal ex post levels of fine and detection.

15.   This simple attitude toward "law" differs significantly from that of a typical economic model which assumes a "frictionless" legal system. The contingent claims contracts of general equilibrium analysis, for example, *cannot* be breached. If one agrees to do X, one must in fact do X.

16.   On this account, all economic models of legal rules are three-stage games in which, first, the policymaker chooses a legal rule; second, the agents choose actions of some sort; and third, if the agents' choices engender a dispute, the agents play a bargaining game.

In fact, some legal institutions create games more complex that this. An important difference exists between primary rules such as those of tort law and secondary rules of empowerment such as the rules of contract law. The rules of empowerment add another stage to the game. Two individuals must first decide whether to avail themselves of the rules. For example, in the contract law case, the individuals must first decide whether to contract at all. If they choose to contract, each must then decide whether to perform. These performance decisions may conflict and engender the bargaining game.

On the distinction between primary and secondary rules, see reference [27].

17. This measure of expectation damages implicitly assumes that the value to the buyer of nonperformance is 0.

18. The following discussion is informal only; Peter Cramton and I are attempting to model more rigorously the heuristic argument of the text.

19. The relation of reasons and motives for action is highly controversial. See, for example, reference [33].

20. Indeed, a little reflection on this simple, traffic regulation example reveals how complex the difficulties in disentangling the effects of a legal rule on behavior may be. A posted speed limit gives some information on the safety of the road. The conduct of other drivers provides additional and perhaps different information to an uninformed driver.

21. One might explain the discrepancy in distributions as due to imperfect information on the part of drivers. That is, some drivers might regard the speed limit as a signal about the safety of particular road conditions so that changing the legal regime changes their beliefs about the costs of their conduct.

I am unsure how to evaluate this suggestion. Certainly, on unfamiliar mountain roads, a sign specifying 30 mph for the next curve carries different information than one specifying 20 mph, and we would expect drivers to respond differently even though the structure of legal penalties was the same. The two hypothetical legal regimes, however, apply to all interstate highways in the jurisdiction, and we might imagine that all drivers have experience with the roads. The intuition of the text still, I think, holds.

On the other hand, drivers may have a very poor idea of the relative risks of accidents at varying speeds. Perhaps the speed limit does serve to alter however slightly and inchoately their beliefs about these risks. Moreover, one might mean by a claim that the law has normative force precisely that the law modifies beliefs though one should distinguish beliefs from values (or preferences).

22. In fact, the behaviors induced are not quite identical. The tax creates a game with multiple equilibria, only one of which is efficient. On this point see reference [34].

23. The "legal intuition" that these two legal regimes should be treated differently was articulated by Judge Friendly in, for example, reference [35], NLRB v. Majestic Weaving Co. 355 F. 2d 854, 860 (1966).

This example arose in discussions with Richard Revesz who graciously supplied the citation.

24. A third modification might impute to agents a preference for a high reputation in their community and tie reputational level to adherence to the norm. Akerlof, in reference [36], offers a model of custom along these lines. In it, reputation depends on compliance and the percentage of people who believe in, as opposed to conform to, the norm. Belief in the norm varies over time, however, as a function of prior compliance. This formulation of the model merges the two suggestions of the text in that it postulates two types of agents— believes and nonbelievers—and that believing, but nonconforming, agents suffer a disutility.

This modification is open to an additional criticism. The disutility suffered varies with the extent of compliance to the required conduct within the population.

References

1. Coase, Ronald, "The Problem of Social Cost," *Journal of Law and Economics*, Vol. 3, No. 1 (October 1960), pp. 1–44 (appearing in 1962).

2. Calabresi, Guido, "Some Thoughts on Risk Distribution and the Law of

Torts," *Yale Law Journal*, Vol. 70, No.4 (March 1961), pp. 499–553.
3. Calabresi, Guido, and Melamed, A. Douglas, "Property Rules, Liability Rules, and Inalienability: One View of the Cathedral," *Harvard Law Review*, Vol. 85, No. 6 (April 1972), pp. 1089–1128.
4. Hohfeld, Wesley N., "'Some Fundamental Legal Conceptions as Applied in Judicial Reasoning," *Yale Law Journal*, Vol. 23, No. 1 (November 1914), pp. 16–59.
5. Kornhauser, Lewis A., "L'Analyze Economique du Droit," *La Revue de Synthese* IIIe Serie, Nos. 118–119 (avril-septembre 1985), pp. 313–329, appearing in English, as "Economic Analysis of Law," *Materiali per una storia della cultura giuridica*, Vol. 16, No. 1 (guigno 1986), pp. 233–247.
6. Kornhauser, Lewis A., "The Great Image of Authority," *Stanford Law Review*, Vol. 36, Nos. 1–2 (January 1984), pp. 349–389.
7. Posner, Richard A., "Economics, Politics, and the Reading of Statutes and the Constitution," *University of Chicago Law Review*, Vol. 49, No. 2 (Spring 1982), pp. 263–291.
8. Posner, Richard A., "Statutory Interpretation in the Classroom and in the Courtroom," *University of Chicago Law Review*, Vol. 50, No. 2 (Spring 1983), pp. 800-822.
9. Dworkin, Ronald, *Law's Empire* (Cambridge: Harvard University Press, 1980).
10. Veljanovski, Cento, "Economic Theorizing About Tort," *Current Legal Problems*, Vol. 38 (1985), 117–140.
11. Veljanovski, Cento, "Legal Theory, Economic Analysis and the Law of Torts," pp. 215–237 in Twining, William (ed.), *Legal Theory and Common Law* (Oxford: Basil Blackwell Publishers, 1984).
12. Veljanovski, Cento, "The Role of Economics in the Common Law," *Research in Law and Economics*, Vol. 7 (1985), pp. 41–64. (1985).
13. Leff, Arthur, "Some Realism about Nominalism, *Virginia Law Review*, Vol. 60, No. 3 (March 1974), pp. 451–492.
14. Brown, John P., "Toward an Economic Theory of Accident Law," *Journal of Legal Studies*, Vol. 2, No. 2 (June 1973), pp. 323–349.
15. Shavell, Steven, *Economic Analysis of Accident Law* (Cambridge: Harvard University Press, 1987).
16. Myerson, Roger B., "Mechanism Design by an Informed Principal," *Econometrica*, Vol. 51, No. 6 (November 1983), pp. 1767–1797.
17. Graetz, Michael J., Reiganum, Jennifer F., and Wilde, Louis L., "The Tax Compliance Game: Toward an Interactive Theory of Law Enforcement," *Journal of Law, Economics, & Organization*, Vol. 2, No. 1 (Spring, 1986), pp. 1–32.
18. Ackerman, Bruce, *Reconstructing American Law* (New Haven: Yale University Press, 1984).
19. Wittman, Donald, "Prior Regulation versus Post Liability: The Choice between Input and Output Monitoring," *Journal of Legal Studies*, Vol. 6, No. 1 (January 1977), pp. 193–211.

20. Becker, Gary, "Crime and Punishment: An Economic Approach," *Journal of Political Economy*, Vol. 76, No. 2 (March/April 1968), pp. 169–217.
21. Shavell, Steven, "Damage Measures of Breach of Contract," *Bell Journal of Economics*, Vol. 11 No. 2 (Autumn 1980), pp. 460–490.
22. Kornhauser, Lewis A., "An Introduction to the Economic Analysis of Contract Remedies," *University of Colorado Law Review*, Vol. 57, No. 4 (Summer 1986), pp. 683–725.
23. Shavell, Steven, "Suit, Settlement, and Trial: A Theoretical Analysis under Alternative Methods for the Allocation of Legal Costs," *Journal of Legal Studies*, Vol. 11, No. 1 (January 1982), pp. 55–81.
24. Bebchuck, Lucian A., "Litigation and Settlement under Imperfect Information," *Rand Journal of Economics*, Vol 15, No. 3 (Autumn 1984), pp. 404–415.
25. P'ng, Ivan P. L., "Strategic Behavior in Suit, Settlement, and Trial," *Bell Journal of Economics*, Vol. 14, No. 2 (Autumn 1982), pp. 539–550.
26. Mnookin, Robert and Kornhauser, Lewis A., "Bargaining in the Shadow of the Law: The Case of Divorce," *Yale Law Journal*, Vol. 88, No. 5 (April 1979), pp. 950–997.
27. Hart, H. L. A., *The Concept of Law* (Oxford: Oxford University Press, 1961).
28. Rubinstein, Ariel, "Perfect Equilibrium in a Bargaining Model," *Econometrica*, Vol. 50, No. 1 (January 1982), pp. 97–109.
29. Samuelson, William, "A Comment on the Coase Theorem," pp. 321–339 in Roth, Alvin E. (ed.), *Game-Theoretic Models of Bargaining* (Cambridge: Cambridge University Press, 1985).
30. Myerson, Roger B., and Satterthwaite, Mark A., "Efficient Mechanisms for Bilateral Trading," *Journal of Economic Theory*, Vol. 29, No. 2 (April 1983), pp. 265–81.
31. Kydland, Finn E., and Prescott, Edward C., "Rules Rather than Discretion: The Inconsistency of Optimal Plans," *Journal of Political Economy*, Vol. 85, No. 3 (June 1977), pp. 473–491.
32. Craswell, Richard, and Calfee, John E., "Deterrence and Uncertain Legal Standards," *Journal of Law, Economics, & Organization*, Vol. 2., No. 2 (Fall 1986), pp. 279–303.
33. Darwall, Stephen, *Impartial Reason* (Ithaca: Cornell University Press, 1983).
34. Cooter, Robert, "The Cost of Coase," *Journal of Legal Studies*, Vol. 11, No. 1 (January 1982), pp. 1–33.
35. *NLRB* v. *Majestic Weaving Co.* 355 F.2d 854, 860 (1966).
36. Akerlof, George, "A Theory of Social Custom," *Quarterly Journal of Economics*, Vol. 94, No. 3 (June 1980), pp. 749–75, reprinted in Akerlof, George, *An Economic Theorist's Book of Tales* (Cambridge: Cambridge University Press, 1984).

3 LAW AND ECONOMICS: AN INSTITUTIONAL PERSPECTIVE

A. Allan Schmid

The study of law and economics has as its goal the identification of the instrumental variables and the fundamental issues and processes in the operation of legal institutions of economic significance. This has been an interest of classical political economy since its inception. The contemporary institutional approach has its roots in the work of such economists as Henry Carter Adams on economics and jurisprudence [1], Richard T. Ely on the role of property and contract in the distribution of wealth [2], and John R. Commons on the legal foundations of capitalism [3]. It can also be found in work of such legal scholars as Walton Hamilton [4], Karl Llewellyn [5], Jerome Frank [6], and Roscoe Pound. [7] These scholars constitute a tradition focusing on the interrelation between the processes of the state and the economy, rather than simply an application of economics to law.

The purpose of this chapter is to integrate a system of ideas for the

Thanks to Warren Samuels, James Shaffer, and Terrence Daintith for a critical review of this chapter. A version of this chapter was presented as the Parsons' Lecture at the University of Wisconsin, May 1986.

study of the legal-economic nexus which has exhibited vigor and wide use traversing any one school of thought and thus has promise for even wider application in the future. I have chosen the term *institutional approach* to demonstrate a continuity and evolution rather than to insist on a precise boundary of a school of thought [8]. I do not mean to suggest that everyone who uses these ideas is an institutionalist or that anyone who doesn't subscribe to all of them can't use the title.

Some studies of law and economics specialize in a particular kind of property right, but the subject here includes both private and public law, tort and contract, common and statutory law, and civil rights or what might be called the rules for making rules. It includes market, administrative, and status-grant transactions. Commons defined property rights or institutions as "collective action in control, liberation, and expansion of individual action" [9]. Contemporary scholars such as Eirik Furubotn and Svetozar Pejovich are complimentary when they say "property rights are the sanctioned behavioral relations among men" [10]. My own Hohfeldian definition emphasizes the sets of ordered relationships among people that define their rights, exposure to the rights of others, privileges, and responsibilities [11].

1. Types of Theory

Several types of institutional theories will be distinguished: evolutionary, impact, and welfare [12]. It is also useful to distinguish theories of behavior versus theories of advantage and to note the place of institutional analysis in a more general policy analysis. Institutional analysis is a complementary good for much law and economics, at the same time that it is a substitute or antidote for some inadequate theory.

Evolutionary theory is long run and involves learning, while impact theory is short run where the human response to incentives is fixed and only the amount and kind of incentive are altered. In evolutionary theory, institutions are both independent and dependent variables [13]. It involves such tensions as that between continuity and change. This theory is practiced by many who teach comparative systems but who do not see themselves as members of any school [14].

Many theories of institutional change are theories of advantage; they explain institutional change by reference to wealth maximization and changing profitability generated by changing tastes or technology which may or not be endogenous to the model [15]. It is easy to slip from this to welfare economics, legitimating certain paths of institutional change and condemning others. This is not the approach to be discussed here.

Impact theory is concerned with predicting the likely substantive performance of alternative proposed institutions. In comparing institutional alternatives, the theory asks which one causes the most change in selected performance variables of interest to a given group. It is not concerned with whether this change is better in any global sense, nor is it concerned with predicting what institutions are coming next. However, if we believe that intelligence guides choice of institutions, then the product of impact theories will eventually affect the evolutionary path of change. This is the link between impact and evolutionary theories.

Welfare theory is not concerned with predicting anything substantive. That is its beauty, since nothing that happens can directly and conclusively challenge its deductions as to what is better to do. A broader definition of welfare economics refers to a framework that determines the analytic questions to be asked. The framework of the institutional approach will be outlined below. Each of the three types of institutional theory will be illustrated in detail below after noting some of the concepts that institutionalists have used which are common to all types of theory. For another but overlapping list, see Kenneth Parsons [16].

2. Themes of Institutional Analysis

No single chapter could capture all of the themes and theoretical constructs of the institutional approach. While each of the three types of theory emphasizes different concepts, a sample of themes useful in all three types of theory will be noted.

2.1. Economy as a Universe of Human Relations (Not Just a Universe of Commodities)

Property rights are a relation of one person to another (rather than a person-thing relationship). This conception is fundamental to develop both evolutionary and impact theories as well as to critique a value-presumptive welfare economics.

2.2. Transactions as the Unit of Analysis

Establishment and transfer of legal control is central. Movement across a technological interface is secondary. This is a complement to seeing the economy as a universe of human relations. Wesley Hohfeld's [17] conception of jural correlatives on both sides of a transaction insists that when interests conflict, one person's opportunities are another's limits and obligations [18]. The state is a participant in every transaction.

2.3. Search for the Instrumental Limiting Factors

This search is at the heart of a pragmatic methodology. It is a search for the limiting factor to achieve a given objective and not for the efficient factor or the factor restoring equilibrium. Efficiency is a derivative of the choice of rights and not a guide to these rights. The focus on instrumentalities contrasts this approach to some Marxian views which point to the inevitable.

2.4. Contract and Hierarchy—Boundaries

Scholars have used a number of conceptions to distinguish different types of transactions. Commons [19] contrasted bargained, managerial, and rationing transactins, which has been evolved by many such as Karl Polanyi [20], Robert Heilbroner [21], Kenneth Boulding [22], and Robert Solo [23]. The different types of transactions come together in the going concern with its working rules and standard operating procedures. The scope and definition of the firm has been of interest to economists of all schools. The consequences of the mix of bargained contract compared with managerial or hierarchical transactions has been explored by many including Ronald Coase [24], Oliver Williamson [25], Terrence Daintith [26], and Gunther Teubner [27]. They hypothesize that the firm's boundaries (choice of type of transaction) are determined by transaction costs. In this conception there is no issue of power. Each party chooses what is best for him/her and can bargain over the mutual gains. There is another perspective to be explored below.

2.5. Recognizing Conflict and Issues of Power

If one doesn't presume some natural harmony, one is led to the question of what right makes whose will effective. Failure to understand this theme leads to a lot of confusion where the only conflict is seen to be that of driving a hard bargain rather than the question of what one has to bargain with. Out of conflict comes the chosen order with its rules, opportunities, and exposures—or it brings war and the current near-wars with which we are so familiar.

Externalities are seen as the ubiquitous substance of human inter-dependence [28]. Externalities can be shifted by choice of law, not abolished. Law is the instrument of securing gains and losses (who can create externalities for whom). Government is an arena of power play and an object of legal control. Law is something made, not discovered. Law is the result of the resolution of social conflicts and not some deduction from universal principles that rational people accept. This theme runs from the earlier schools of institutional economics and legal realism to today's critical legal studies movement [29].

If conflict is recognized, it is not surprising that bureaucrats and private agents pursue their own interests and not necessarily the preferences of their principals. The big question for rights is who gets defined as the principal. Often the agent pursues the interests of some other would-be principal as well as him/herself.

2.6. Importance of Collective Action

Collective action is the instrument to increase someone's power over nature as well as the instrument of someone's power over other people. Markets depend on some prior agreement on the assignment of rights. Calculations of efficiency rest on a noneconomic foundation [30]. There is no such thing as a free market in the sense that its outcome is independent of collective choice of rights. The conflicting freedoms of the parties are always channeled and constrained.

2.7. Uncertainty and Expectations

The costs of uncertainty are one of the major facts of life which must be accounted for in the prediction of the effects of institutional change. Some degree of security of expectations as to the acts of others seems necessary. The institutions of credit and debt instruments are fundamental.

2.8. Evolutionary Interrelation of Economy, Polity, and Technology

Analysis stresses evolutionary change rather than equilibrium. This is more relevant to evolutionary theory than impact analysis. The concern is not only with resource allocation given the technology but with how institutions affect technological change and adaptation [31]. History is important in the process of cumulative causation [32].

Most models of law and economics contain variables relating to human behavior, the character of the good, and the instrumental character of the law. In the institutional view these can be summarized by saying that people matter, the specific goods and their situation matter, and the detail of the law matters.

2.9. People Matter

The generalization of utility maximization is not very helpful. This must be given specific content. Observation is necessary to determine how the content of what is perceived as producing utility differs among individuals [33]. For example, it might appear that people could maximize their utility by being freeriders with respect to high exclusion cost goods. But if some people derive satisfaction from participation in providing a good separate from its actual provision, then free ridership would not maximize their utility. Such people may still be said to maximize utility, but such a characterization does not help predict their behavior unless the content of their utility is known. The concept of bounded rationality and the uncertainty of relating activity in the future to utility is part of this content.

Prediction of behavior associated with legal change will go wrong unless the analyst can account for forbearance. Not using one's opportunities may be due to altruism or lack of knowledge.

Particularly important for evolutionary analysis is the role of rights in defining areas for creative choice by people. The universe-of-commodities perspective misses the fact that the marginal value product of labor is affected by people's sense of participation and fairness.

Law both reflects and shapes preferences. Guido Calabresi [34] observes the "law, unlike economics, is not concerned only, or even primarily, with reduction of cost, 'given tastes.' It is fundamentally concerned with shaping tastes." He then cautions, "We must be on guard that those allocations which lesson short run costs by reducing moralisms or offense do not mindlessly lead us, in the long run, to tastes and values which today we would find appalling." Institutional economics shares this perspective.

This approach emphasizes learning and socialization. One of the tensions in this field is what kind of psychological models to employ. Some would dispense with the whole notion of maximization of preferences and look at the process of learning and reinforcement of behavior. In this view there is no preexisting preference map that interacts with a new set of prices affected by law. Preferences are formed in the act of choosing and negotiation with legal equals and superiors. This is consistent with the view that other people are not just the objects of contract but are subjects for the learning of values [35].

2.10. Goods Matter

Different kinds of goods cause different kinds of human interdependence or opportunities for one person to affect another. The same law or type of transaction applied to different kinds of goods causes different performances.

2.11. Legal Detail Matters

If law is an instrument of power to apportion opportunities and their correlative exposures, then adequate description of the legal variable is critical. Highly abstract dichotomies are likely to produce inconclusive predictions. Because the characteristics of goods create many different types of interdependence, kinds of rights that control this interdependence are also necessarily complex. Pure competition and factor ownership do not control all sources of interdepence. Money income is an inadequate way to describe endowments. Richard Posner makes a good point when he says that knowledge of the law distinguishes law and economics as a field of study [36].

2.12. Methodology

Central to the methodology of an institutional approach is the observation that most economic activity takes place in groups. People make their living in a number of overlapping going concerns—family, church, club, union, corporation, nation—whose essence is their working rules or standard operating procedures, some of which are formed internally (private governance) and some externally. So while individuals are acting, the focus is the holistic going concern with its rules and negotiations. The models employed are never counterfactual. Comparisons are made between real, discrete, institutional alternatives. Concern is with identification of legal instrumentalities (limiting factor) and substantive performance measured in terms of real goods and human states such as income and its distribution, employment rates, disease rates, etc., and not whether the result can be termed efficient, productive, or marked by freedom. One rule is better than another in its effectiveness in furthering a given interest. Qualitative and directional predictions are sought [37].

3. Evolutionary Theory

Institutional analysis will be more coherent if the research agenda of evolutionary theory is distinguished from other types of theory. To add to what has already been said, several propositions of evolutionary theory are discussed.

1. *Rights have their origin in the settlement of disputes stemming from conflicts of interest.* The mandated behavior, when repeated over time, becomes habitual and is experienced as voluntary and natural. Nevertheless, new conflicts arise from many sources including technological change, resource discoveries and depletions, ideological learning, and unintended effects of past institutional change. Groups struggling for power are both trying to change the rules for making rules as well as working within the current political rules to change rights as they apply to the economy.

2. *People are uncertain as to the effect of any proposed institutional change and the ability of any political representative to serve their interest.* In turn, politicians are uncertain how to maximize voter support. In this context Randall Bartlett hypothesizes, "To the extent that interested parties can alter the relative prices of information favorable and unfavorable to their desired end, they can influence this acquisition and with it the outcome of the decision" [38].

3. *Intangible property is exposed in a market economy.* Pecuniary diseconomies hurt as much as any physical trespasser or thief and require different kinds of rights to control them. Property rights cannot be fully described only with reference to control of physical things, such as in the law of trespass and liability. Commons [39] studied the evolution of shoemakers from itinerant to factory worker over a period of 250 years. In the era of custom work, the shoemaker performed every function, and the only competitive threat was inferior products that undersold the price received for the traditional high quality product because consumers could not always distinguish quality. Later, as the market widened, the worker lost control of determining quality and was exposed to receiving wages equivalent to what the marginal worker would accept in distant markets. The consumer surplus was captured by employers and merchants. The

shoemakers organized protective associations, and the courts had to affirm or deny their power.

One is reminded of today's issues of the menace of foreign competition. Shoemakers and many industrial workers are protectionist, while those service occupations not subject to foreign competition favor the downward pressure on industrial wages engendered by foreign competition. Commons describes the process in a nonpresumptive manner avoiding terms like *exploitation*, simply noting the conflict of interests and the legal instruments involved. One of the lessons he drew from the experience was that institutions could change as a result of market extension without any change in technology.

4. *The marginal value product (MVP) of labor is not a given, but is influenced by institutions.* Parsons [40] argues that development has a lot to do with whether people feel that what they do can make a difference in their lives. How hard and creatively people work is not just a matter of fear of lower wages and the transaction cost of supervision to prevent slacking. It depends on what Commons called willing participation.

Lester Thurow [41] notes that the MVP and work stoppages are related to people's learned sense of the fairness of their wages relative to others. Instead of hypothesizing that people are paid according to their MVP, or noting institutional barriers thereto, Thurow turns it on its head and suggests that MVP depends on what people are paid. It is an evolutionary question as to how people form their concept of what is fair. It is an impact question as to whether a particular rights change, which would result in different relative wages, would today change MVP. A good example would be to ask, if women were given the right to comparable worth, how would it affect their productivity and the productivity of men? (And, of course, those rights would help determine what is to be regarded as productive.) Thurow observes that relatives wages of many occupations can't be explained by anything except that certain jobs have rights attached. Cost is not something naturally determined but institutionally determined. Commons invited us to shift our attention from costs to shares. A major institutional theme is that prices and allocations derive from more than references and production functions—power and collective choice must be noted.

5. *Experience with collective action builds trust which contributes to control of opportunistic behavior in the face of high exclusion costs.* Albert Hirschman [42] has observed that groups successful in obtaining a high exclusion cost good have had previous experience in collective action. Even if past attempts were unsuccessful, they increase the probability of future success. This is a good example of an evolutionary theory which involves learning.

6. *The economy and polity are interrelated and change is marked by evolution rather than movement to an equilibrium.* One illustration of this is known as the political business cycle [43]. Governments do not just compensate for the business cycle but contribute to it by manipulation of government spending and transfers prior to presidential elections.

7. *Rights related to the credit system are a major institutional theme.* Individual saving is much celebrated as the key to economic growth. But seeing credit as a system of property rights reveals than when banks are given the right to create money via new loans, there is a collective saving [44]. Nonborrowers find that they consume less as new money reallocates current consumption to investment. The individual piggy bank is not necessary in a system of fractional reserves. Commons and the famed institutional monetary theorist, Irving Fisher, went on to advocate zero interest public debt during periods of unemployment [45]. Roberto Unger [46] has suggested that government act as its own bank and make loans for purposes it wishes to further and then use the interest to finance other government expenditures.

8. *Institutional creativity and innovation are a hallmark of the institutionalist* [47]. This tradition did not stop with innovations in workmens' compensation, social security, or New Deal agricultural programs. Some modern examples are people like Joseph Sax [48] who created and got the Michigan legislature to adopt a citizen-suit law to stop environmental damage and Julian Levy [49] who did the same for enforcement of housing codes in Chicago. There are many lawyers and agricultural extension specialists who are practicing institutional analysis by helping groups design and implement collective action [50].

9. *Order and willing participation are a major social achievement.* Since conflict is inevitable, what can be said about maintaining participation and loyal opposition? When beliefs conflict, someone has to lose. Calabresi [51] offers this testable hypothesis: people can accept losing some of the time if they are told that their values are worthy of consideration but just did not prevail in the case at hand. If this is violated, he would predict violent and revolutionary behavior. This is a substantive prediction requiring knowledge of psychology beyond any notion of welfare maximization. With this prediction, Calabresi is critical of the Supreme Court reasoning in *Roe* v. *Wade*, 410 U.S. 113 (1973) where the court declared that the fetus is not a person and thus anti-abortionists had unreasonable beliefs and were outside of constitutional protection.

This is only a sample indicating the continuity of a body of ideas and theory of evolving institutions. There are many other scholars working on these and similar themes such as Richard Norgaard [52], Willard Hurst

[53], Bruno Frey [54], Dan Bromley [55], and Don Kanel [56], whether or not they see themselves as institutionalists.

4. Welfare Theory

Welfare theories are those from which the analyst deduces that one institution is globally better than another. Some economists speak of maximizing welfare and production and some lawyers speak of adhering to legal principles. The reader of the works of the founders of American institutional economics have reason to be confused, and conclude that institutionalists are confusing since Thorstein Veblen and Commons are so different in regard to welfare theory [57].

Veblen [58] and Clarence Ayres [59], while critical of neoclassical welfare economics, had a substitute. For the neo-Veblenians, see reference [60]. Veblen was quite willing to pronounce certain (in fact, most) contemporary institutions as bad. While he saw tools and social organization as an interrelated process [61], there is much to suggest that he saw a natural imperative in technology and the instinct of workmanship. If you got rid of ceremonial institutions, the good would win out. This has certain parallels with neoclassical theory which sees costs as natural phenomena rather than derivatives of rights. If technology and workmanship are natural, there is no need for chosen institutions to select among them or organize them. This sounds a lot like the Chicago school's insistence that if government were minimized, the good in mankind would jump out to the benefit of all. It is also similar to Mancur Olson's [62] idea that if there were no rent-seeking interest groups, there would be no productivity-inhibiting institutions and all would be nirvana. While my own values are sympathetic with many of Veblen's, it is hard to go from nature to values. The words "ceremonial" and "rent-seeking" remain little more than labels for what one doesn't like [63].

The Commons branch of institutional economics and scholars in the legal realism and critical legal studies tradition are quite different. To be sure, Commons was a reformer, but forthright. When he suggested workman's compensation and liability laws, he did not argue that it would increase global efficiency, but rather that it would achieve a certain substantive performance of fewer accidents. Law always selects what to be efficient about, and Commons wanted more output per worker, including injured workers in the denominator. Commons' view of reality and his research agenda were influenced by his social preferences, but he did not have a welfare economics that made a general argument for what is better to do on the basis of grand efficiency or freedom.

The continuity in this line of analysis from the classical institutionalists to contemporary scholars is illustrated by Calabresi's latest analysis of tort law. Earlier he argued that liability should be placed to minimize accident avoidance costs and thus maximize wealth. But in his 1985 work he argues that "who is the cheapest avoider of a cost, depends on the valuations put on acts, activities, and beliefs by the whole of our law and not on some objective or scientific notion" [64]. This is very much in the holistic tradition of institutional analysis. He continues by saying that "what is efficient, or passes a cost-benefit test, is not a 'scientific' notion separated from beliefs and attitudes, and always must respond to the question of who we wish to make richer or poorer."

Michael Carter's [65] discussion of yellow dog contracts also makes the point that costs are selected by law and not a determinant of law. The neoclassical analysis of labor contracts which allowed workers to be discharged for joining a union would defend them as Pareto-better trades. The contract would not have been made if both parties were not better off than before. Any change is seen as a welfare-decreasing restriction.

Commons proceeded differently. First, he did some evolutionary institutional economics by analyzing why the impact of the law of "exclusive holding for self" was different in an interdependent market economy than in self-sufficiency. Next, he was an open reformer with announced sympathy for workers. Then he had to expose the presumptiveness of the neoclassical analysis both as to how the law evolved and its correctness. As Carter puts it, "Commons was not preoccupied with the question of whether exchange was Pareto efficient. The more salient question...is, What determines the reservation utility" of the workers [66]. In other words, the issue is what one has to trade in the first place, and just because people trade, it does not mean that they voluntarily accept what they brought to the trade.

C. Edwin Baker argues, "Starting points are crucial, and policy use of economic criteria, unless one can describe and defend appropriate starting points, is often indeterminate and incoherent" [67]. Baker notes, "Pareto superiority is not at home in the context of making initial assignments." Care must be taken not to speak of re-assignment of rights (which accepts the starting place) when the issue is initial assignment.

Adam Smith had a great insight when he noted that voluntary exchange is mutually advantageous to the individuals in a transaction. But this can be misleading if we presume the question of rightful participation in the transaction. Overzealous interpretation of Smith leads to recommendations that the market be extended to every commodity and opportunity in the name of gains from trade. Inalienability is often the vehicle for some people's opportunities that cannot be served as well otherwise [68].

An argument for a given efficient solution (from among many) is also an argument for the interests to which its rights give effect. A claim for compensation is a claim to the legitimacy of a certain starting place (assignment of rights). Don't presume either a stance of willingness to pay or willingness to sell when that is the question to be decided. In Commons' words, a court's decision can be explained "not as a matter of logic but as a matter of beliefs and this belief is none other than the habitual wish of the judge who decides and who. . . can always find precedents and logic to back up what he wishes" [69]. The same point is made by David Kairys [70] when he says there is nothing within the law that determines which rationalization a judge should choose from in a particular situation.

A fundamental policy question is efficiency version one versus efficiency version two. It is presumptive of whose interests count to frame the issue as one of efficiency versus waste or the tradeoff between efficiency and equity. Some radical economists cast the argument in terms of exploitation and force. They would object to the neoclassicals' description of yellow dog contract as being a voluntary acceptance of the result. But since the essence of any right in the face of scarcity is that someone is forced, this argument cuts both ways. We can't label something as exploitative or not without an explicit value judgment of who in the particular case can force whom (i.e., who has what to sell and can "force" a bid from nonowners) [71].

Carter [72] goes on to offer a critique of Avishay Braverman and Joseph Stiglitz's [73] presumption of the legitimacy of certain sharecropper-landlord contracts as Pareto-efficient solutions to a high information cost situation. Similar analysis in other contexts is made by numerous scholars [74], Demolition of these presumptive neoclassical arguments should not be interpreted as proving that these sharecropper contracts were exploitative. Getting rid of one presumption should not give license to another. To recommend one right over another, analysts must take their stand as naked normativists without the comfort of the Pareto-better cloak or any other formalism [75].

If institutional analysis destroys the old welfare economics of Veblen, Marx, and the Kaldor-Hicks criterion, what will take its place? It is critical to understand that the destruction was not made to erect another presumption in its place. Indeed, the whole point is that global welfare maximization is meaningless. In the words of that eminent post-Keynesian, Joan Robinson, "there is no better 'ole to go to" [76]. The pragmatic naked normativist says, this is my moral judgment informed by reason and experience, but with no pretense of global maximization of anything.

This is increasingly the implication of what is becoming mainstream welfare economics which leaves behind counterfactual assumptions and instead reasons from a second-best real world. Robin Boadway and Neil Bruce say, "To obtain a measure of welfare change in many-consumer economies which serves to rank all alternatives, there appears to be no alternative but to employ a social welfare function. This, of course, was what the compensation test literature was trying to avoid" [77]. Boadway and Bruce demonstrate that the basic directional moral choices behind the social welfare function cannot be avoided. The social welfare function is shorthand for resolution of all of the sources of interdependence and conflict which institutional analysis ferrets out. The same theme is reflected in Robert Tresch who states that "recent work has made it painfully obvious just how hopelessly intertwined distributional and efficiency terms become in many second-best tax (and expenditure) decision rules" [78]. The mainstream is moving toward the formerly heterodox institutional analysis.

Unger observes that "real markets are never just machines for instantaneous transactions among economic agents equally knowledgeable and equally able to await the next offer or to withdraw from current courses of dealing. Continued success in market transactions shows partly in the buildup of advantages of power or knowledge that enable their beneficiaries to do much better in the next round of transactions" [79]. When shall these inequalities be corrected? One way the issue is joined is in the law of contract, and the definition of duress which can void a contract. Some argue that law can't establish a principle of duress without judging the terms of fairness of exchange. Labor law frequently states the principle of requiring good faith bargaining, but good faith can't be practically implemented without defining duress. A failure to negotiate may be because the other party has made an absurd demand or offer.

If society had agreed on the initial starting place (social welfare function), there could be no question of duress since each party is just using its rightful opportunities. But did the choosers of any particular set of rights anticipate cumulative causation over time? If they were capable of doing that, they should be capable of judging duress which requires a definition of fairness at a particular moment. Either both or neither can be done. A person who accepts (had judged) the fairness of the starting place for contract cannot then object that it is beyond human judgment (too subjective and messy) to determine if a contract has at any particular point in history been agreed to under duress and is therefore unenforceable.

Commons made it clear whose side he was on. But he wanted to get things done and not just be known as being on the right side by his friends. That made him a pragmatist in public policy. He needed to use knowledge to suggest a compromise among conflicting interests that had a good probability of being acceptable (workable). This is where evolutionary analysis is useful in suggesting continuity with past trends and identifying the best of existing practice. Pragmatic suggestions can be offered to the conflicting parties who may consider them without fear of being labeled irrational. Legal resolution is something to be created by the parties, not discovered by high priest analysts [80].

There is a tension among law and economics scholars at this point. While they agree that society, through political negotiation and learning, must fashion its compromises, they differ with respect to the necessity to state their own preferences for the good society. Some scholars in the institutional economics tradition such as Philip Klein [81] or the critical legal studies movement such as Unger [82] put forward their own personal vision, albeit still quite abstract and mostly procedural. Unger puts great value on the weakening of social hierarchies and the fixed order of society so that a person's life chances and experiences are freed and it is possible to overcome and revise every social or mental structure. This has to be negotiated with others, which involves a theory and practice of democracy. While these objectives might be embraced by many, one does not find such explicit arguments for one vision versus another in the work of many other leading institutional scholars (such as Warren Samuels) [83].

5. Institutional Impact Theory

Impact theory predicts the substantive consequences of institutional alternatives, i.e., who gets what. The notion of substantive performance is central to distinguish this theory from welfare economics. The results of alternative institutions (structures) are compared in such terms as changes in income and its distribution, rate of soil erosion, accident rates, etc., rather than in terms of such abstractions as efficiency or equilibrium. It is related to the Keynesian conception that equilibrium is possible at less than full employement. The level of employment is a substantive performance.

This theory is composed of a three-part sequence of situation, structure, and performance [84]. While there are many roots in neoclassical economics, industrial organization, and classical institutional studies, the main contemporary element is an explicit classification of the situational characteristics of goods that cause human interdependence, and a wider range of structural (legal) variables [85].

The situational categories include incompatible use, economies of scale, joint impact goods, high exclusion cost goods, high information cost goods, prisoners' dilemma, and surpluses (rents). While these concepts are familiar, to some they imply market failure and exceptions to deductive logic showing that competitive markets maximize global welfare. But here they are features of goods causing human interdependence which is given direction by law. The identification of legal instrumentalities depends on understanding the different sources of interdependence.

In evolutionary theory, these features are the dynamic result of social and technical change, but for impact analysis, they are given. They are inherent in the nature of goods and separate from the structural institutional alternatives being analyzed. The theory posits that if one understands what it is about a good that makes it possible for one person's acts to affect another, one can hypothesize how this is controlled by the institutional structure and thereby predict performance. It follows that the same structure will have different effects when combined with different situations. The utility of the situational classification is that if one understands how one member of a situational class performs when combined with a given type of structure, one has the basis for hypothesizing how another member of the class will perform with the same institution. This is what theory is for—namely, to make it possible to learn more from our experience.

Industrial organization studies are a type of impact analysis ranging from the classical studies of Adolf Berle and Gardener Means to the neoinstitutional work of Willard Mueller and Bruce Marion [86]. Classical studies in land economics that asked of the impact of alternative tenures on income and its distribution are impact analyses. These studies implicitly considered different characteristics of the resources being analyzed. Institutional impact theory would be more unified and we would learn more from it if these characteristics of goods were made more explicit. There is not space enough here to enumerate all of these situational variables, but a sample will be presented. This sample will include completed work and a yet-to-be-tested hypothesis for the future development of law and economics.

Structural variables include the mix of bargained, administrative, and grant transactions. In industrial organization, structure refers to competitive conditions, concentration, and barriers to entry. Here the relevant variables are much broader. Structure is a synonym for rights. Much theoretical work is still to be done to develop a meaningful classification of structural variables consistent with the observation above that legal detail matters.

5.1. Economies of Scale

Goods produced under economies of scale have always been given special attention in economics [87]. The term *natural monopolies* is applied to instances where the low point on the average cost curve is not reached for a single firm within the relevant range of demand. Multiple firms and competition result in duplicate facilities and increase total costs. But a single firm requires regulation to avoid monopoly pricing. Commons devoted much time to predicting the consequences of public utility regulation such as whether a franchise contract granted by a city was temporary or could be repurchased by the public and at what valuation. The modern industrial organization literature is concerned with alternative rights that control the tradeoffs between achieving economies of scale and the accompanying implications for economic and political power.

One aspect of the interdependence created by the situation of economies of scale is illustrated by the case of copyright structure applied to computer operating systems and applications software. Copyright has usually been a very limited grant of monopoly power. It gave exclusive rights to a particular expression of an idea, but many near-substitutes were possible. When faced with an extension of this institution in the modern world of computers, copyright was granted for applications software. When the issue of extending this further in the case of computer operating systems was before the court, the court evidently applied its past experience and predicted that the copyright of disk operating systems would encourage their development at the small price of a limited monopoly in *Apple Computer* v. *Franklin Computer*, 714 Fed. Rep. 2nd 1240 (1983).

Institutional impact theory would predict that the same right applied to both applications and operating systems software will produce a different performance because the goods situation is different [88]. Operating systems, because of their unique linkage to applications programs, have extreme economies of scale. The cost of developing an applications program for another brand of computer is zero if it uses the same operating system. In other words, it is very costly to write applications programs for more than one operating system. This means that a copyrighted operating system, such as Apple incorporated into their computers, could have a substantial monopoly even if that system was only slightly different than a host of competitors. That slight difference, with a unique fit to available applications programs, gave Apple a great competitive advantage. Either this relationship of situation, structure, and performance was not understood by the court or their policy objective was to distribute income toward Apple. Note that this was not described as redistribution because this would be presumptive of the starting place.

In the above case, the institutional design problem was how to control the distributive consequences of economies of scale when they have been achieved. There are a host of situations where the problem is how to achieve economies of scale in the first place. Unrooted cost minimization cannot be uncritically accepted since law is concerned with what costs to minimize. Still, standardization of some products is one of the major opportunities and limiting factors in modern economic growth. A good example is the cost savings that could be achieved in the transportation and warehousing of food products if everyone used a common shipping container (carton) so it would fit on the standard pallet [89].

Policy analysis requires both microeconomics and institutional economics. The microeconomics of shipping containers is straight-forward. Incidentally, there is no institutional economics to replace calculation of least-cost resource combinations. But the institutional analysis problem is to consider what costs are to be made relevant and to understand how incentives work to achieve a given performance. And in this case the problem is to predict how alternative distributions of the cost of change affect the pattern of change. Food manufacturers have investments in current packing box and pallet size which would be lost if they had to change. While the cost savings in total may be great enough to exceed these losses, there is no institution available for sharing them to which enough agree. A study of other similar situations where industry standards have been achieved seems in order. This illustrates the role of theory to know what to look for. To help the food industry, scholars may have to study other goods with similar situational features, such as the history of the railroad or communications industry as they have achieved economies of scale through standardization.

5.2. Exclusion Cost

The interdependence created by high exclusion cost goods is troublesome for isntitutional design. If a market structure is chosen, free riders may prevent the good from being produced. If an administrative structure is chosen, a tax may mean unwilling riders pay who truly do not want the good and are not being opportunistic. If one ignores their welfare economics, some public choice theorists such as Olson [90] have explained why the substantive performance of lobby groups such as the American Medical Association or the Farm Bureau are more successful than consumer groups. One of the best pieces of empirical work is that by Jonathon Pinus [91] who tried to explain the structure of tariff rates implemented in 1824. Since a tariff is available to everyone in an industry whether or not they helped pay for the lobbying effort, Pincus tried to explain relative tariffs by group size, location, etc., which affect the group's ability to control opportunistic behavior.

While this work is very useful in explanation, it doesn't solve many problems of institutional design if one wants to change performance. In fact, Olson regards the person who voluntarily contributes to a high exclusion cost good as irrational. The institutional analyst includes sociological variables as needed. Hirschman argues that participation in providing a high exclusion cost good makes a person "feel more like a person" even if not instrumental in providing a physical good [92]. The person who forbears the opportunity to be a free rider gains utility from striking a blow for a good cause. And if enough do it, the good may be realized. Since reform has utility it may be realized. Since reform has utility it may be interpreted so as to retain an assumption of utility maximization, but the real question is how people conceive of their utility. There is much relevant literature here [93]. But much work remains. This may be one area where there may not be any short-run answers, and evolutionary institutional theory is needed to suggest what learning environments produce Olson's "irrational person" or what might be more neutrally termed nonopportunistic participants. Prospects seem good for research in the direction of Hirschman's work on cumulative collective experience noted above.

5.3.   Information Costs

Information is not perfect, and different people have different information costs. People also have different preferences for different product mixes. How do institutional alternatives affect who gets what? Take the case of Arnold, Schwinn & Co. who in 1951 required their franchised bicycle dealers to provide minimum services and also resale price maintenance (refrain from reselling to nonauthorized discount houses)—*United States* v. *Arnold, Schwinn & Co.*, 388 U.S. 365 (1967). How would a rule allowing or prohibiting this practice affect substantive performance?

Some buyers with high opportunity cost and no mechanical skill want a full service product that minimizes their costs. On the other side, there are buyers who want the Schwinn machine but prefer to assemble and maintain their own. In a world of imperfect information, a new buyer may hear of a buyer who was dissatisfied with a Schwinn product, but not know that it was due to improper home assembly. The handy buyer is denied the product to prevent loss of reputation by Schwinn. Such a buyer may not have perfect substitutes available from other brands (particularly if location is a factor). Schwinn may locate its franchisees with an eye to economies of scale. There is a conflict between those who would like the lowest cost per unit and those who prefer variety in the packaging of Schwinn machines and services.

Cost minimization provides no guide, contrary to the claim by Williamson [94]. The issue is whose costs count. Where interests conflict there is an issue of power [95]. There is a subsequent efficient result associated with each power resolution. The two different efficient results then cannot be a guide to power giving rights to the all thumbs versus handy buyers. Another problem of imperfect information is that investors can make mistakes in creating immobile assets. John K. Galbraith's [96] technological imperative for planning is a recognition that modern industry can't afford too much uncertainty. Neoclassical theorists with selective perception accept capital losses (pecuniary externalities) as the cost of signaling resource allocation and a needed learning so people make fewer mistakes in the future. This misses the point of the longer run dynamic of the situation: understanding requires a combination of evolutionary and impact analysis.

Consider a Schumpeterian change introduced into meat distribution by Gustavus Swift at a time when beef was shipped to Eastern markets live and then slaughtered [97]. Swift thought it would be cheaper to kill the animals in the West and ship the meat in refrigerated cars. This would cause losses in the fixed investments of the railroads and Eastern slaughterhouses. Both interest groups fought to avoid the loss but did not prevail.

Swift apparently had the right to create pecuniary externalities for others. If transaction costs had kept the fixed assets losers from making an effective bid to Swift, it is possible that Swift was never aware of the size of the losses. If transaction costs did not overwhelm the railroad's bid, impact analysis to predict use of the innovation would require knowledge of Swift's perception of the uncertain future transport saving when compared to the losses of the railroad. The latter would influence the bid of the railroad to lessen its net damages. See Lucian Bebchuck [98] for discussion of how uncertainty affects the meaning of consent in trade. If the railroad owned the right to be free of this externality, the impact analyst would need to know the perception not only of Swift but also that of his bankers if Swift needed a loan to make a bid for the railroad's permission to innovate.

Some suggest that the choice of the court could be explained and predicted by reference to wealth maximization. If the court didn't care about income distribution, it would have to have the information noted above to guess what Swift would do, or it could eschew Swift's potential mistakes and substitute its own perception of the uncertain future. To give a right is to determine whose perception of the future counts. Wealth maximization can't be a guide to predicting court choice since whatever it chooses will maximize wealth according to the perception of the party the rights give effect to. Firms will try to do the best they can given their options. What is the effect of giving all beef raisers, railroads, and packers the right to integrate? They would not invest in livestock cars and Eastern slaughterhouses if they thought a new technology and distribution system would make them obsolete before the cost could be recovered. If these firms had minimized their transaction cost, Swift would never have gotten started because there would have been no rancher from which to buy beef since all would have been committed to the integrated firm. And if this super integrated firm were lethargic, it may never have innovated. Whose vision of the future and whose costs are considered is part of the rights and power problem. It is law that determines what goes into the cost-minimization equation.

The substitution of rayon for silk is another example of the cost of adjusting to a new technology [99]. Some market rules mean that the security provided by the previous caste, feudal, or other nonmarket system is no longer available. The issue is sometimes seen as a conflict between consumers who benefit from technological change and the investors and workers who lose. But one wonders if the consumer is well served if the response of investors is to reduce investment in immobile capital or fight political battles to get subsidies or to protect themselves from competition. This may be part of the answer to why the Japanese, with their longer planning horizons and coordination of public and private investments in complementary fields, were so successful in automobiles and electronics [100]. Those scholars working in what is now called industrial policy are part of a long line of institutional impact analysts.

The 1986–1987 federal policy of buying out dairy farmers is a laboratory to test the effect of alternative institutions for distributing the costs of what is now seen to be investment mistakes. If the substantive performance objective is taken to be prevention of continuing asset losses in agriculture, then farmer incentives will have to be modified. These incentives are now provided by the use of supported market prices combined with the situation of unpredictable demand and supply and immobile assets. The owners of immobile assets try to meet objectives by further investments in new technology. Unless policy adopts explicit rights to market sharing, farmers will remain caught in a social trap (prisoners' dilemma) with some producers going broke while others are still adding to surplus supplies [101]. Another alternative is forward deliverable contract markets [102]. Some institutional creativity is needed here.

In the natural resources field, one of the major problems is due to imperfect information on the long-run consequences of irrigation on soil and water salinity. Major portions of Western irrigated land are becoming dangerously close to crop salinity tolerance, and the runoff is polluting drinking water and killing wildlife, such as in the Kesterson Marsh in California. If irrigation is reduced, some very large farmers are going to lose some big fixed assets.

Could evolutionary theory be used to predict what will happen? One hypothesis would be that these big farmers will get the government to build some very expensive engineering works to forestall the problem. In seeking a high exclusion cost good like legislation, small groups with concentrated payoffs have an advantage over large diffuse groups where benefits are large in the aggregate, but individually small. Could impact theory suggest some institutional alternatives? One answer lies in consumers sharing some of the costs of these past mistakes—buy out some of the irrigators and don't allow any new ones. The interrelation of income distribution and performance is a continuing institutional theme. The big problem with empirical impact analysis is to find any institutional variation to observe. Can we find any industries that have created institutions for sharing the costs of mistakes from imperfect information? The institutional analyst may have to go far afield to find a relevant comparison of alternative structures and related performances.

6. Conclusion

Institutional theory is a system of ideas that provides insight into the complementary and strategic factors affecting performance. To get the most from that theory it will be useful to carefully distinguish evolutionary and impact analysis. Further theoretical work and standardization of terms such as those suggested above for impact theory would be useful so we can see that common themes are being investigated and can learn more from our experience.

Not everyone working in these fields wants to carry any particular label. Old labels have unavoidable, excess, symbolic baggage. Perhaps we should just speak of modern political economy [103] though a term with which both lawyers and economists could be comfortable would be better. Progress would be enhanced if more realized they were working on some common themes. Undue product differentiation should not keep us from making probabilistic and directional predictions and pragmatic suggestions based on an understanding of how institutions affect what and how much is produced and who gets it (impact theory). In addition, I would emphasize the creative enlargement of the supply of new institutions from which to choose. Institutions do not just arise from nature when the price is right (evolutionary theory). And, since pseudo-scientific obfuscation is a fact of life, there will be a continuing role for a critique of presumptuous welfare theories, though the prospect is good that mainstream welfare economics will move toward the formerly heterodox institutional analysis.

References

1. Adams, H. C., *Relation of the State of Industrial Action and Economics and Jurisprudence*, Joseph Dorfman, ed. (New York: Columbia University Press, 1954).
2. Ely, R. T., *Property and Contract in Their Relation to the Distribution of Wealth*, 2 vols. (New York: Macmillan, 1914).
3. Commons, J. R., *Legal Foundations of Capitalism* (New York: Macmillan, 1924) Reprinted by Madison: University of Wisconsin Press, 1957.
4. Hamilton, W. H., "Property According to Locke," *Yale Law Journal*, Vol. 4 (1932), pp. 964–980.
5. Llewellyn, Karl N., "What Price Contract? An Essay in Perspective," *Yale Law Journal*, Vol. 40 (1931) pp. 704–751; "The Effect of Legal Institutions on Economics," *American Economic Review*, Vol. 15 (1925), pp. 665–683.
6. Frank, Jerome, *Law and the Modern Mind* (New York: Coward, 1930).
7. Pound, Roscoe, "The Scope and Purpose of Sociological Jurisprudence," *Harvard Law Review*, Vol. 24, pp. 591–619; Vol. 25 (1911–1912), pp. 140–168 and pp. 489–516.
8. Veljanovski, Cento, in discussing economic approaches to law denotes one as an "institutionalist approach" in *The New Law-and-Economics, A Research Review* (Oxford: Centre for Socio-Legal Studies, 1982). See also, Mercuro, Nicholas, "Contributions to Law and Economics: A Survey of Recent Books," *Journal of Economic Education*, Vol. 17, No. 4 (1986) pp. 295–306.
9. Commons, John R., *Economics of Collective Action* (New York: Macmillan, 1950), p. 21.
10. Furubotn, Eirik, and Pejovich, Svetozar, "Introduction: The New Property Rights Literature," in Furubotn and Pejovich (ed.), *The Economics of Property Rights* (Cambridge: Ballinger, 1974), p. 3.

11. Schmid, A. Allan, *Property, Power and Public Choice: An Inquiry Into Law and Economics*, 2d ed. (New York: Praeger Publishers, 1987), ch. 1.

12. Terrence, Daintith, Tuebner, and Gunther, suggest a similar classification: 1) interrelation between legal norms and social structures and developmental tendencies; 2) legal impact analysis; and 3) policy analysis of prescriptions. *Contract and Organization: Legal Analysis in the Light of Economic and Social Theory* (Berlin: Walter de Gruyter, 1986), pp. 11–12.

13. Samuels, Warren J., "Interrelations Between Legal and Economic Processes," *Journal of Law and Economics*, Vol. 5 (1971), pp. 435–450.

14. An example is Wiles, P. J. D., *Economic Institutions Compared* (New York: Halsted, 1977).

15. An example is North, Douglass C., and Thomas, Robert P., *The Rise of the Western World* (New York: Cambridge University Press, 1973). For a critique see, Field, Alexander J., "The Problem with Neoclassical Institutional Economics: A Critique with Special Reference to the North/Thomas Model of Pre–1500 Europe," *Explorations in Economic History*, Vol. 18 (1981) pp. 174–198.

16. Parsons, Kenneth H., "John R. Commons: His Relevance to Contemporary Economics," *Journal of Economic Issues*, Vol. 19 (1985), pp. 755–78.

17. Hohfeld, Wesley N., "Some Fundamental Legal Conceptions as Applied in Judicial Reasoning," *Yale Law Journal*, Vol. 23 (1913), pp. 16–59.

18. See also, Hale, Robert, "Coercion and Distribution in a Supposedly Non-Coercive State," *Political Science Quarterly*, Vol. 38 (1923), pp. 477–478; Samuels, Warren J., "The Economy as a System of Power and Its Legal Bases: The Legal Economics of Robert Lee Hale," *University of Miami Law Review*, Vol. 261 (1973).

19. Commons, John R., *supra* note 3, at ch. 3.

20. Polanyi, Karl, *Trade and Market in the Early Empires* (Glencoe, IL: Free Press, 1957).

21. Heilbroner, Robert L., *The Making Of Economic Society* (Englewood Cliffs, NJ: Prentice Hall, 1962), ch. 1.

22. Boulding, Kenneth, *The Economy of Love and Fear* (Belmont, CA: Wadsworth, 1973).

23. Solo, Robert A., *Economic Organizations and Social Systems* (Indianapolis: Bobbs-Merrill, 1967).

24. Coase, R. L., "The Nature of the Firm," *Economica*, Vol. 4 (1937), pp. 386–405.

25. Williamson, Oliver E., *The Economic Institutions of Capitalism* (New York: Free Press, 1985).

26. Daintith, Terrence, "The Design and Performance of Long-Term Contracts, in Daintith, Terrence, and Teubner, Gunther (eds.), *Contract and Organization* (Berlin: Walter de Gruyter, 1986).

27. Teubner, Gunther, "Industrial Democracy Through Law? Social Functions of Law in Institutional Innovations," in Daintith and Teubner (ed.), *supra* note 26.

28. Samuels, Warren J., "Welfare Economics, Power and Property," in Samuels, Warren, and Schmid, Allan (eds.), *Law and Economics: An Institutional Perspective* (Boston: Martinus Nijhoff, 1981), pp. 9–75; Mercuro, Nicholas, and Ryan, Timothy P., *Law, Economics and Public Policy* (Greenwich, CT: JAI Press, 1984).

29. Unger, Roberto M. *The Critical Legal Studies Movement* (Cambridge: Harvard University Press, 1986).

30. Klevorik, Alvin K., "Legal Theory and the Economic Analysis of Torts and Crimes," *Columbia Law Review*, Vol. 85 (1985), pp. 905–921; Heller, Thomas C., "The Importance of Normative Decision-making: The Limitations of Legal Economics as a Basis for a Liberal Jurisprudence," *Wisconsin Law Review*, Vol. 1976 (1976), p. 385.

31. Langlois, Richard N., "The New Institutional Economics: An Introductory Essay," in Langlois (ed.), *Economics as a Process* (Cambridge: Cambridge University Press, 1986), pp. 1–25.

32. Myrdal, Gunnar, "What is Development," *Journal of Economic Issues*, Vol. 8 (1974), pp. 729–736.

33. Simon, Herbert A., "Rationality as a Process and as a Product of Thought," *American Economic Review*, Vol. 68 (1978), pp. 1–15.

34. Calabresi, Guido, *Ideals, Beliefs, Attitudes, and the Law* (Syracuse: Syracuse University Press, 1985), p. 84.

35. Tushnet, Mark V., "Introduction to Perspectives on Critical Legal Studies," *George Washington Law Review*, Vol. 52 (1984), p. 240.

36. Posner, Richard A., "The Law and Economics Movement," *American Economic Review*, Vol. 77, No. 2 (1987), pp. 3–4.

37. Simon, Herbert A., *supra* note 33.

38. Bartlett, Randall, *Economic Foundations of Political Power* (New York; Free Press, 1973).

39. Commons, John R., "American Shoemakers, 1648–1895," *Quarterly Journal of Economics*, vol. 25 (1909), pp. 39–84.

40. Parsons, Kenneth H., "Transforming the Economic Order in Agricultural Development" (Unpublished, Dept. of Agricultural Economics, University of Wisconsin, 1982).

41. Thurow, Lester, *Dangerous Currents, The State of Economics* (New York: Random House, 1983).

42. Hirschman, Albert, *Getting Along Collectively: Grassroots Experience in Latin America* (New York: Pergamon Press, 1984). See also, Favero, Philip, *The Processes of Collective Action: Small Electric Companies in Michigan* (Unpublished Ph.D. Thesis, Michigan State University, 1977).

43. Frey, Bruno, *Modern Political Economy* (New York: John Wiley, 1978).

44. Schmid, A. Allan, "Broadening Capital Ownership: The Credit System as a Locus of Power," in Alperovitz, Gar, and Skurski, Roger (eds.), *American Economic Policy: Problems and Prospects* (Notre Dame, IN: University of Notre Dame Press, 1985), p. 119.

45. Commons, John R., *Institutional Economics* (New York: Macmillan, 1934),

pp. 589–590; Fisher, Irving, *100% Money* (New York: Adelphi, 1935).

46. Unger, Roberto, *supra* note 29, at p. 35.

47. Shaffer, James D., "On Institutional Obsolescence and Innovation—Background for Professional Dialogue on Public Policy," American Journal of Agricultural Economics, Vol. 51 (1969), pp. 245–267.

48. Sax, Joseph, "Michigan's Environmental Protection Act of 1970: A Progress Report," *Michigan Law Review*, Vol. 70, (1972), pp. 1003–1106.

49. Levy, Julian, "Focal Leverage Points in Problems Relating to Real Property," *Columbia Law Review*, Vol. 66 (1966), pp. 275–285.

50. McDowell, George R., "Political Economy of Extension Program Design," *American Journal of Agricultural Economics*, Vol. 67 (1985), pp. 717–725.

51. Calabresi, Guido *supra* note 34, at ch. 5.

52. Norgaard, Richard, "Coevolutionary Development Potential," *Land Economics*, vol. 2 (1985), pp. 160–173.

53. Hurst, Willard, *Law and Social Process in United States History* (Ann Arbor: University of Michigan Law School, 1956).

54. Frey, Bruno, *Democratic Economic Policy* (Oxford: Martin Robertson, 1983).

55. Bromley, Daniel, "Resources and Economic Development: An Institutionalist Perspective," *Journal of Economic Issues*, Vol. 19 (1985), pp. 779–96.

56. Kanel, Don, "Property and Economic Power as Issues in Institutional Economics," *Journal of Economic Issues*, Vol. 8 (1974), pp. 827–840.

57. Rutherford, Malcolm, "J. R. Commons Institutional Economics," *Journal of Economic Issues*, Vol. 17 (1983), pp. 721–44.

58. Veblen, Thorstein, *The Theory of Business Enterprise* (New York: Charles Scribner, 1904).

59. Ayres, C. E., *The Theory of Economic Progress*, 2nd ed. (New York: Schocken Books, 1962).

60. Tool, Marc, *The Discretionary Economy: A Normative Theory of Political Economy* (Santa Monica: Goodyear Publishing, 1979).

61. Hamilton, David, "Technology and Institutions," *Journal of Economic Issues*, Vol. 20, No. 2 (1986), pp. 525–532.

62. Olson, Mancur, *The Rise and Decline of Nations* (New Haven: Yale University Press, 1982).

63. Samuels, Warren J., and Mercuro, Nicholas, "A Critique of Rent-Seeking Theory," in Colander, David (ed.), *Neoclassical Political Economy* (Cambridge: Ballinger, 1984).

64. Calabresi, Guido, *supra* note 34; see also Horwitz, Morton J., "Law and Economics: Science or Politics?" *Hofstra Law Review*, Vol. 8, No. 4 (1980), pp. 905–912; Farjat, Gerard, "The Contribution of Economics to Legal Analysis: The Concept of the Firm," in Daintith and Teubner, (ed.), *supra* note 12.

65. Carter, Michael, "A Wisconsin Institutionalist Perspective on Microecono-

mic Theory of Institutions: The Insufficiency of Pareto Efficiency," *Journal of Economic Issues*, Vol. 19 (1985), pp. 797–813.

66. *Ibid.*, p. 808.

67. Baker, C. Edwin, "Starting Points in the Economic Analysis of Law," *Hofstra Law Review*, Vol. 8, No. 4 (1980), pp. 939–972. See also, Coleman, Jules L., "Efficiency, Utility, and Wealth Maximization," *Hofstra Law Review*, Vol. 8, No. 3 (1980), pp. 509–551, Seidman, Robert B., *The State, Law and Development* (London: Croom Helm, 1978); Langlois, *supra* note 31.

68. Rose-Ackerman, Susan, "Inalienability and the Theory of Property Rights," *Columbia Law Review*, Vol. 85, (1985), pp. 931–969.

69. Commons, John R., *Legal Foundations of Capitalism* (New York: Macmillan, 1924), reprinted by Madison: University of Wisconsin Press, 1957.

70. Kairys, David, "Law and Politics," *George Washington Law Review*, Vol. 52 (1984), pp. 243–262.

71. Samuels, Warren J., "A Critique of the Discursive Systems and Foundation Concepts of Distribution Analysis," *Analyse & Kritik*, Vol. 4 (1982), pp. 4–21.

72. Carter, Michael, *supra* note 65.

73. Braverman, Avishay, and Joseph Stiglitz, "Sharecropping and the Interlinking of Agrarian Markets," *American Economic Review*, Vol. 72 (1982), pp. 695–715.

74. Randall, Alan, "Welfare, Efficiency and the Distribution of Rights," in Wunderlich, Gene, and Gibson, W. L., Jr. (eds.), *Perspectives of Property* (University Park: Pennsylvania State University, 1972), pp. 25–31; Bromley, Daniel, "Land and Water Problems: An Institutional Perspective," *American Journal of Agricultural Economics*, Vol. 64 (1982), pp. 834–844; Lang, Mahlon, "Economic Efficiency and Policy Comparisons," *American Journal of Agricultural Economics*, Vol. 62 (1980), pp. 772–777; Samuels, *supra* note 28; Schmid, *supra* note 11, at ch. 11; Hutchison, T. W., *'Positive' Economics and Policy Objectives* (Cambridge: Harvard University Press, 1964); Kennedy, Duncan, and Michelman, Frank, "Are Property and Contract Efficient?" *Hofstra Law Review*, Vol. 8, No. 3 (1980), pp. 711–770.

75. Ramstad, Yngve, "Institutional Existentialism," *Journal of Economic Issues*, Vol. 21, No. 2 (1987), pp. 661–672; Tushnet, *supra* note 35. Martin Brofenbrenner notes that several institutional economists were fired between 1885 and World War I by universitities responding to conservative business interests. These open normativists were more exposed than their mainstream brethren whose recommendations were cast as natural findings with which no rational person could disagree. See Brofenbrenner, Martin, "Early American Leaders—Institutional and Critical Traditions," *American Economic Review*, Vol. 75, No. 6 (1985), p. 14. There is some parallel in today's tenure battles of scholars in the critical legal studies movement.

76. Robinson, Joan, *Economic Philosophy* (Chicago: Aldine, 1963), p. 146.
77. Boadway, Robin, W., and Bruce, Neil, *Welfare Economics* (New York: Basil Blackwell, 1984), p. 272.
78. Tresch, Richard W., *Public Finance: A Normative Theory* (Plano, TX: Business Publications, 1981), pp. 350–351.
79. Unger, Roberto, *supra* note 29, at p. 67.
80. Dewey, John, *The Public and Its Problems* (Denver: Allan Swallow, 1927). Bogholt, Carl M., "The Value Judgement and Land Tenure Research," in Ackerman, Joseph et al. (eds.), *Land Tenure Research Workshop* (Chicago: Farm Foundation, (1956); Unger, Roberto, *supra* note 29.
81. Klein, Phillip A., "The New Classical Economics," *Journal of Economic Issues*, Vol. 20, No. 2 (1986), pp. 313–324.
82. Unger, Roberto, *supra* note 29, at pp. 22–25.
83. Samuels, Warren, *supra* notes 13, 28, 63 and 71.
84. Schmid, A. Allan, *supra* note 11.
85. Kiser, Larry L., and Ostrom, Elinor, "Three Worlds of Action: A Meta-theoretical Synthesis of Institutional Approaches," in Ostrom, E. (ed.), *Strategies of Political Inquiry* (Beverly Hills: Sage 1982), pp. 195–198.
86. Mueller, Willard F., "The Anti-Trust Movement," in Cravens, John V. (ed.), *Industrial Organization and Public Policy* (Boston: Kluwer-Nijhoff, 1983); pp. 19–40; Marion, Bruce W. (ed.), *The Organization and Performance of the U.S. Food System* (Lexington, MA: Lexington Books, 1985).
87. Glaeser, Martin G., *Public Utilities in American Capitalism* (New York: Macmillan, 1957).
88. Schmid, A. Allan, *A Conceptual Framework For Organizing Observations on Intellectual Property* (Washington, DC: U.S. Congress, Office of Technology Assessment, 1985).
89. Abdalla, Charles W., *Problem in Interindustry Coordination and System-Wide Productivity* (Unpublished Ph.D. Dissertation, Michigan State University, 1985).
90. Olson, Mancur, *The Logic of Collective Action* (Cambridge Harvard University Press, 1965).
91. Pincus, Jonathon, *Pressure Group and Politics in Antebellum Tariffs* (New York: Columbia University Press, 1977).
92. Hirschman, Albert, "Against Parsimony: Three Easy Ways of Complicating Some Categories of Economic Discourse," *American Economic Review*, Vol. 72, No. 2 (1984), pp. 89–96.
93. Morrison, Denton, "Some Notes Toward a Theory of Relative Deprivation, Social Movements and Social Change," *American Behavioral Scientist*, (May/June 1971), pp. 675–90; Rich, Richard C., "A Political Economy Approach to the Study of Neighborhood Organizations," *American Journal of Political Science*, Vol. 24 (1980), pp. 559–592; Sproule-Jones, Mark, "A Description and Explanation of Citizen Participation in a Canadian Municipality," *Public Choice*, Vol. 17 (Spring 1974), pp. 73–83.

94. Williamson, Oliver E., *supra* note 25, at pp. 185–189.
95. Weiss, Terry R., "The Dealer-Services Rationale for Resale Price Mainten-
    ance: Does the Manufacturer Really Know Best," *Saint Louis University
    Law Review*, Vol. 30, No. 2 (1986), pp. 517–535.
96. Galbraith, J. K., *The New Industrial State* (Boston: Houghton Mifflin,
    1967). See also, Daintith, Terrence, *supra* note 26.
97. Williamson, Oliver E., *supra* note 25, at pp. 236–237.
98. Bebchuck, Lucian A., "The Pursuit of a Bigger Pie: Can Everyone Expect
    a Bigger Slice?" *Hofstra Law Review*, Vol. 8, No. 3 (1980), pp. 671–710.
99. Kanel, Don, "Institutional Economics: Perspectives on Economy and
    Soceity," *Journal of Economic Issues*, Vol. 19 (1985), pp. 815–828.
100. Solo, Robert A., "Lessons From Elsewhere," in Alperovitz, *supra* note 44,
    pp. 43–55.
101. Cochrane, Willard W., *The Development of American Agriculture: A His-
    torical Analysis* (St. Paul: University of Minnesota Press, 1979).
102. Kaufmann, Daniel E., and Shaffer, James D., *Forward Contract Markets:
    Can They Improve Coordination of Supply and Demand?* (East Lansing:
    Michigan State University, 1985).
103. Frey, Bruno, *supra* note 43.

4 THE LAW AND ECONOMICS AND CRITICAL LEGAL STUDIES MOVEMENTS IN AMERICAN LAW

Gary Minda

1. Introduction

One of the most striking new developments in American legal thought has been the almost simultaneous emergence of *two* new intellectual "movements" in law—*law and economics*, and *critical legal studies*. The title, law and economics, as used in this chapter describes the work of legal-economic scholars who appeared on the academic scene in the early 1970s located primarily at the University of Chicago. There they developed a "new" methodology for doing economic analysis of law. What is new about law and economics is that its practitioners apply concepts developed in the theory of microeconomics, and in a branch of microeconomics called welfare economics, to systematically describe, reformulate, and critique nearly every aspect of law and the legal system. A central claim of the new law and economics is that the entire legal system can be analyzed and reformed through the application of a relatively small number of fundamental economic concepts [1].

The research for this essay was supported by Brooklyn Law School's summer research fund.

At about the same time law and economics began to attract the attention of legal scholars, a rival movement in legal studies established itself as a major critic of both traditional and law and economics scholarship. This rival academic movement—critical legal studies (CLS)—surfaced in the late 1970s when a group of younger legal scholars formed a social and professional network called The Conference on Critical Legal Studies and began publishing critical essays on various legal subjects [2]. Like the law and economic scholar, the CLS scholar seeks to develop a systematic or totalistic critique of legal theory and doctrine but does so by using different nonlegal methodologies and insights.

As academic movements, both law and economics and critical legal studies are interdisciplinary "schools," working within fundamentally diverse worlds and methodologies [3]. While the law and economics movement draws upon the quasi-scientific methods of economics, critical legal studies purports to employ its insights and methods from eclectic sources and disciplines such as critical theory, literary criticism, feminism, structuralism, and Marxism. Each movement has thus introduced a new form of legal scholarship which departs radically from the perspectives and methods of mainstream legal thought. It is commonly believed, not without foundation, that these two movements are *fundamentally* different movements in that their methodologies project different visions about the nature of law and the legal system. Law and economic scholars argue that judge-made law should be structured to promote legal outcomes that maximize wealth; CLS scholars argue that the law should be "transformed" to create real democratic decisionmaking. These differences are without doubt the source of deep disagreement about values and politics.

Despite their many differences, there have been some who have claimed that law and economics and critical legal studies share a great deal in common. For example, Martha Minow, a feminist and fellow traveler of the CLS movement at Harvard University, has recently observed in an article, Law Turning Outward [4], that behind each of these trends in legal scholarship "is a brooding doubt about whether law deserves a privileged place in resolving conflict and ordering society" [5]. In her view, "[e]ach of the different movements search outside of law to address the question of law's legitimacy" [6]. Minow concludes that the debate generated by law and economics and critical legal studies has raised serious questions concerning "the legitimacy of law within a culture that suspects politics and believes in science or science-like methods for securing truth" [7].

A somewhat similar view has been expressed by a leading liberal scholar, Owen Fiss, of Yale Law School. In a recent lecture delivered at

Cornell Law School, Fiss argued that "[b]oth law and economics and critical legal studies are united in their rejection of the notion of law as public ideal" [8]. In his view, "[b]oth movements can be understood as a reaction to a jurisprudence, confidently embraced by the bar in the sixties, that sees adjudication as the process for interpreting and nurturing a public morality" [9].

Finally, one of the leading spokespersons for the law and economics movement, Richard A. Posner, has echoed a similar theme. In a recent essay commemorating the hundredth anniversary of the *Harvard Law Review*, Posner argued that "[t]he supports for the faith in law's autonomy as a discipline have been kicked away in the last quarter of Century," partly as a result of "a boom in disciplines that are contemporary to law, particularly economics and philosophy" [10]. Posner argued that the recent progress of law and economics and critical legal studies in "illuminating law" has "undermine[d] the lawyer's (especially the academic lawyer's) faith in the autonomy of his discipline" [11]. As Posner explained: "A purely verbal, purely lawyer's scholarship, in which the categories of analysis are the same as, or very close to, those used by the judges or legislators whose work is being analyzed—a scholarship moreover in which political consensus is assumed and the insights of other disciplines ignored—does not fit comfortably into today's scholarly *Zeitgeist*" [12].

The idea that law and economics and critical legal studies might be united in some way is also reflected in the common antagonism that some legal scholars have shown toward both movements. For some, law and economics and critical legal studies have been a welcomed new development, bringing a renewed sense of intellectual excitement to the legal academy. For others, however, these new trends in legal thought are naive, wrongheaded, threatening, and even *dangerous*. Legal scholars have criticized these movements for being either too "theoretical" or too "simplistic" in their claims or methods. At least one distinguished legal scholar and law school dean has suggested that one of these movements, CLS, should be banned from the legal academy because its message is too "radical" or "subversive" for legal education [13]. More recently, Fiss has argued that law and economics *and* CLS are dangerous "jurisprudence movements" because they may "mean the death of the law, as we have known it throughout history, and as we have come to admire it" [14].

This chapter develops a somewhat different account, one that is perhaps more hopeful and optimistic, for why law and economics and CLS are developing at this time and what they may mean for law and the legal system. It claims that the new developments in legal jurisprudence are generating a more complex and rich understanding of what "law" and "adjudication" means—an understanding which is making it increasingly difficult to accept the liberal jurisprudence of mainstream legal scholars.

While the methods and approach of law and economics and critical legal studies are not beyond criticism, neither are they responsible for creating the current malaise in mainstream legal scholarship and legal theory [15]. The competition between these movements and the controversy they have sparked can be understood as part of an ongoing intellectual struggle that began in the 1920s and 1930s with the legal realist movement and which is now being waged by new critical discourses offering new ways for understanding law and new methods for utilizing that understanding. The debate that has been generated by the new movements in legal theory has relevance to an older debate involving some of central questions raised by the legal realists concerning the nature of power and meaning, and the role of law in American society. The current debate also raises new theoretical questions concerning the limits of scientific reasoning and rational investigation. Before addressing these questions I will seek to characterize law and economics and critical legal studies by focusing on the major differences that these academic movements are known to exhibit.

2. Understanding the Differences Which These Academic Movements Exhibit

Most legal scholars today have come to understand law and economics and critical legal studies as radically different academic movements working on the boarder of traditional legal studies. These perceptions have now become folklore generated by literally thousands of informal conversations at faculty cocktail parties and academic social gatherings. It is not uncommon to overhear established legal scholars refer to law and economics and CLS as if they were fierce political rivals—law and economics is commonly assoicated with the conservative economic philosophy of the Chicago school; whereas, CLS is usually type-casted as the New Left intellectual offspring of the radical counterculture of the 1960s. Law and economics is thus characterized in the profession as the reactionary movement of the right, and CLS is known as the radical movement of the left. Such stereotypic thinking has been responsible for creating the impression that these two academic movements are marginal or fringe schools working outside the established academic tradition of the profession.

There is, of course, at least some basis for such stereotypes. Law and economics has become closely associated with the conservative Chicago school of economics and its basic methodology (an undying quest for efficiency together with the *Coase theorem*) which has served to undermine the confidence in the "interventionist" programs of welfare economics of the 1960s [16]. Without doubt, the dominant message of the law and economics movement has served to strengthen the influence of the free market conservatives at the University of Chicago and elsewhere. The CLS movement, on the other hand, seeks to provide intellectual support for a new form of radical and critical scholarship. The central focus of this movement is "to explore the manner in which legal doctrine and legal education and the practices of legal institutions work to buttress and support a pervasive system of oppressive, inegalitarian relations" [17]. CLS scholars thus seek to show how the dominant tradition in legal scholarship (as well as the emerging tradition represented by the law and economics movement) has served to create a powerful justification for ignoring and hence concealing economic and political inequality.

One must, however, go beyond generalization and stereotypes in order to obtain a more realistic understanding of the relation between these two movements. Indeed, there has been a recent effort devoted to the task of "characterizing" the movements. Lewis Kornhauser, for example, has argued that the economic analysis of law commits law and economic scholars to a particular conception of law and human behavior [18]. He asserts that the economic analysis of law can be understood in terms of four claims or theses: 1) a "behavioral claim" which asserts that economic theory can provide a sufficient "good theory for predicting how people will behave under rules of law"; 2) a "normative claim" which asserts that the "law ought to be efficient"; 3) a factual or "positive" claim which provides that the "(common) law is in fact efficient"; and 4) a "genetic" claim which argues that the "common law tends to select efficient rules, although not every rule will, at any given time, be efficient" [19]. These "theses" or economic claims about law are defended by other law and economic scholars on the normative justification that they will allow judges to shape legal principles to create rights that maximize the wealth of society [20].

Critical legal studies, on the other hand, is commonly viewed as merely a "negative" movement that criticizes without offering either a constructive program or specific standard of reference for determining whether the subject of criticism is more or less inferior [21]. The "negative" tone to the CLS movement does not mean that it lacks either a distinctive method or approach. Minow, for instance, has argued that the CLS "school is recognizable in its commitment to explain both that legal principles and doctrines are open-textured and capable of yielding contradictory results, and that legal decisions express an internal dynamic of legal culture contingent on historical preferences for selected assumptions and values" [22]. She identifies four "activities" in which CLS scholars are known to engage: 1) "[t]he critical scholar seeks to demonstrate the indeterminacy of legal doctrine: any given set of legal principles can be used to yield competing or contradictory results"; 2) "[t]he critical scholar engages in historical, socioeconomic analysis to identify how particular interest groups, social classes, or entrenched economic institutions benefit from legal decisions despite the indeterminacy of the legal doctrines"; 3) "the critical scholar tries to expose how legal analysis and legal culture mystifies outsiders and legitimates its results"; and 4) "the critical scholar may elucidate new or previously disfavored social visions and argue for their realization in legal or political practice in part by making them part of legal discourse" [23].

Characterizations such as these suggest that law and economics and CLS scholars project different conceptions about the nature of law and human behavior. Law and economic scholars argue that human beings are fundamentally rational creatures, that they behave in ways that tend to maximize their self-interests. In the economic perspective, law serves essentially an incentive function in rewarding efficiency-enhancing conduct and punishing inefficient aberrations. CLS scholars argue that the economic concept of rational behavior is dependent upon an underlying ideological perspective which seeks to justify and explain disadvantage and privilege as the consequence of rational private choice. These scholars argue that behavior is "rational" only because it conforms to a particular political ideology. The "normative" and "genetic" claims of law and economics are thus seen by CLS scholars as merely highly refined statements of a particular world-view or political viewpoint.

These differences are reflected in the slogans, perspectives, and styles of the two movements; impressionistic characteristics which in turn influence the way legal academics have come to understand how the two movements engage in their unique form of criticism [24]. Critical legal scholars, for example, argue that traditional legal thought performs an ideological or political function which helps to create and legitimate social and economic inequalities within society. A central goal of CLS scholarship is to reveal how traditional modes of legal analysis help create a system of beliefs or *legal consciousness* that presumes the autonomy, permanence, and objectivity of legal rules. CLS argues that the creation of shared perceptions of legal actors has served to conceal and minimize the political and social premises of law and legal practice [25]. This form of criticism is by nature negative in tone.

While law and economic scholars appear to agree that traditional legal thought is flawed by ambiguity in purpose and method, these scholars, unlike their counterparts in CLS, argue that the current doctrinal justifications of the law can be *grounded* by economic analysis to achieve determinacy and formal equality. They argue that the economic value of efficiency or the principle of "wealth maximization" [26] can be utilized "instrumentally" by judges as an ethical standard for determining whether a particular legal outcome is "just" [27]. The criticism of law and economics thus appears *constructive* in that a specific methodological proposal is offered for legal decisionmaking.

There is also deep disagreement between these movements over the possibility of constructing objective and coherent explanations of how law operates within society. Critical legal scholars are known to argue that traditional liberal modes of legal analysis are flawed because fundamental choices about the necessity and desirability for the intervention of the coercive power of the state over the free will of the individual are incoherent. While law and economic scholars appear to agree that traditional legal thought is inadequate, these scholars argue that the conflict between regulation and the market can be "solved" by judge-made rules that make sharp distinctions between allocational and distributional issues, by adopting behavioral assumptions that presume rationality and by encouraging judges to ignore distributional concerns in favor of decision-making standards that seek to maximize the value of competing preferences.

These differences are reflected in the slogans of the two movements. By far the most popular slogan of the law and economics movement is that "law is efficient."[1] Indeed, much of the work in law and economics has been devoted to the single task of demonstrating why judges usually choose decision-relevant standards in common law cases that assign rights and impose liabilities in a manner that would be efficient in the sense of maximizing the total satisfaction of preferences. In cases where judges have failed to select rules that maximize preferences, advocates of the economic approach argue that judges should favor rules that do in fact maximize preferences. In making descriptive and normative claims about legal efficiency (or what some have called the *wealth maximization criterion*), advocates of the movement challenge the liberal notion that law is distinct from economics, that justice does not and should not depend on wealth.

For example, it is said that the new law and economics is different from the old because it promises a new *systematic* method for achieving a comprehensive understanding of legal issues. If economic analysis can be applied "across the board" to nearly every legal subject, as some have argued [28], then lawyers would have a powerful new method for understanding the complexity of law and legal development. This new method, however, would call into question the idea that law could be studied "autonomously" through traditional legal analysis. It would also challenge the perception of law as an embodiment of fair process for achieving public values. According to the message of law and economics, law is merely an instrument for increasing the size of the economic pie; if a "value" is to be achieved it is the sole value of "wealth maximization."

Scholars who identify with CLS, on the other hand, practice a form of *oppositional existence* in that they seek to challenge and transform the very practices that define their profession [29]. Most, but not all, reject the idea that legal analysis and argumentation can be grounded in, or rendered determinant by, a mode of discourse claiming to be objective, neutral, and apolitical. Nearly everyone within this movement has sought to demonstrate the *indeterminacy* or *incoherence* of many of the traditional beliefs and theories of the legal profession. The "hallmark" of CLS is relentless *critique*, sometimes called "*trashing*," of liberal claims that seek to establish the coherence and benevolence of established theory and doctrine [30]. In attacking the idea that it is possible to demonstrate objectively the "truth" of abstract claims about law and the legal system, CLS challenges the liberal notion that law is distinct from politics. A popular slogan of this movement is that "law is politics."

While both movements can be understood to be challenging established liberal notions of mainstream legal scholars, this does not mean that both movements oppose *liberalism*. Law and economics can be understood to be a liberal movement which is seeking to build on the vision of the liberal state. Indeed, many of the arguments which these scholars advance are in reality a justification for the existing institutional practices of the modern liberal state such as the allocation of functions between the legislature and the judiciary as well as the doctrinal legal categories which support the notion of what is public and what is private, and so forth [31]. Critical legal studies, on the other hand, is characteristically nonliberal in its methodology and approach. CLS scholars seek to critique as well as transcend the abstract categories of liberal legalism. While they fall short of advancing a positive program, they do because this is part of their form of criticism. CLS practitioners seek to open up the professional dialogue so that other voices can be heard in the discussion about whose interests and what values should figure in any program for future change.

3. The Intellectual Bond Between Law and Economics and CLS

If law and economics and the CLS movement are different in so many fundamental respects, which they are, then why have some argued that they share a common ground? Of course, one point of intersection can be found in the fact that both are distinctively dissident academic movements revolting against the mainstream. There is, in fact, a deep source that unites these movements as oppositional academic movements in the legal academy. It is significant, for example, that both law and economics and CLS legal scholars claim, somewhat ironically, to be rooted in the same intellectual jurisprudential tradition—the tradition of *American legal realism* [32]. Legal realism was an earlier intellectual movement in law, dominant during the 1920s and 1930s, which attempted to transform and undermine the assumptions of American jurisprudence [33]. The body of work that gave rise to the American legal realist movement is, without doubt, marked by committed engagement and struggle [34]. The realist movement was itself comprised of conflicting impulses and alternative strands of oppositional thought [35].

As an oppositional movement, legal realists revolted against forms of so-called "mechanical jurisprudence," namely *formalism* and *conceptualism*, which prevailed and dominated the judicial imagination during the so-called formalist era of American legal thought [36]. The legal realist movement was also a reaction against the Liberty of Contract Era of constitutional law; a time when the Supreme Court routinely invalidated federal and state social welfare legislation [37]. The realists claimed the liberty of contract cases of the Supreme Court were decided by methods of legal analysis which concealed or deflected attention away from the social consequences of judicial decisionmaking.

Legal educators commonly invoke the legal realists, as a group, to signify some truism about legal decisionmaking, for example, the proposition that a "legal decision depends less on precedent that on what the judge ate for breakfast" [38]. But legal realism was much more than just a crude belief in the subjectivity of judicial decisionmaking; it was a "many-layered attack on formalism: on *empirical ignorance, doctrinal abstraction*, and *oppressive social values*" [39]. As Gary Peller has recently argued, there were in fact different critical strands of legal realist thought which generated different attitudes and perspectives about legal formalism [40].[2]

One strand of legal realist thought was reflected in the scholarship of

Felix Cohen who emphasized a "deconstructive approach" [41] to legal criticism; an approach that focused on the indeterminacy and the circularity of legal reasoning as a basis for "debunking" Liberty of Contract discourse. Legal realists like Cohen taught that legal scholars should be skeptical about claims of legal objectivity, that many of the key categories of legal doctrine were incoherent, and that the paradigm of "applying the law" through the formal logic of legal syllogisms was insufficient as a model or legal theory of law. As Cohen put it: "[T]he question of whether the action of the courts is justifiable calls for an answer in nonlegal terms. To justify or criticize legal rules in purely legal terms is always to argue in a vicious circle" [42].

But the realists also taught that law must be studied as "it works in practice by making use of the social sciences" in order to establish what became known as a new "realistic jurisprudence" [43]. In this second understanding, realism became associated with a "post-formalist" method of law study and practice which was influenced by the belief in the empiricism of the scientific method and the pragmatism of "skilled craftsmanship." Karl Lewellyn's empirical approach, for example, focused on human behavior as the basis for understanding what "official do about disputes" [44]. Jerome Frank took Llewellyn's approach one step further in arguing his case for a psychoanalytic understanding of the judicial method [45]. Other realists sought to defend the social engineering of the New Deal by articulating a coherent conception of the public interest and then developing legal policies to that interest [46]. These efforts ultimately led to the reconstruction of a new Public Interest Law dedicated to public values and social justice created by the melding of the craftsmanship skills of the older formalism with new policy instrumentalism.

While the legal realists stopped short of developing a *systematic* critique of American legal thought, they did provide at least two powerful examples of how one might critique formal legal arguments and how to practice oppositional forms of legal scholarship. A subsequent generation of legal scholars could thus claim the legal realists as "inspirational heroes" for demonstrating that law could not be divorced from politics; that the logical methods of legal analysis could never "justify" legal decisions without reference to nonlegal considerations. At the vary same time, a different group of legal scholars could "celebrate" the work of the legal realists for demonstrating how one might seek to apply scientific methods and technocratic craftsmanship to law study. These two different ways of understanding the work of the legal realists help explain why today both law and economics and critical legal studies scholars might "claim" legal realism as a source of their intellectual inspiration and legacy.[3]

4. Mainstream Legal Thought

What united the deconstructive and the realistic jurisprudence strands of legal realist thought was a common opposition to the political visions, ideas, and social images of the jurisprudence of formalism that came to characterize the liberty of contract discourse of the 1930s Supreme Court. The strand of critical realism associated with the work of the "radical" realists pursued a pure form of relentless critique of deconstruction of the argumentative structure of the liberty of contract cases in order to show how judges were essentially unrestrained in legal decisionmaking. The other strand of critical realism, "realism as science," sought to ground the radical critique of the deconstructive approach in the determinate theories of the social sciences. Both strands were united in their rejection of the political vision of a jurisprudence which viewed adjudication as a mechanical process of logical manipulations of legal abstractions.

Subsequent developments in legal theory illustrate how a new generation of legal scholars reacted to the challenge posed by the realists. A new group of modern doctrinal scholars began to construct a theory of adjudication which accepted the public interest or social engineering strand of legal realism but rejected the extreme claims of the deconstructionists. The deconstructive strand of legal realism was dismissed by modern doctrinal scholars as "nihilistic, morally relativistic, and nominalist" [47]. The fear was that the skepticism of legal realism might lead legal scholarship to a "dead end" [48]. This was also a time when there was a new confidence in the scientific method and the rational ability of man to solve social problems [49].

Indeed, by the end of the 1930s many of the best well-known realists eventually embarked on a new effort to "reconstruct" an objective theory of law by turning to the social sciences and pragmatic social engineering [50]. The concerns of intellectual discovery and social improvement led a number of the realists to look to the social sciences for guidance in developing a new public interest law. Others gave up law teaching and law practice and joined the New Deal effort established by the Roosevelt administration. Ultimately, the rise of fascism in Europe and World War II made it difficult, if not impossible, for legal academics to sustain the realists' assault on the legitimacy of American law. While the recollections of the misadventures of Justice McReynolds and the 1930 Supreme Court remained "vivid" in the minds of legal scholars, there was a renewed sense of optimism that an alternative jurisprudence could be found to "answer" the questions posed by the radical challenge of legal realism.

By the 1950s a *new pluralism* in legal methodology was established with the "uneasy marriage" [51] of the formalist and realist traditions. The resulting new paradigm in legal analysis, known as the "legal process" school, promised once again to preserve legal objectivity by a process of "reasoned elaboration" which combined both principle and policy.[4] The purpose of law was thus to provide an objective "process" for resolving subjective questions of public policy and thus avoid the dangers which were exemplified by the "misadventures" of the 1930 Supreme Court.[5] The hope was that judicially conceived notions of self-restraint, the need for workable standards of general application, and the duty to render a "reasoned decision" would impose constraints on the freedom of a judge in deciding substantive issues of subjective value. The realist critique of "subjectivity" in decisionmaking would thus be avoided by a new understanding of "legal reasoning" and the process of adjudication.

Thus, H. L. A. Hart argued that there were "characteristically judicial virtues" that potentially constrained judges in legal decisionmaking [52]. These constraining virtues were described in terms of values such as "impartiality" and "neutrality" in surveying the alternatives, "fair consideration" for the interest of all who will be affected, and "judicial rationality" that some acceptable general principle be deployed as a resoned basis for decision. Herbert Wechsler [53] and Henry Hart, Jr. [54], in turn, argued that judicial authority rests on "principle neutrality" or "reasoned principle." The thrust of their argument was that judges should be constrained from interjecting too much ideology into the process of decisionmaking at the expense of consistency and principled reasoning. The underlying idea was that judges were supposed to decide "like cases alike" and to base their decisions on reasons that have general application. While judges may be required to make difficult choices between conflicting values, they should make those choices in a fair and impartial manner by applying neutral principles.[6]

An alternative paradigm born out of the legal realist tradition thus seemed possible: one that is more mainstream and less oppositional in its understanding of the legal realist's project. This alternative paradigm is a product of the view of traditional legal scholars who have accepted the skeptical, functional approach of the realists but who have rejected the political and ideological ramifications of their critique [55].[7] This alternative paradigm accepted the view of the legal realists that law must look outward for legal justifications, but rejected the radical implications of the realists' assault on the objectivity of law [56]. It has become the view that proclaims that there are genuine public values shared within the community under which questions of public policy can be settled through the faithful observance of "legal process" virtues—the virtues of reasoned judgment and rational technique.

5. How Each Movement Critiques the Mainstream

The idea of law as process sees the task of judging as an "interpretative process" of "reading" legal texts for the purpose of explicating meaning. But interpretation also requires the decisionmaker to decide upon a underlying *method* for choosing between different interpretative criteria as well as different modes of interpretation in reaching *judgment*. A fundamental source of difficulty posed by the legal process concept of adjudication is that it fails to offer a principled *method* for determining the bounds of discretion which must be allowed in order for judges to perform their duty of choosing between different techniques of interpretation.[8] Even if one were to accept the existence of "reasoned elaboration," "neutral principles," or "rationality of law," judges would still need to know how to choose between any number of possible different meanings ascertainable from different interpretations, any one of which might be defended on rational grounds.

In eschewing ideological preferences, judges in the legal process school were supposed to preserve the integrity of the legal system by preventing individual biases and preferences from influencing the resolution of disputes. The belief in the "characteristically judicial virtues" of rationality, neutrality, and respect for the institution simply fails, however, to instruct judges what to do when they are faced with subtle choices between different modes of interpretation in adjudication. The most careful of legal process scholars would now seem to agree that it would be difficult to "evaluate the consistency of a judge from case to case, and difficult even for the judge who aims for consistency to be sure that he was not being swayed by non-relevant factors in particular cases" [57]. Indeed, it is now recognized that "occasional compromises" of legal process virtues must be made in judicial decisionmaking; that the neutral principles and reasoned decision might have to be "sacrificed" for other social goals in making choices about different modes of legal interpretation.

The now classic illustration of this can be found in the liberal jurisprudence of the Warren era in civil rights. Indeed, it was the Warren Court activism in civil rights culminating in such celebrated decisions such as *Shelley* v. *Kramer* [58] and *Brown* v. *Board of Education* [59] which presented serious challenge to the dominant ideology of the legal process school. The Warren Court decisions on race were particularly troublesome because while they "seemed obvious victories for truth and right," they "were under sharp attack" by well-respected legal scholars such as Herbert Wechsler, Alexander Bickel, and Philip Kirkland. These scholars launched "widesweeping indictments of the Warren Court's performance, claiming that the Court had constitutionality enshrined its own egalitarian sentiments without adequate justification," [60].

Law and economics and CLS can be seen today as offering substantially different modes of legal interpretation, interpretative modes which directly challenge the views of the legal process school. Indeed, it is the intellectual opposition to the legal process school that unites the law and economic and the CLS movements. Specifically, law and economics and critical legal studies can be understood to be post-realist oppositional movements which are reacting against the dominant ideology of legal process much in the same way that the legal realists reacted against the formalism of the liberty of contract era in constitutional law.[9] Like the legal realists of the 1920s and 1930s, practitioners of law and economics and critical legal studies have raised fundamental questions about the way mainstream legal scholars have come to understand their subject—law and adjudication. Law and economics builds on the idea of realism as science.in its effort to reconstruct a new determinant theory of legal analysis developed from the "science" of economics [61]. Critical legal studies has developed that strand of legal realist thought that pursued the deconstructive approach to legal criticism [62]. Both law and economics and CLS can be seen to be practicing merely a different form of legal criticism—forms of critique that draw upon the legacy of legal realism— in opposing mainstream legal thought.

In identifying legal realism as the intellectual source of each movement it becomes possible to understand the fundamental interrelationships bonding these two academic movements. Each movement has presented the traditional legal scholar with the need for considering nonlegal methodologies for gaining insight about the nature of law and adjudication [63].[10] Both law and economics and CLS scholars utilize nonlegal methodologies to question the view of modern liberal legal scholars who claim that the virtues of "principled decisionmaking" can give determinant and consistent expression to the true meaning of shared values [64].[11] Members of each movement assert that the judicial process, as it works in practice, is far too inconsistent and unstable to support the claims of liberal scholars who advocate principled, consistent approaches [65]. Finally, each movement, in its own way, rejects the liberal notion that judges can rely upon an objective legal methodology for choosing between hotly contested positions in controversial matters involving politics and economics.

Law and economics scholars, for example, argue that the dominant methodology of the legal process school is inadequate because it lacks both scientific rigor and a realistic understanding of the "facts of life" [66]. These scholars argue that "hopes for a better society do not justify unreflective treatment of the tradeoffs we must make in a world of scarcity" [67]. Law and economic scholars take issue with the traditional wisdom of liberal legal scholars who argue that the legal process should be concerned with *moral* values and *distributive* goals [68]. In place of the legal process values of "harmony," "stability," and "shared-values," law and economic scholars argue that in the "real world" what counts is scarcity, choice, and self-interested conduct [69].

Critical legal studies scholars make somewhat similar claims. They, too, attack the dominant ideology of the legal process school. CLS scholars argue that the current plea of legal scholars for a reaffirmation of the "virtues" and "morality" of the legal process school is merely an apology for protecting the professional status of a particular conception of the judicial process which has dominated the profession since the 1950s [70]. CLS scholars argue that objectivity in legal interpretation is but an illusion; that mainstream scholars can defend their claims of rationality only by establishing a theory of law which projects false and misleading visions about the nature of law in American society [71]. In place of the virtues of the legal process school, these scholars argue that law and adjudication are the product of "conflict," "struggle," and "politics."

Both law and economic and CLS scholars also challenge the pragmatic and antitheoretical stance of traditional doctrinal scholars who argue that questions of public policy can be settled by an autonomous and neutral "legal process" [72]. Law and economic scholars argue that modern liberal scholars have internalized a "political" view of "law as an autonomous discipline"—a view which assumes that law is "a subject properly entrusted to persons trained in law and in nothing else."[12] Law and economic scholars assert that this way of thinking is "old-fashioned, passe', tired" [73]; it ignores the insights of other disciplines, and assumes that a political consensus can be reached for deciding upon an official method for legal decisionmaking [74]. These scholars argue that it is "wrong" to assume that legal problems can be "informed by one set of premises and one method of argument" [75].

CLS scholars challenge the notion that legal texts contain meanings which can be "correctly" discovered by utilizing "authoritative" interpretive methods [76]. They argue that the claims made by modern liberal scholars in defense of their methods is merely political rhetoric in the guise of neutral analysis. They argue that the class of law interpreters is simply too elite and privileged to be relied upon to be representatives of the values and interests of those within the larger society [77]. CLS scholars argue traditional methods of legal analysis resist and ignore the significane of *contingency and difference*.

Both law and economics and critical legal studies thus reject a number of the central premises of the legal process school—the assumption that judges *or* legislators can discover shared-values [78], the idea that a political consensus on fundamental issues exist [79], or the belief that American society consists of a harmonious, conflict-free citizenry who share profound values [80]. Practitioners of each movement argue for a new realism that takes into account the deep conflict and tension existing in a world comprised of sharp political and economic differences; a world where scarcity, privilege, and disadvantage is ubiquitous.

What is *new* about law and economics and critical legal studies is that they offer a theoretical approach that goes beyond the approach of the legal realists in establishing a systematic or totalistic critique and analysis of the structure of American law [81]. The legal realists were mainly concerned with critiquing individual cases and particular methods of legal reasoning. Law and economics and critical legal studies offer more than just a new way to critique cases or analyze law. Each of the new movements has attempted to develop a new theoretical approach for analyzing American law "across the board." Law and economic scholars seek to show how the various legal subjects such as contract, property, or criminal law *or* how different styles of legal reasoning (common law, statutory law) can be approached from the context of a unified approach developed from the logic of economic analysis of law. Critical legal scholars seek to demonstrate a somewhat similar point in deconstructing the common argumentative structures that pervade legal discourse. CLS practitioners practice a totalistic critique in their demonstration of how American law supports and defends hierarchies of power and privilege.

Law and economics and critical legal studies scholars have also transcended the critique of legal realism in pushing the two strands of legal realist thought to new levels of understanding. In developing a new systematic understanding of the economic analysis of law, law and economic scholars offer a much more sophisticated basis for establishing a new "rational" approach to legal analysis [82]. The new developments in law and economics represent significant advances when compared to "social science" scholarship of the legal realists. Law and economics, in this respect, offers a new "constructive" understanding of the legal process school. Indeed, as Mark Kelman has recently observed, law and economics may represent "the best worked out, most consummated liberal legal ideology of the sort that modern liberal scholars have sought to defend and CLS scholars have tried to understand and critique" [83]. From this perspective, one can come to see the law and economics movement as "an academic school which has advocated, normatively, a certain general vision of state function as well as particular implementing practices *and* a movement that purports to present a general descriptive theory of existing legal practice" [84].

Critical legal studies scholars have also gone beyond the legal realists in developing a new deconstructive practice of American law. Critical legal theorists have first "pushed beyond realism" in developing a deeper understanding of "law as politics" [85]. While the radical strand of legal realist thought sought to demonstrate how judges employed "class bias and bad logic" in legal decisionmaking, CLS theorists seek to reveal how the myth of "neutral law" is sustained by a "set of contradictions that beset the liberal view of the state" [86]. These critics have argued that law must be understood in terms of the "belief-clusters" or the "legal consciousness" which underlie the way traditional legal scholars perceive the world. In rejecting claims of neutral law, CLS scholars also disagree with law and economic scholars who argue that the inconsistencies of the traditional methods of the law can be rendered determinant by the so-called "scientific" method of economics [87].

CLS scholars also raise new theoretical questions in bringing to bear a criticism that raises serious questions about the concept of rationality and the limits of scientific reasoning. In pushing the realists' deconstructive approach to the limits, a number of CLS practitioners have developed a theoretical critique that transcends law in its attempt to demonstrate the "politics of reason" [88]. Critical legal studies scholars have argued that the realization of the liberal ideal of "a government of law and not men" requires an understanding of the "metaphysics of twentieth-century thought and the politics of reason itself" [89].

These scholars have thus analyzed the manner in which legal discourse is constructed and the ways in which claims of legal rationality seek to distinguish legal discourse from other ways of thinking and communicating about the social world [90]. The deconstructive study of American law is thus an attempt to show how the "purported distinction between rational legal argumentation and irrational emotional appeal is incoherent" [91]. The objective of such work is to reveal how claims of rationality exclude other ways of understanding the world, other knowledges, and other ways of being.[13] The goal of such analysis is to demonstrate the underlying openness in the legal system for experimenting with new ways in responding to the complexities of the pressing issues of the day [92].[14]

6. Why These New Trends in Legal Scholarship Are Developing

Law and economics and critical legal studies movements promise to be successful because they both offer new insights for understanding the complexity of law in modern society. In arguing their case for an economic approach to legal decisionmaking, law and economic scholars have been successful in persuading judges that it makes sense to consider the *opportunity cost* of their decisions; that in the real world there is "scarcity," and legal actors, like people generally, tend to engage in "self-interested conduct." These scholars have thus been successful in advocating a new economic "metric" for making choices about sharply divided public policies because they have presented a new methodology which accepts and responds to the modern realities of scarcity, choice, and tradeoffs.[15] While one may find the underlying values of law and economics distasteful, disagree with its underlying assumptions or empirical assertions, retain a skepticism as to the use of efficiency as a judicial decisional rule, and reject its political orientation, it is difficult to ignore the realism of an approach which reminds us that in a world of scarcity, tradeoffs are inevitable and that "[g]iven scarcity, judicial decisions ...create, transfer, or destroy valuable things and affect people's decisions" [93].

Critical legal scholars offer yet another message about law and adjudication. These scholars have fueled a deep skepticism about the possibility of authoritative and rational interpretations of legal texts [94]. The arguments of these critics are bound to be unsettling to both traditional liberal and modern law and economic scholars. If their claims about the limits of scientific reasoning and rational discourse are correct, then much of the current thinking about law and adjudication would be placed in jeopardy by a crisis which transcends law by questioning the distinction between rationality and politics [95]. What critical legal scholars have been successful in doing is that they have advanced a "new realism" about the way knowledge and power are reproduced and reinforced by law and adjudication.

Modern liberal legal scholars have found it difficult to counter the law and economics and CLS rhetoric because they have been unable to develop a firm rhetorical basis for advancing their own vision of law and adjudication. This is in part a result of the fact that liberal scholars have sought to defend legal process values which are now largely out of touch with modern realities. While the belief in a shared political consensus might have seemed sensible in the 1950s when the legal process school was established, that view is "oddly out of touch" with the realities of social events following the Vietnam war and Watergate [96]. Law, like the larger society, is composed of a wide spectrum of conflicting views which, as Posner has noted, "runs from Marxism, feminism, and left-wing nihilism and anarchism on the left to economic and political libertarianism and Christian fundamentalism on the right" [97]. We no longer live in a world of shared values, where ideology is at an "end" [98].

Lacking a rhetorical basis for defending their particular vision of the world, modern liberal legal scholars have adopted essentially a defensive posture. Some traditional legal thinkers have sought to counter the critique of the new movements by objecting on the grounds that the new critics are practicing unacceptable or uncollegial forms of criticism. Hence, they have argued that CLS scholars should leave the legal academy because they have failed to "keep the faith of the secular religion" by making a public commitment to "the law" [99]. While others have found the idea of a purge distasteful, they have nevertheless agreed with the intellectual position of those who have criticized law and economics and CLS for lacking a "commitment" to the "Rule of Law" [100].

For example, in his essay, "The Death of the Law?," Fiss has argued that law and economics and CLS are "dangerous jurisprudential movements" because the practitioners of these movements "distort the purposes of law and threaten its very existence" [101]. Law and economics is criticized because its arguments and methodology depend upon "contestable assumptions" about law and adjudication [102]. Fiss goes on, as others have, to argue that the new economic analysis of law "fails to supply the explanatory mechanism needed to give [the movement's claims] predictive validity, or even descriptive credibility" [103]. He further argues that the "normative" claims of the movement rests upon a "crude instrumentalism" which would lead to the "relativization of all values" [104]. He claims that the law and economics movement fails to reflect the way the judiciary understands its own role—"judges do not see themselves as instruments of efficiency, but rather as engaged in a process of trying to understand and protect the values embodied in the law" [105].

In the case of the critical legal studies, Fiss argues that practitioners of this movement "critique without a vision of what might replace that which is destroyed"—a form of critique which he finds "politically unappealing and politically irresponsible" [106]. He also asserts that the claims of CLS scholars about the openness of the normative concepts used in the law have not been empirically established or defended [107]. He argues that this form of legal criticism is threatening to both law and morality because there is no way of confining the bite of the CLS critique [108]. He claims that the CLS movement has generated a dangerous form of new *nihilism* which threatens the ability of law to sustain or generate a public morality [109].

What is missing from Fiss' argument is an affirmative justification for believing that *his* particular professional conception of law and adjudication is superior to the ones he criticizes. Nor for that matter does he persuasively establish even the power of the criticisms he has made in rejecting the approaches he disfavors. Law and economic scholars argue that the judges should be concerned with the consequences of their decisions and that as a normative matter the preferences of the parties affected by the legal process should trump the preferences of judges. In the view of law and economics, judges should seek to maximize the preference of legal actors. Fiss argues just the opposite in establishing that judges should utilize their preferences in deciding upon shared values. One must confront the negative implications which Fiss' conception of law raises in light of the liberal ideal of "a government of law, not men." Certainly, law and economics scholarship cannot be found inappropriate merely because it provides a new libertarian basis for critiquing the particular professional conception of law advanced by Fiss.

Fiss' objections to CLS are even more difficult to understand in light of what they imply for the shared-value perspective of the legal process school. Fiss argues that the CLS critique of law is dangerous because it undermines the law's belief in shared public values. Like other modern liberal legal scholars, he believes that the law should give expression to our public values. CLS does not deny the ideal that law should give expression to fundamental human values. Indeed, many, if not most, practitioners share the liberal values which Fiss seeks to protect through his conception of law and adjudication. What CLS does argue is that there is a *dialectical* relationship between the law and values; that our dreams and visions for a better world are *shaped* and *limited* by traditional legal discourse. CLS scholars thus argue that it is the forces of conformity in the profession that are the true obstacles impeding the critical reflection needed for the development of law and the legal profession. The fact that someone or some group has claimed the authority to define the appropriate legal standards and values is too often the excuse for blocking or dominating alternative experiences and understandings. How can we expect to have shared experiences or understandings if only one particular perspective is given the power and authority to define meaning?

Of course, Fiss might still object to the recent jurisprudential movements on the ground that they depend upon unfounded empirical assertions about law and adjudication. But these questions could also be asked for Fiss. Where is the proof that "our legal culture is sufficiently developed and textured so as to yield a body of disciplining rules that constrains judges and provides the (rational) standards for evaluating their work" [110]? The problem is that in law, like so many areas of human endeavor, one can never know with any degree of certainty that our views about the world are empirically verifiable. Any requirement establishing that legal change can be implemented only after empirical proof would be a paralyzing standard which few, if any, reformist projects could satisfy. CLS scholars would argue that the real problem with the view expounded by Fiss and others is that he assumes that both law and legal criticism must proceed on the basis of some "objective," "rational," or "pure" form of professional discourse. The irony in such a position is that it cannot surmount the problem of knowledge and politics [111]. Fiss' argument leads him to accept legal discourse as a neutral, unproblematic method for distinguishing truth from ideology, fact from opinion, or politics from interpretation. Ultimately, it will be the lingering doubts about method that will undermine Professor Fiss' strategy [112].

7. Conclusion

Academic discussions about American law have always been the subject of debate and controversy. Discussions about law are bound to be controversial because law is fundamentally a controversial subject. But today academic discussions about law have reached a new level of heightened hyperbole. It does seem apparent that the legal academic profession is "more openly politicized and more polarized that ever before" [113]. For some, the new developments in legal theory have resulted in a "pseudo critical posturing" at the legal academy which has erupted into a "shouting match pairing outrageous and self-congratulatory Chicagoans against obscure and critical Ungero-Marxists" [114]. In reacting to the possibilities of sheer incomprehensibility of different discourses, some legal scholars have called for the creation of a new "constructive" or "comprehensible" discourse.

Minow has thus argued the new interdisciplinary movements in law are making it increasingly difficult for members of the profession to speak together or to speak to members of other disciplines [115]. Minow calls for a new *"comprehensible discourse"* which would allow legal academics to engage in a public debate about their differences in methodology and outlook. In asserting her "feminist commitment to communication," Minow argues that we need a new discourse which would "relinquish the claim of exclusive truth, and (evince) a willingness to hear competing vantage points, all of which are partial" [116]. She asserts that "[r]ather than creating some new distanced categories and methods of legal analysis removed from popular understanding, legal scholars [should] look to local, specific problems that crop up in their experiences" such as "problems grounded in the experiences of particular groups, like women, or like the residents of the Jamaica Plain area in Boston" [117]. Here, the underlying idea would be that "legal scholarship should look outward by looking inward to how it has insulated law from communication with nonlawyers, and cut off the sound of legal meaning in people's daily lives" [118].

Other legal academics have made similar proposals for the creation of a new form of legal discourse. Bruce Ackerman, for example, has recently argued that the legal profession needs a "common language" that will enable its practitioners to engage in a "main line of conversation in a more constructive direction" [119]. Unlike Minow's feminist commitment to a new discourse of differences, Ackerman calls for a new "technocratic" discourse which will provide a new source of authority for stabilizing the rhetoric of lawyers so that they can "translate their clients' grievances into a language that powerholders find persuasive" [120]. As it turns out, the new "common language" which Ackerman advocates is based on the language of "law and economics" [121].

These two different proposals for a new common discourse suggest that the decision to use a particular "descriptive" discourse—say, feminism—or the discourse of difference, or the language of law and economics, would be just as controversial and perhaps as polarizing as the current substantive debate now being waged by different discourses. Legal scholars probably could never agree on a common language because whoever has the power to define the official language for the profession will have the power to entrench particular conceptions of law and adjudication.

Even a language that seeks to glorify difference may fall subject to the abuse of power in cutting off alternate conversations which may be necessary for presenting new and contrary perceptions of the world. In short, the call for a new common or comprehensible form of legal discourse probably will fail to escape the very conflict it is designed to avoid. The notion of a pure descriptive discourse for communication ignores the fact that social power is always at stake, that change can only come about through struggle and conflict, and that "there is no such metadiscourse that is itself immune to being placed within its particular 'interpretative framework'" [122]. The fact that someone or some group has the power to define the acceptable form of professional discourse is too often submerged and not expressed or appreciated. If different discourses are allowed to coexist and compete, then perhaps other perspectives can be acknowledged and appreciated or least tolerated.

Whether law and economics and critical legal studies are to be praised, condemned, or replaced by new forms of "comprehensible discourse" will, in my view, depend on how successful these movements are in hastening the death not of law, but rather the particular methods legal scholars have traditionally utilized to think about their subject. The proliferation of new forms of competing discourses, the willingness of some to try new methods, the expression of discontent and resistance signify neither the end of professional discourse nor law as we have known it—all are symptomatic of change from the old to the new [123].

Notes

1.   Advocates of the movement justify applying economic analysis in law by premising their arguments on descriptive and normative claims which seek to establish the relationship between economic concepts of efficiency and the common law.

2.   Boyle sets out a somewhat similar description of different "traces" of legal realist thought. He argues that at least three different traces or themes of critical thought can be discovered in the work of the realists which are structured by the binary opposition between what he calls the "structuralist" and "subjectivist" strands of critique (Ibid., p. 740). Boyle's thesis is "simply that these two strands represent a good way of getting at'...the most important philosophical issues and some of the most important existential experiences with which social theory and political action have to deal" (Ibid., pp. 740–741).

3.   Critical legal scholars can argue that they are "heirs" of "*Realism as Critique*"; Law and Economic scholars can claim that they are the "heirs" of "*Realism as Science*." See Peller, *supra* note 32, *infra*, at pp. 1226–1259. But see Kelman, *supra* note 83 at p.12 (arguing that CLS presents a critique of law which is different than the deconstructive realist critique).

4.   This post-realist movement is commonly associated with the scholarship of Hart, Henry M. and Sacks, Albert M. *infra* note 54. Hart and Sacks articulated the new pluralism of legal process by suggesting that it was possible to identify a legal method of "reasoned elaboration" for resolving controversial issues of public policy in a determinant manner. The idea of "reasoned elaboration" assumed that decisionmakers could employ a neutral process for reaching legal solutions in a way that would give effect to fundamentally shared values.

5.   As one recent account of this period has explained:

Stressing the nonrational aspects of judicial decision, some realists had talked as if judicial decision, some realists had talked as if judicial decisions were essentially indistinguishable from other decisions, as if all one could reasonably hope for was a "mature" decisionmaker, as if the process of "reasoned justification" merely conceals the emper-

or's nakedness. The realist portrayal of judges as essentially unrestrained conflicted disturbingly with democratic ideals which place legislative authority in popularly elected and politically responsible bodies. The portrayal was particularly trouble-some in the context of constitutional law, given the direct clash between the judicial and political branches and constitutional invalidation involves and the then still vivid recollections of the misadventures of the 1930's Supreme Court. If judges in constitutional cases were really no different from legislators, one of two obvious lessons could be drawn: either Justice McReynolds and his brethren had made no fundamental mistakes about judicial authority and constitutional interpretation but had erred, if at all, only in their "legislative" wisdom, or judicial "legislators" should defer to elected legislators when the latter have expressed themselves.

Greenawalt, *infra* note 53).

6.   In response to the question of the legal realists who questioned the ability of judges to render neutral decisions, Wechsler stated: "The answer...inheres primarily in that they (judges) are—or are obliged to be—entirely principled. A principled decision...is one that rests on reasons with respect to all the issues in the case, reasons that in their generality and their neutrality transcend any immediate result that is involved" (Wechsler, *supra* note 53).

7.   For example, it is not uncommon to hear traditional legal scholars reject the legal realist project as "a naive attempt to do empirical social science" and yet at the same time proclaim that "we are all realists now."

8.   This has been the source of the current debate in Constitutional law about whether the Supreme Court should give effect to the original meaning of the framers in interpreting the clauses of the constitution. That debate has involved a host of interpretative theories about constitutional adjudication such as "originalism," "textualism," and "intentionalism" [124].

9.   These new movements are post-realist movements because they build upon the critiques of legal realism in order to criticize the legitimacy and coherence of the prevailing conception of law and adjudication within the legal profession. Hence, while right-wing law and economics and left-wing critical legal studies represent different ideological camps, they are united in their opposition to some of the central premises of mainstream legal thought.

10.   Each movement argues the necessity for turning to new methods in resolving the critical issues of the day.

11.   Each movement challenges the liberal jurisprudence which has been identified with the Warren Court era—namely, the presupposition that legal process and legal reasoning can be a vehicle for expressing and preserving fundamental values shared within the larger society.

12.   Posner, *supra* note 3, p. 762.

13.   "The point is that the attempt to exclude other discourses from the legal world because they are "merely" myths, poems, or opinions is mistaken. Legal reasoning itself depends on metaphor and myths of origin" (Peller, *supra* note 32, p. 1156).

14.   The hope would be that by exposing the contingency of legal rationality, it would be much more opportunity for other voices to be heard and alternative views to be considered.

15.   As one leading law and economic scholar has proclaimed:

We can nowhere by listing values unless we have both a metric by which to assess the claims the parties make and a legitimate rule of decision. Economic analysis sometimes suggests a metric and a rule of decision; a list of values along with an aspiration to improve life in all its fullness does not (Easterbrook, *supra* note 66).

References

1. By far the most influential work seeking to demonstrate the idea that economic analysis can be instrumentally applied to law "across the board" is Posner, Richard A., *Economic Analysis of Law* (Boston: Little, Brown and Company, 1986).

2. Critical legal studies emerged as an identifiable movement in American law with the foundation of the Conference on Critical Legal Studies in 1977. For a social history of the critical legal studies movement see Schlegal, John H., "Notes Toward an Intimate, Opinionated and Affectionate History of the Conference on Critical Legal Studies," *Stanford Law Review*, Vol. 36, Nos. 1 & 2 (January 1984), pp. 391–411. For psycho-social history commenting on the "state of the movement," see Kennedy, Duncan, "Psycho-Social CLS: A Comment on the Cardozo Symposium," *Cardozo Law Review*, Vol. 6 (1984–85), pp. 1013–1031. The intellectual component of CLS is described in Unger, Roberto M., "The Critical Legal Studies Movement," *Harvard Law Review*, Vol. 96, No. 3 (January 1983), pp. 563–675. For a bibliography of CLS scholarship see Kennedy, Duncan, and Klare, Karle E., "A Bibliography of Critical Legal Studies," *Yale Law Journal*, Vol. 94 (1984–85), pp. 461–463.

3. Law and economics and critical legal studies are richly diverse intellectual movements involving a multitude of individual views, methodologies, "schools," and diverse theoretical traditions. For a recent attempt to describe the different views of the two movements in a preliminary way see, Fiss, Owen M., "The Death of the Law?," *Cornell Law Review*, Vol. 72, No. 1 (November, 1986), pp. 1–16; Minow, Martha L., "Law Turning Outward," *Telos*, Vol. 73 (Fall, 1987), pp. 79–100; Kornhauser, Lewis A., "The Great Image of Authority," *Stanford Law Review*, Vol. 36, Nos. 1 & 2 (January 1984), pp. 349–389. See also, Posner, Richard A., "The Decline of Law as an Autonomous Discipline: 1962–1987," *Harvard Law Review*, Vol. 100, No. 4 (February 1987), pp. 761–780.

    The law and economics movement is frequently identified with the Chicago school of economics which is associated with the work of *conservative* economists trained or working at the University of Chicago. Practitioners of the Chicago school tend to view law and the legal system as merely a supplement to the market, a necessary but minor vehicle for perfecting market-like solutions. See Minda, Gary, "The Lawyer-Economist at Chicago: Richard A. Posner and the Economic Analysis of Law," *Ohio State Law Journal*, Vol. 39 (1978), pp. 439–475. See also Ackerman, Bruce A., "Symposium of Law and Economics—Foreward: Talking and Trading," *Columbia Law Review*, Vol. 85, No. 5 (June 1985), pp. 899–904. There are, however, other "schools" within law and economics that exhibit different perspectives. The New Haven school, of Yale University, for instance, has attracted liberal practitioners who adopt the common methodology of the Chicago school but believe that there is a larger need for state intervention in order to cure problems involving market failure. See Fiss, *supra* note 3. What is common about the Chicago and New Haven schools, however, is that both can be seen to be working within the *liberal* tradition of economics. Attempts to describe the general themes and vision of the law and economics movement have also been more successful in that these scholars seem to agree on a common methodology.

Critical legal studies is even harder to pin down since practitioners of this movement do not appear to share a common methodology, but are united instead by their political and social alliances. The intellectual basis for this movement includes a number of diverse theoretical traditions. The common thread within this movement which distinguishes itself from law and economics is that CLS explicitly adopts methodologies and approaches which are characteristically *nonliberal* in their origin and orientation. For a description of the views expressed within the CLS movement see Fitzpatrick, Peter, and Hunt, Allen (eds.), *Critical Legal Studies* (New York: Basil Blackwell, 1987).

4. See Minow, *supra* note 3, pp. 79–100.
5. *Ibid.*, p. 89.
6. *Ibid.*, pp. 90–91. Minow argues that the group of scholars within each movement have been "preoccupied with the apparent loss of certainty and determinability within legal reasoning and legal institutional decision-making." *Ibid.*, at p. 91.
7. *Ibid.*, p. 90.
8. Fiss, *supra* note 3, p. 2.
9. *Ibid.* In Minow's view, law and economics and critical legal studies signify that the legitimacy of law is now open to question. For Fiss, these two movements signify the "death of law."
10. Posner, *supra* note 3, pp. 766, 768.
11. *Ibid.*, p. 769.
12. *Ibid.*, p. 773.
13. Paul Carrington, Dean of Duke University Law School, argued in a widely publicized journal that members of CLS should leave legal education because they failed to "keep the faith" in their commitment to "the law." Carrington, Paul D., "Of Law and the River," *Journal of Legal Education*, Vol. 34 (1984), pp. 222–228. For responses to Dean Carrington's article, see Martin, Peter W., "'Of Law and the River,' and of Nihilism and Academic Freedom," *Journal of Legal Education*, Vol. 35 (1985), pp. 1–26. My views are discussed in Minda, Gary, "The Politics of Professing Law," *Saint Louis University Law Journal*, Vol. 31, No. 1 (1986), pp. 61–71.
14. Fiss believes that the new "jurisprudential movements of the seventies" are threatening because they are "united in their rejection of the law as public ideal." Fiss, *supra* note 3. Fiss' views are more fully developed in Fiss, Owen M., "The Supreme Court, 1978—Foreword: The Forms of Justice,"

Harvard Law Review, Vol. 93, No. 1 (November 1979), pp. 1–58. See also Fiss, Owen M., "Objectivity and Interpretation," *Stanford Law Review*, Vol. 34 (1981–82), pp. 739–763. For a critical review of the view expressed in these papers see Brest, Paul, "Interpretation and Interest," *Stanford Law Review*, Vol. 34 (1981–82), pp. 765–773; Fish, Stanley, "Fish v. Fiss," *Stanford Law Review*, Vol. 36 (July 1984), pp. 1325–1347. For Fiss' reply to Fish see Fiss, Owen M., "Conventionalism," *Southern California Law Review*, Vol. 58 (1985), pp. 177–197.

For nearly a decade now Fiss has been warning of the dangers of new jurisprudential trends which depart from the style of jurisprudence characterized by the Warren Court era in constitutional law. He asserts that during the Warren Court era of the 1960s, judges sought to provide "structural reform" by giving "meaning to our public values." Fiss (1979), *supra* note 14, p. 2. According to Fiss, Earl Warren symbolizes the "great judge"—"someone whom the specter of authority both disciplines and liberates, someone who can transcent the conflict." Fiss (1982), *supra* note 14, p. 758. The public values which "great judges" are supposed to give effect (values such as equality, liberty, due process, etc.) are thought to have a "true and important meaning" such that by a process of "reasoned elaboration" judges can "discover" these values and make them meaningful in decisionmaking. Fiss (1979), *supra* note 14, p. 17. ("The task of a judge, then, should be seen as giving meaning to our public values and adjudication as the process through which that meaning is revealed or elaborated." *Ibid.*, p. 14.)

15. For discussion of the current "crisis" in legal scholarship and legal theory see Posner, *supra* note 3, p. 3; see also Brest, Paul, "The Fundamental Rights Controversy: The Essential Contradictions of Normative Constitutional Scholarship, *Yale Law Journal*, Vol. 90, No. 5 (April 1981), pp. 1063–1109; Gordon, Robert W., "Historicism in Legal Scholarship," *Yale Law Journal*, Vol. 90, No. 5 (April 1981), pp. 1017–1056, Posner, Richard A., "The Present Situation in Legal Scholarship," *Yale Law Journal*, Vol. 90, No. 5 (April 1981), pp. 1113–1130; Stone, Christopher D. "From a Language Perspective," *Yale Law Journal*, Vol. 90, No. 5 (April 1981), pp. 1149–1192; Tushnet, Mark, "Legal Scholarship: Its Causes and Cure," *Yale Law Journal*, Vol. 90, No. 5 (April 1981), pp. 1205–1223; Note, "Legal Theory and Legal Education," *Yale Law Journal*, Vol. 79, No. 6 (May 1970), pp. 1153–1178.

16. Kennedy, Duncan, "Cost-Benefit Analysis of Entitlement Problems: A Critique," *Stanford Law Review*, Vol. 33 (1981) pp. 387–445.

17. Statement of Critical Legal Studies Conference *quote in* Fitzpatrick & Hunt (eds.), *supra* note 3, p. 1.

18. Kornhauser, *supra* note 3, p. 352.

19. *Ibid.*, pp. 353–357.

20. See Posner, Richard A., "Utilitarianism, Economics, and Legal Theory,"

Journal of Legal Studies, Vol. 8 (1979), pp. 103–140; Posner, Richard A., "The Ethical and Political Basis of the Efficiency Norm in Common Law Adjudication," *Hofstra Law Review*, Vol. 8 (1980), pp. 487–507.

21. See, e.q., Fiss, *supra* note 3, p. 10. ("Critical legal studies scholars want to unmask the law, but not to make law into an effective instrument of good public policy or equality."

22. Minow, *supra* note 3, p. 83.

23. *Ibid.*, pp. 84–85.

24. These differences are also said to characterize the aspirations and personal style exhibited by members of each group. For example, Fiss has observed that "[t]he practitioners of law and economics tend to be better behaved; their mission more nearly accords with the traditions of the academy than does than of critical legal studies scholars." Fiss, *supra* note 3, p. 2. See also, Kornhauser, *supra* note 3, p. 352 (describing the criticism of law and economics as "constructive" and that of CLS as "destructive"). See, e.g., Granetz, Marc; "Duncan the Doughnut," *New Republic*, March 1, 1986, at p. 22 (describing the personal style of one well-known member of CLS, Duncan Kennedy, as the Abbie Hoffman of CLS). See also, Kennedy, *supra* note 2 ("CLS is a real-life revenge of the nerds, and nerds by definition have trouble in groups.").

  Certainly law and economic scholars have *not* suffered the degree of scorn that some traditional legal scholars have exhibited toward practitioners of CLS. See Frug, Gerald, "McCarthyism and Critical Legal Studies," *Harvard Civil Rights Law Review*, Vol. 22 (1987), p. 665. No one, for example, has suggested that practitioners of law and economics should leave the legal academy because they believe in a different legal vision or fail to share a particular creed. See Posner, *supra* note 3. Nor have the law and economics scholars experienced the tyep of tenure problems that CLS scholars have recently encountered. See, Kuttner, Robert, "Free Ideas at Harvard Law School Aren't So Free," *The Boston Globe* (May 18, 1987). See also, Bernstein E., "Profs Say Dalton Was Treated Unfairly," *The Harvard Crimson* (May 13, 1987); Colodny M., "Bok Reluctant to Enter Dalton Tenure Dispute," *The Harvard Crimson* (May 27, 1987). Indeed, while law and economic scholars are tolerated because they fit the traditional mold, CLSers are put down and ridiculed because they are thought to be nontraditional in their beliefs and life styles.

25. The two movements also project vastly different views about the nature and purpose of legal scholarship. CLS members, for example, have claimed that traditional legal scholarship has helped create and legitimate a world that tolerates wide discrepancies in wealth, class and social position. See Kennedy, Duncan, "Cost-Reduction Theory as Legitimatation," *Yale Law Journal* Vol. 90 (1981), p. 1275. These scholars seeks to develop a new form of radical legal scholarship which is committed to a form of theory that shares a dialectical relation with radical practice. The objective of such work is to transform the prevailing legal consciousness of traditional scho-

lars. Law and economic scholars, on the other hand, are much more traditional in their views about scholarship. These scholars argue that legal scholarship should be more like the *natural sciences*—that legal scholarship should concentrate on formulating and then testing falisifiable, law-like generalizations about social life. See generally, Tushnet, *supra* note 15, pp. 1211–1223.

26. When applied to judicial decisionmaking, the criterion of wealth maximization provides that the decisionmaker should choose the set of decision-relevant standards that will assign rights and impose liabilities in a manner designed to bring about an increase in social wealth as measured in dollar equivalents. See Posner, *supra* note 20, p. 119.

27. Posner (1979), *supra* note 20, p. 103, and Posner (1980), *supra* note 20, p. 487.

28. Posner, *supra* note 1, p. 19.

29. Unger, Roberto M., *Knowledge and Politics* (Free Press, 1975); p. 217 (describing the "paradox of sociability" as the "problem posed by the relation between self and others").

30. Kelman, Mark G., "Trashing," *Stanford Law Review*, Vol. 36, Nos. 1 & 2 (January 1984), pp. 293–348.

31. See, e.g., Posner, Richard A., "Wealth Maximization and Judicial Decision-Making," *International Review of Law and Economics*, Vol. 4 (December 1984), pp. 131–135.

32. See, e.g., Boyle James, "The Politics of Reason: Critical Legal Theory and Local Social Thought," *University of Pennsylvania Law Review*, Vol. 133, No. 4 (April 1985), pp. 685–780 at 691–705; Peller, Gary, "The Metaphysics of American Law," *California Law Review*, Vol. 73, No. 4 (1985), pp. 1151–1290, at 1220–1259; Kitch, Edmund D., "The Intellectual Foundations of Law and Economics," *Journal of Legal Education*, Vol. 33 (1983), pp. 184–196, Freeman, Alan D., "Truth and Mystification in Legal Scholarship," *Yale Law Journal*, Vol. 90, No. 5 (April 1981), pp. 1229–1237; Tushnet, Mark, "Post-Realist Legal Scholarship," *Journal of the Society of Public Teachers of Law*, Vol. 15 (March 1980), pp. 20–32, at 21; Tushnet, Mark, "Critical Legal Studies: An Introduction to Its Origins and Underpinnings," *Journal of Legal Education*, Vol. 36 (1986), pp. 505–517, at 505; Note, "Round and Round the Bramble Bush: From Legal Realism to Critical Legal Scholarship," *Harvard Law Review*, Vol. 95, No. 7 (May 1982), pp. 1669–1690; Note (1970), *supra* note 15. See also Mensch, Elizabeth, "The History of Mainstream Legal Thought," ch. 2 in Kairys, David (ed.), *The Politics of Law* (New York: Pantheon Books, 1982); Unger, Roberto M., "The Critical Legal Studies Movement," *Harvard Law Review* , Vol. 96 (January 1983), pp. 561–675. For a critical review of the relation between CLS and the legal realist movement, see White, G. Edward, "The Inevitability of Critical Legal Studies," *Stanford Law Review*, Vol. 36, Nos. 1 & 2 (January 1984), pp. 649–672.

For general background of the American legal realism movement see,

Purcell, Edward A., "The Rise of Legal Realism," ch. 5 in *The Crisis of Democratic Theory* (Lexington: University of Kentucky Press, 1973); Schlegel, John H., "American Legal Realism and Empirical Social Science: From the Yale Experience," *Buffalo Law Review*, Vol. 28, No. 4 (Fall 1979), pp. 459–586. See also Mensch, *supra* note 32, pp. 26–29.

33. Legal realism has been described as a "broad and dynamic attempt during the twenties and thirties to alter singificantly the assumptions of American Jurisprudence." Purcell, *supra* note 32, p. 188. Peller has, in turn, argued that "it is apparent that the realists felt an immediacy and urgency to their work, a belief that they were part of a larger transformation extending across disciplines, a historic undermining of the dominant ideology." Peller, *supra* note 32, p. 1220.

34. Peller, *Ibid.*, p. 1212.

35. Legal realism has been said to have emerged from such early nineteenth-century traditions as pragmatism, instrumentalism, and progressivism. See White, Morton G. (ed.), *Social Thought in America: The Revolt Against Formalism* (Boston: Beacon Press, 1957).

36. Kennedy, Duncan, "Toward a Historical Understanding of Legal Consciousness: The Case of Classical Legal Thought in America, 1850–1940," *Research in Law and Sociology*, Vol. 3 (1980), pp. 3–24.

37. Peller, *supra* note 32, p. 1193. As Peller has explained: "This era is associated with the well-known decisions in *Coppage* v. *Kansas*, 236 U.S. 1 (1915); where the Supreme Court struck down a Kansas statute forbidding employers to make nonunion affiliation a condition of employment; and in *Lockner* v. *New York*, 198 U.S. 45 (1905); where the Court struck down a New York statute limiting the workday of bakers to ten hours." *Ibid.*, pp. 1193–4.

38. Minow, *supra* note 3, p. 93.

39. Note (1970), *supra* note 15.

40. Peller, a critical legal studies scholar, has recently demonstrated how one might come to understand the critique of legal realism in two different ways. See Peller, *supra* note 32, pp. 1219–1259. For a similar discussion of the different "traces" of legal realist thought, see Boyle, *supra* note 32, pp. 691–705, at 746–756.

41. Cohen, Felix S., "Transcendent Nonsense and the Functional Approach," *Columbia Law Review*, Vol. 35, No. 6 (June 1935), pp. 809–849, for example, is a classic illustration of the work of a legal realist as "critic." Felix Cohen demonstrated in his article how legal principles such as *corporations*, *trade marks*, or *property rights*, were flawed by contradiction and circularity of reasoning. Cohen's effort was to deconstruct the legal concepts and arguments of the dominant discourse of the law in order to reveal how the legal abstractions were indeterminate and incoherent. See also Peller, *supra* note 32, p. 1227. Peller also reveals how the "deconstructive" strand of legal realism can be found in the work of other legal realists including Holmes and Robert Hale. *Ibid.*, pp. 1230–40.

The deconstructive method seeks to reveal how legal rules and principles are indeterminate. Deconstruction was a method utilized by the legal
realist to critique formalism. Deconstruction is also one of the main themes
of critical legal studies. See Tushnet, Mark, "Introduction, Perspectives on
Critical Legal Studies," *George Washington Law Review*, Vol. 52, No. 3
(March 1984), pp. 239–242. See also Peller, Gary, "Reason and the Mob:
The Politics of Representation," *Tikkun*, Vol. 2, No. 3 (July/August 1987),
pp. 28–31; Text & Notes *infra*, at notes 90–92.

42.   Cohen, *supra* note 41, p. 810. See also Peller, *supra* note 32, p. 1229.
43.   The idea of "Realistic Jurisprudence" comes from Llewellyn's famous
      article: Llewellyn, Karl N., "A Realistic Jurisprudence—he Next Step,"
      Columbia Law Review, Vol. 30, No. 4 (April 1930), pp. 431–465. Llewellyn
      argued that realistic jurisprudence would require judges to look beyond
      abstract legal verbalism and instead focus on behavioral factors—"the area
      of contact, of interseaction, between official regulatory behavior and the
      behavior of those affecting or affected by official regulatory behavior...."
      Ibid., 464. The idea of realistic jurisprudence made the social sciences,
      including economics, relevant for law study. As Llewellyn put it: "When one
      approached the law, not with the idea of formulating its rules into a system,
      but with an eye to discovering how much it does or can effect...economic
      theory offers in many respects amazing light." *Ibid.*
44.   Llewellyn, *supra* note 43, pp. 431–465. See also Purcell, *supra* note 32, p.
      126 ("Llewellyn's empirical approach concentrated on behavior as the
      proper subject of study for the legal scholar."); Note (1970) *supra* note 15,
      p. 1169 wherein it's stated: "Llewellyn based his realist approach on the
      possibility of formulating instrumental concepts or rules, flexible doctrines
      with specific purposes informed by broad intellectual inquiry and precise
      attention to behavior and consequences."
45.   Frank, Jerome, *Law and the Modern Mind* (New York: Brentano's 1930)
      pp. 140–141. As Purcell has explained: "Accepting most of Llewellyn's
      ideas, Frank went far beyond them in earning his reputation as one of the
      most extreme realists. Whereas Llewellyn believed that rules and prece-
      dents were relevant and of some importance, Frank did not even consider
      them a meaningful part of the law....To him law meant a particular
      judicial determination upon a particular and singular set of facts. Reducing
      law to what he considered an unequivocal empirical minimum, Frank
      equated it solely with the specific individual judicial decision." Purcell,
      supra note 32, pp. 126–127.
46.   Note (1982) *supra* note 32, p. 1674. An example of such an effort can be
      found in Lassell, Harold D., and McDougal, Myres S., "Legal Education
      and Public Policy: Professional Training in the Public Interest," *Yale Law
      Journal*, Vol. 52, No. 2 (March 1943), pp. 203–295.
47.   Peller, *supra* note 32, p. 1222; Cohen, Morris C., "Justice Holmes and the
      Nature of Law," *Columbia Law Review* Vol. 31, No. 1 (January 1931), pp.
      352–367, at 357–58; Dickerson, John, "Legal Rules: Their Function in the

Process of Decision," *University of Pennsylvania Law Review*, Vol. 79, No. 7 (May 1931), pp. 833–868; Fuller, Lon L., "American Legal Realism," *University of Pennsylvania Law Review*, Vol. 82, No. 5 (March 1934), pp. 429–462; Harris, Rufus C., "Idealism Emergent in Jurisprudence," *Tulane Law Review*, Vol. 10 No.2 (February 1936), pp. 169–187; Kantorowicz, Hermann, "Some Rationalism About Realism," *Yale Law Journal*, Vol. 43, No. 8 (June 1934) pp. 1240–1253; Mechem, Philip, "The Jurisprudence of Despair," *Iowa Law Review*, Vol. 21, No. 4 (May 1936), pp. 669–692, 672; Miltner, Charles C., "Law and Morals," *Notre Dame Lawyer*, Vol. 10, No. 1 (November 1934), pp. 1–10, 8; Pound, Roscoe, "The Future of Law," *Yale Law Journal*, Vol. 47, No. 1 (November 1937), pp. 1–13, at 2; Pound, Rescoe, "The Call for a Realist Jurisprudence," *Harvard Law Review*, Vol. 44, No. 5 (March 1931), pp. 697–711.

48. *Ibid.*, pp. 697–711. See also Note (1982) *supra* note 32. at p. 1669, fn. 4.

49. See, e.g., Lasswell and McDougal, *supra* note 46. See also Purcell, *supra* note 32, pp. 74–94.

50. Such well-known realists as Thurmon Arnold, Charles Clark, Felix Cohen, Walton H. Hamilton, Jerome Frank, Rexford G. Tugwell, and William O. Douglas left teaching or practice careers for public service. See Note (1982) *supra* note 32 at p. 1675, fn. 41. See also, Mensch, *supra* note 32; Minow, *supra* note 3, p. 93. She stated: "Many of the Legal Ralists....sought to establish anew the bases for law's legitimacy...by trying through the New Deal to reorder through law. That New Deal experience launched the infusion of policy analysis into law; pragmatic social engineering with reliance on the good intentions of the social engineers supplied one route toward re-establishing law's legitimacy. Others shifted the intellectual focus from substantive aims, now properly the domain of political conflict, and process values, the central preserve of law."

51. Note (1982) *supra* note 32 at p. 1669.

52. Hart, H. L. A., *The Concept of Law* (London: Oxford University Press, 1961).

53. Wechsler, Herbert H., "Toward Neutral Principles of Constitutional Law," *Harvard Law Review*, Vol. 73, No. 1 (November 1959), pp. 1–35, reprinted in Wechsler, Herbert, *Principles, Politics, and Fundamental Law: Selected Essays*, 3rd ed. (Cambridge: Harvard University Press, 1961). See also Greenawalt, Kent, "The Enduring Significance of Neutral Principles," *Columbia Law Review*, Vol. 78, No. 5 (June 1978), pp. 982–1021.

54. Hart, Henry M., and Sacks, Albert M (tent. ed.), *The Legal Process: Basic Problems in the Making and Application of Law* (Unpublished manuscript, Harvard University Law School, 1958).

55. See Schlegel, *supra* note 32, pp. 459–460.

56. See Minow, *supra* note 3, p. 93.

57. Greenwalt, *supra* note 53, pp. 982–983.

58. 334 U.S. 1 (1948). In *Shelley* v. *Kramer*, the Supreme Court invalidated a

racially restrictive covenant in a private contract for the same of law which discriminated on the grounds that the enforcement of the convenant constituted impermissible state action under the fourteenth amendment.

59. 349 U.S. 294 (1954). In *Brown*, a unanimous Supreme Court declared that the equal protection clause of the fourteenth amendment forbid racial segregation in the public schools.

60. See Greenwalt, *supra* note 53, p. 983; Wechsler, *supra* note 53, p. 1. Bickel, Alexander, *The Supreme Court and the Idea of Progress* (New Haven: Yale University Press, 1978); Kirkland, Philip, *Politics, The Constitution and the Warren Court* (Chicago: University of Chicago Press, 1970).

61. See Note (1970), *supra* note 15.

62. *Ibid*.

63. See Minow, *supra* note 3, p. 94. Both law and economics and critical legal studies reject the widely held view of lawyers and judges that legal problems can be analyzed and studied "autonomously" by objective methods of legal reasoning and analysis.

64. See Fiss, *supra* note 3.

65. See, e.g., Easterbrook, Frank H., "Foreword: The Court And The Economic System," *Harvard Law Review*, Vol. 98, No. 1 (November 1984), pp. 4–60, at 8–9 (law and economic scholar arguing that the dominant methods of the judicial process are unprincipled and inconsistent); Brest, *supra* note 15 (CLS scholar arguing that liberal theories of constitutional scholarship are essentially incoherent and indeterminate).

66. See, e.g., Easterbrook, Frank H., "Method, Result, and Authority: A Reply," *Harvard Law Review*, Vol. 98, No. 3 (January 1985), pp. 622–629, at 622. (Arguing that "scarcity," "choice," and "self-interested conduct" are "the facts of life" to which judges must respond in legal decisionmaking). See also Peller, Gary, "The Politics of Reconstruction," *Harvard Law Review*, Vol. 98, No. 4 (February 1985), pp. 863–881, at 864 (describing how "liberal reformist legal thinkers" are challenged by "law-and-economics adherents' claims to scientific rigor and hardheaded realism about the way things are").

67. Easterbrook, *supra* note 66, p. 629.

68. See, e.g., Tribe, Lawrence H., "Constitutional Calculus: Equal Justice or Economic Efficiency?," *Harvard Law Review*, Vol. 98, No. 3 (January 1985), pp. 592–621.

69. Easterbrook, *supra* note 66.

70. See, e.g., Gordon, *supra* note 15 (describing the various "responsive modes" of traditional legal scholarship in *denying* "the historical and cultural contingency of law") ; Hutchinson, Allen C., and Monahan, Patrick J., "Law, Politics, and the Critical Legal Scholars: The Unfolding Drama of American Legal Thought," *Stanford Law Review*, Vol. 36. No. 1 (January 1984), pp. 199–245, at 202–8.

71. See, e.g., *Ibid*. ("The central thrust of the Critical critique is that all such

efforts to reconstruct American legal thought in the wake of the Realists' challenge are doomed to failure, and that they simply offer more cogent evidence of the bankruptcy of mainstream legal thought.") See also Schlegel, John H., "Introduction," *Buffalo Law Review*, Vol. 28, No. 4 (Fall 1979), p. 203; Mensch, *supra* note 32, pp. 29–37.

72. See, e.g., Posner, *supra* note 3; Easterbrook, *supra* note 65; Tushnet, Mark, "Critical Legal Studies: An Introduction to Its Origins and Underpinnings," *Journal of Legal Education*, Vol. 36, No. 4 (December 1986), pp. 505–517; Unger, *supra* note 32.

73. *Ibid.*, p. 773.

74. *Ibid.*

75. Easterbrook, *supra* note 65, p. 4.

76. Borrowing from the field of *literary criticism*, critical theorists have challenged the notion that legal texts contain meanings which can be "correctly" discovered by utilizing "authoritative" interpretative methods. See, e.g., Kennedy, David, "The Turn to Interpretation," *Southern California Law Review*, Vol. 58, No. 1 (January 1985), pp. 251–275; Frug, "Henry James, Lee Marvin and the Law," *New York Times Book Review Magazine* (February 16, 1986). See also, Minda, Gary, "Phenomenology, Tina Turner and the Law," *New Mexico Law Review*, Vol. 16, No. 2 (Fall 1986), pp. 479–493, at 487, fn. 34. By deconstructing legal texts into equally plausible countermeanings, these educators have sought to illustrate how a community of legal interpreters have performed an ideological function by creating legal meanings that fail to perceive honest differences and alternative ways of being. Their goal is to empower the reader so that he/she can evaluate the inescapably ideological character of legal thought. For a general introduction to deconstruction as a new critical attitude toward interpretation see Peller (1987), *supra* note 41, pp. 28–31, 92–93.

77. See, e.g., Brest, *supra* note 14, p. 771.

78. See, e.g., Posner, *supra* note 3, p. 773–774.

79. *Ibid.* See also Freeman, Alan, "Truth and Mystification in Legal Scholarship," *Yale Law Journal*, Vol. 90, No. 5 (April 1981), pp. 1229–1237, at 1233–1234.

80. See, e.g., Mensch, *supra* note 32, p. 406.

81. See Boyle, *supra* note 32; Note (1982), *supra* note 32, p. 1667.

82. See, e.g., Boyle, *supra* note 32. Peller, *supra* note 32.

83. Kelman, Mark M., *A Guide to Critical Legal Studies* (Cambridge, Harvard University Press, 1987).

84. *Ibid.*, p. 184.

85. See Boyle, *supra* note 32, p. 707.

86. *Ibid.*, p. 706.

87. Indeed, there is now a growing body of critical legal scholarship which seeks to critique law and economics scholarship. See, e.g., Kelman, Mark G., "Misunderstanding Social Life: A Critique of the Core Premises of

"Law and Economics," *Journal of Legal Education*, Vol. 33, No. 2 (1983), pp. 274–284; Kelman, Mark G., "Consumption Theory, Production Theory and Ideology in the Coase Theorem," *Southern California Law Review*, Vol. 52, No. 3 (March 1979), pp. 669–698; Kelman, Mark G., "Choice and Utility," *Wisconsin Law Review*, Vol. 1979, No. 3 (1979), pp. 769–797. Kennedy, Duncan, "Distributive and Paternalist Moves in Contract and Tort Law, with Special Reference to Compulsory Terms and Unequal Bargaining Power," *Maryland Law Review*, Vol. 41, No. 4 (1982), pp. 563–658. Kennedy, *supra* note 16. Kennedy, Duncan, and Michelman, Frank, "Are Property and Contract Efficient?" *Hofstra Law Review*, Vol. 8, No. 3 (Spring 1980), pp. 711–770. These CLS critiques of the law and economics scholarship advance the general form of critique CLS scholars utilize in critiquing mainstream scholarship. Thus, CLS scholars argue that there is simply no politically neutral, coherent way to talk about whether a legal decision is efficient, wealth-maximizing, or whether benefits outweigh costs. For a summary of the specific critiques see Kelman, *supra* note 83.
88. Boyle, *supra* note 32, p. 707.
89. *Ibid.*, p. 705.
90. Peller, *supra* note 32, p. 1154.
91. *Ibid.*, p. 1155.
92. See Minda, *supra* note 76, p. 490.
93. Easterbrook, *supra* note 66, p. 622.
94. Posner, *supra* note 3, p. 768.
95. Unger, Roberto M., *Passion: An Essay on Personality* (New York: The Free Press, 1984).
96. See, e.g., White, *supra* note 32.
97. Posner, *supra* note 3, p. 766.
98. See Bell, Daniel, "The End of Ideology" (Glencoe IL: The Free Press, 1960).
99. See Carrington, *supra* note 13.
100. See Fiss, *supra* note 3, Hegland, Kenney, "Goodbye to Deconstruction," *California Law Review*, Vol. 58, No. 5 (July 1985), pp. 1203–1221.
101. Fiss, *supra* note 3, p. 1.
102. *Ibid.*, p. 4.
103. *Ibid.*, p. 5.
104. *Ibid.*, p. 5.
105. *Ibid.*, p. 8.
106. *Ibid.*, p. 10.
107. *Ibid.*, p. 12.
108. *Ibid.*, p. 13.
109. *Ibid.*, p. 15.
110. *Ibid.*, p. 11, where Fiss also acknowledges that his assumptions are "open to a factual challenge, as any empirical claim must be."
111. See Unger, *supra* note 29.

112. See also Minda, *supra* note 13.
113. Peller, *supra* note 66.
114. Ackerman, Bruce A., *Reconstructing American Law* (New Haven: Yale University Press, 1984), p. 44. See Peller, *supra* note 66.
115. See Minow, *supra* note 3.
116. *Ibid.*, p. 97.
117. *Ibid.*, p. 97.
118. *Ibid.*, p. 99.
119. Ackerman, *supra* note 114, pp. 44–45.
120. *Ibid.*, p. 3.
121. *Ibid.*, p. 42. Ackerman argues that there are two structures to his new discourse: one for establishing "facts"; the other for establishing "values." The language of law and economics would be used to determine facts, and common discourse of the "people" would be used to determine "values." *Ibid.*, pp. 29, 79-80. See also, Peller, *supra* note 66, pp. 867–868. "Ackerman's strategy for the liberal-reformist center is to incorporate conservative law-and-economic discourse into the 'main line of conversation' for the legal description of *facts* yet preserve traditional liberal discourse for the discussion of values," at p. 869.
122. *Ibid.*, pp. 880–881.
123. See Kuhn, Thomas S., *The Structure of Scientific Revolutions* (Chicago: University of Chicago Press, 1970).
124. Lyons, David, "Constitutional Interpretation and Original Meaning," *Society Philosophy and Policy*, Vol. 4, No. 1 (Autumn 1986), p. 75.

5 PUBLIC CHOICE AND THE ECONOMIC ANALYSIS OF LAW

Charles K. Rowley

"What Can Economics Contribute to Its Neighbors?
To Law—Limitations
To Political Science—A Theory
What Can Economics Learn from its Neighbors?
From Law—A Framework
From Political Science—Data"
—J. M. Buchanan [1966]

1. Introduction

In 1966, when James M. Buchanan [1] signaled important inter-dependencies between economics and law and economics and political science, portents for a new political economy already amounted to more than "the wind blowing through the rocks at Delphi.[1] *The Coase Theorem* [2] had introduced exchange catallactics into the analysis of

I wish to acknowledge the editorial contribution of Nicholas Mercuro and the excellent secretarial support of Helen Rusnak.

the law, and *The Calculus of Consent* [3] had already alerted political scientists to the impending imperialistic invasion of their discipline by economists.

Yet in 1966, even Buchanan could not have foreseen the full force of the research program that was to emerge and to consolidate not just throughout North America but also throughout Western Europe, Australia, and Japan; a research program that was to receive, only 20 years later, the ultimate accolade, by the Swedish Royal Academy through the award of the Nobel Prize in Economic Science in recognition of Buchanan's own contributions to the new political economy, a political economy that rightly bears the "Virginian Blend" insignia. The essay charts the development of the new political economy, outlines tensions that have emerged between this research program and the new law and economics, and identifies prospects for future interactions between those vibrant and still advancing disciplines.

Arguably, there is only one basic brand of Virginia political economy, pioneered by Buchanan and his erstwhile colleague, Gordon Tullock, and consolidated by the faculty associated with the Center for Study of Public Choice, first at Blacksburg and now at George Mason University. On the other hand, there are several, not always harmonious, strands to the new law and economics, each with its own interface with public choice. Despite a widerspread belief that the new law and economics in some sense is "right-wing," because it employs market analysis in the evaluation of the legal process, the research program in reality is ideologically neutral, just as are markets themselves in the hands of sophisticated scholars. A research program that has penetrated economic scholarship at institutions as ideologically disparate as Chicago and Yale is not easily or wisely to be categorized by reference to some political issue space location.

Section 2 outlines the central features of the law and economics research program, noting tensions within that program over issues of methodology, and controversies concerning the relevance of such issues as efficiency, liberty, and justice. Section 3 outlines the central features of the public choice research program, identifies sources of tension within that program, and centers attention upon crucial differences that have emerged from research in the new law and economics and in public choice relevant to an understanding of the law and legal institutions. Section 4 briefly applies public choice analysis to specific areas of the law, identifies significant differences of insight between this approach and that of the new law and economics, and signals the opportunity that exists, through beneficial interaction, for the emergence of a new, far-reaching political economy.

2. The Law and Economics Research Program

The term *law and economics* is here defined as the application of economic theory and econometric methods to examine the formation, structure, processes, and impact of law and legal institutions. As such, the discipline has been divided, albeit somewhat arbitrarily, into "old" and "new" [4]. The old law and economics, with a pedigree almost as lengthy as that of economics itself, confined itself to the legal subject matter that inescapably affected the operation of the economy and markets. It encompassed such areas as antitrust, regulation, labor, and taxation. The subject matter of the new law and economics, in contrast, is the entire legal system and the doctrines and procedures of the civil, criminal, and public laws, whether or not they appear superficially to regulate explicit economic relationships. It is this wider application of economics that constitutes the essence of the new approach and which makes the subject relevant to all legal scholarship.

Inevitably the new law and economics draws heavily upon neoclassical economics—demonstrably the most powerful predictive approach available to economists—and upon advanced statistical and econometric methods, to evaluate predictions as the basis of its scientific thrust. Nevertheless its distinctive feature is the application of market economics to legal institutions, rules, and procedures which in certain areas (notably in tort and in crime) are not conventionally seen to influence market behavior, but which indeed are defined in terms of market failure. From its early beginnings in 1960, with the application of the Coase theorem to the law of tort, this technique has now been applied to every aspect of the legal system, including contract, property, crime and punishment, enforcement, civil and administrative procedure, legislation, and constitutions. This imperalism could not succeed without controversy in a discipline as conventionally conservative as the law.

2.1. Tensions Over Positive Methodology

Economics, in its application to the law no less than elsewhere, is a science in much the same sense as chemistry, biology, and physics. As such, its practitioners (concerned with what is or with what conditionally will be) are equally as concerned to formulate hypotheses and to test such hypotheses against experience by observation and, where feasible, by experimentation. Although economics prior to David Hume's recognition of the problem of induction—the moving from singular to universal statements—had not infrequently followed the route of inductive logic, slowly it had shaken itself loose from this essentially unscientific method. Following the early writings of Karl Popper [5], economics embraced the approach of deductive logic that emphasizes the moving from universal statements (nets to catch the world) to singular statements (predictions) through a process of logical deduction.

Almost all economists subscribe, in principle if not always in practice, to the deductive approach as outlined above. There is much more controversy, however, concerning the full thrust of Popper's logic, at least as interpreted by Milton Friedman in his important 1953 essay on methodology [6]. Since this particular controversy has remained submerged, for the most part, in the law and economics literature, not least because of the domination of Chicago contributions, it is important to outline the approach of Popper.

According to Popper, the method of critically testing theories, and discriminating between them according to the results of tests, always proceeds along the following lines. From a new idea, anticipation, hypothesis, or theoretical system, more or less tentatively derived, conclusions are drawn by means of logical deduction. It is then possible to distinguish four different ways in which the theory may be tested. First, there is the logical comparison of the conclusions among themselves, by which the internal consistency of the system is evaluated. Second, there is the investigation of the logical form of the theory, with the intent of determining whether it has the character of a scientific theory (i.e., it is falsifiable) or whether it is mere tautology. Third, there is a comparison of the theory's predictions with those of other theories, to determine whether it constitutes a scientific advance. Finally, there is the testing itself, designed to falsify the predictions to the extent feasible. If the theory survives, for the time being, it is not falsified. But, if the outcome is negative and the singular statements are falsified, then so is the theory whence such statments were logically deduced.

Given Popper's emphasis upon falsifying rather than upon defending extant theory, rules are essential. For, in the absence of rules, it is always possible to evade falsification, not least by reinforcing the universal statement ad hoc with suitable auxiliary statements or hypotheses. Indeed, the unscrupulus "scholar" could refuse to acknowledge any falsifying experience whatsoever. To counteract such temptation, and to expose theory to the fiercest struggle for survival, Popper established rules which carried with them significant implications for scientific method.

The universal statements, which provide what Imre Lakatos [7] subsequently was to call the "protected core" of a theory, are not required by Popper to relate directly to reality, or even to be observable in any empirical sense. However, this exemption is not extended to the auxiliary (singular) conditions, which provide the basis for the testing of conditional predictions, and which, in general, must relate to reality. The introduction and/or the modification of such auxiliary conditions is acceptable, furthermore, only when it intensifies the degree of falsifiability of the system.

Rules also are established governing the definition of the empirical statements of science—the basic statements or predictions. The formal requirements for such basic statements are satisfied by all singular statements. In addition, however, Popper requires that such statements also should satisfy a material requirement—they must be testable by observation. Clearly, therefore, they must relate directly to reality.

In order to test a theory, decisions are required as to which predictions are to be evaluated. At this stage, individual perceptions and preferences impinge directly on scientific method, interferences that place a premium on rules that define success and failure at the testing phase. The theoretician is to set out sharply defined predictions, ex ante, before the evidence accumulates. The empiricist is to elicit a decisive answer to those predictions—and to those predictions alone—in evaluating that theory. Once again, however, individual perceptions and preferences play an inescapable role. The procedure is not unlike that of trial by jury. But it is clear that the verdict need not be true merely because a jury has accepted it. In Popper's science, Frank Knight's [8] warning about "the relatively absolute absolute" is always center stage.

Theories may be more or less testable, in this sense of falsifiability; and the degree of such testability is relevant to the choice between competing theories. Specifically, as the area representing the basic statements which it forbids becomes increasingly wide, so the theory becomes increasingly vulnerable to falsification, since it allows the empirical world an ever-narrowing range of possibilities. Such a theory asserts so much about the world of experience—its empirical range is so great—that there is little chance for it to escape falsification. Popper contends that science aims precisely at producing theories which are easily falsifiable in this sense, thus restricting the range of permitted events to a minimum. The empirical content of a statement, therefore, increases with its degree of falsifiability; the more that it forbids, the more that it says about the world of experience. Indeed, Popper defines the empirical content of a statement as the class of its potential falsifiers.

Many scientists attach value to the property of simplicity in a theory. In Popper's view, the properties ascribed to simplicity precisely are those that falsifiability promotes. Simple statements are prized more highly than complex statements "because they tell us more; because their empirical content is greater; and because they are better-testable." As a corollary, theories are described to be complex in the highest degree when they are viewed as unfalsifiable, to be secured at whatever cost by the manipulation of ad hoc auxiliary hypotheses.

The concept of "corroboration," as applied to theory by Popper, denotes the degree to which a theory has proved its fitness to survive by standing up to tests. Popper relies less upon the number of corroborating instances as the overriding criterion than upon the severity of the various tests to which the theory in question can be, or better, has been, subjected. Thus, the simpler the theory, the higher is the degree to which it can be corroborated. A theory which has been well corroborated can be superseded only by a theory of a higher level of universality. Such a method subjects our "ever tentative answers to ever renewed and ever more rigorous tests."

Even among mainstream economists, exposed to Friedman's interpretation of Popper's methodology at the outset of their professional careers, there are many who do not subscribe to its logic [9]. Many dislike its reliance upon universal statements which may not be observable empirically, indeed which Friedman provocatively has stated must be unrealistic. Many do not trust the "as-if" approach to offer any realistic interpretation of observed events, and refuse to rely upon a method that values predictive power exclusively and ignores explanation. Some even reject the notion that positive science is concerned with prediction at all and seek refuge instead in the elegance and/or the mathematical complexity of their modeling. At least, however, all of them have been trained in Popper's deductive logic, are aware of its widespread appeal, and have come to terms with its attractiveness to the editors of the leading scholarly journals.

How much more bewildering, therefore, is the logic of this approach for the large majority of legal scholars and political "scientist" who often have had no formal exposure to Popper's logic, indeed even to the deductive approach, during their professional training [10]. Political science, in the wake of the post-1960s invasion of mathematics and statistical method, to say nothing of public choice, increasingly embraces Popper's method, despite the resistance of many of its senior scholars. The law, in all its mainstream jurisprudence, remains committed to the inductive method as the basis for positive analysis.

Lawyers who specialize in jurisprudence may follow the deductive logic of the philosophers and economists who have tended to dominate this area of scholarship. For the most part, however, lawyers seek out the universal "truth" of the law by a careful selection of a number of singular statements encompassed in judgments pronounced by the higher courts.

For such is the thrust and strength of precedent; such is the indoctrination of the case book method in the law schools of the Anglo-Saxon world. Yet this movement from the singular to the universal—from a single judgment to generalization of the law, at least with respect to the *ratio decidendi* of the case—is anathema to the deductive approach as employed in normal science.

Moreover, in its emphasis upon a case-by-case evaluation, the common law, and indeed the judicial interpretation of public law, moves essentially from observation of facts to the derivation of theory. Once again, this runs counter to the approach of Popper, which emphasizes the role of evidence in evaluating a preconstructed theory (though second-rate econo-metricians breach this requirement more frequently than not). A further consequence of this approach is haphazard development, since legal issues cannot be determined by the courts until suitable cases arise and are adjudicated, often through a time-consuming process of appeals.

Furthermore, lawyers are not enamored, for the most part, of the formal model-building employed in economics, most especially not with the conditional predictions derived from such models. Lawyers, typically are concerned with the detailed facts surrounding a particular case, with the precise formal arguments that encapsulate specific judgments. There is precious little scope for general theory in such circumstances. Lawyers are not accustomed to evaluating partial relationships on ceteris paribus terms, since each case requires a total judgment in which all aspects of the relevant environment are sifted and evaluated.

Given this sharp disparity of methodologies, it is remarkable that law and economics emerged so quickly over the period 1965 to 1980 as a discipline dominated by the method of Popper utilizing the techniques of modern science. Such a shift of emphasis underscores the versatility of gifted lawyers and, itself, is a tribute to the quality of a good legal training. For those who remain behind, however, committed to "black-letter" law, the new law and economics is an enigma, an alien "black-box" discipline which is seen to threaten the legitimacy of a long-developed jurisprudence essential to any well-based social and economic order.

2.2. Tensions Over Normative Methodology

Tensions are evident in the normative methodology of the new law and economics, in deciding what ought to be. The debate over the competing claims of efficiency, liberty, and justice reflects the ubiquity over all areas of scholarship of scholars motivated by conservative, by libertarian, or by socialist ideology—and indeed of some who are unutterably confused or ambivalent between the demands of each.

Because of the preeminence of Richard Posner [11] in normative (as well as positive) law and economics, there is a widespread misapprehension within the legal profession that law and economics is concerned exclusively with the pursuit of economic efficiency, sometimes loosely (and inaccurately) referred to as wealth maximization by Posner himself. The efficiency thrust stems from an excessive reliance by such scholars on Paretian welfare economics, buttressed by the concept of potential compensation and predicated on some acceptance of an implicit distribution of rights.

Paretian welfare economics, like any normative framework for policy evaluation, rests upon a set of significant value assumptions to which its advocates necessarily adhere [12]. Specifically, the concern of this approach is with the welfare of all members of society; for the most part, individuals are considered to be the best judge of their own welfare, though exceptions are made for lunatics, minors, drug addicts, and the like, viewed by the large majority as incapable of effectively pursuing their own interests. If any change in resource allocation is available which would increase the welfare of at least one individual and not reduce the welfare of any other individual, then this change is commended as Pareto-preferred. When all such opportunities are exhausted, a Pareto optimum prevails. The Paretian criteria, which provide only a quasi-ordering, are then silent on issues of further resource reallocation. This last-mentioned value judgment, which precludes the making of interpersonal comparisons over matters of utility, often is referred to erroneously as *the* Paretian assumption.

To understand the rationale of the Paretian approach, it is important to realize its original role, which was to determine just how far policy issues were capable of resolution on the least limiting (or weakest) set of assumptions designed to capture the acceptance of all individuals in society. Not surprisingly, such an approach proved to be limited, not least because of its dependence upon prior acceptance of the primary distribution of income and wealth. Almost all important policy changes involve losers as well as gainers, and thus require the making of interpersonal comparisons of utility.

To handle the latter problem, Kaldor-Hicks-Scitovsky developed the notion of potential compensation, suggesting that a resource shift was Pareto-preferred whenever the gainers potentially could overcompensate the losers without the losers then being able potentially to overcompensate the gainers. By advocating potential rather than actual compensation, Kaldor-Hicks-Scitovsky dramatically extended the policy reach of the amended Pareto criteria. That they did so successfully while violating the contractarian underpinnings of the entire approach demonstrates the collectivist thrust of an economics profession increasingly hungry in the 1950s for policy reach and increasingly ignorant of or ill-disposed toward catallaxy and methodological individualism [13].

Potential compensation, attractive as it was to cost-benefit analysts prepared to write out world welfare functions and anxious to impact upon public policy, did not enter undisputed into the literature of welfare economics. Scholars such as Buchanan writing in the Virginia school tradition of contractarianism, reject as invalid the use of any method of policy reconciliation that involves coercion of losers by gainers. In the absence of actual compensation, there is no exchange nexus, no contract resolution. Even scholars wedded to policy activism and willing to apply potential compensation to that end recognize the high transaction costs of demand revelation, given the public good characteristics of this process. The incentives to lie in the potential compensation case have not been resolved in any practical sense.

The intellectual abyss that separates Paretian welfare economics from the wealth-maximization hypothesis encountered so frequently in the economic analysis of law has been spanned skillfully and strategically in a bid to extend the policy reach of his approach [14]. Kaldor-Hicks potential compensation and distributional neutrality form the twin cantilevers of the bridge. From these assumptions a particular, essentially noncontractarian notion of predictive efficiency is forged Viz:

> Because the conditions for Pareto superiority are almost never satisfied in the real world, yet economists talk quite a bit about efficiency, it is pretty clear that the operating definition of efficiency in economics is not Pareto superiority. When an economist says that free trade or competition or the control of pollution or some other policy or state of the world is efficient, nine times out of ten he means Kaldor-Hicks efficient, as we shall in this book [15].

and

> The dependence of even the Pareto-superiority concept of efficiency on the distribution of wealth...suggests a serious limitation of efficiency as an ultimate criterion of the social good....Thus, the economist's competence in a discussion of the legal system is limited. He can predict the effect of legal rules and arrangements on value and efficiency, in their strict technical senses, and on the existing distribution of income and wealth, but he cannot issue mandatory prescriptions for social change [16].

By relying upon "the spirit" of Kaldor-Hicks potential compensation,

Posner is able to analyze the law from the perspective of efficiency even in situations involving involuntary exchange (crimes and many torts). This approach attempts to reconstruct the likely terms of a market transaction in circumstances where instead a forced exchange took place. Once again, Posner sacrifices precision as an acceptable price for an extended policy reach:

> The choice is between a necessarily rather crude system of legally regulated forced exchanges and the even greater inefficiencies of forbidding all forced exchanges, which could mean all exchanges, as all have some third-party effects [17].

Posner ties this concept of efficiency to constrained utilitarianism by asserting the effectiveness of the measuring rod of wealth:

> The things that wealth makes possible—not only luxury goods but also leisure and modern medicine, and even departments of philosophy—are major ingredients of most people's happiness, so that wealth maximization is an important—conceivably the only effective–social instrument of utility maximization [18].

Posner defined wealth as follows:

> Wealth is the value in dollars or dollar equivalents...of everything in society. It is measured by what people are willing to pay for something or, if they already own it, what they demand in money to give it up. The only kind of preference that counts in a system of wealth maximization is thus one that is backed up by money—in other words, that is registered in a market [19].

Because Posner betrays the Pareto principle in favor of Kaldor-Hicks potential compensation, his entire approach is ambiguous with respect to rights, presenting a "fundamental circularity problem" [20]. Wealth maximization, in a mixed economy such as the United States, cannot be pursued effectively in the absence of some delineation of rights, some prior distribution of income and wealth. The entire "willingness to pay" principle depends upon such a prior event [21]. Yet, as Paretian welfare economics indicates, there is an infinite number of efficiency outcomes, each related to a specific prior distribution. So it is with wealth maximization, Posner's proxy for efficiency. In cases of legal dispute, however, rights themselves not infrequently are in dispute. If wealth maximization is to be the objective of the courts, then the (normatively destructive) circularity between efficiency and rights cannot be ignored, as Nicholas Mercuro and Warren J. Samuels emphasize:

> ...the market prices reflect and give effect to the underlying distribution of wealth (as a means of weighting preferences). More narrowly, insofar as

willingness to pay is a function of the distribution of wealth, the use of offer—versus asking—prices will tend to reflect that distributional choice [22].

Posner's response [23], perhaps muted by his experience on the bench, is that wealth maximization is the only social value that courts can do much to promote. Therefore, in common law fields, where the shaping of policy has been left to the courts, "it makes sense for them to adopt wealth maximization as their goal" [24]. Courts, therefore, should take the distribution of wealth for granted, as a responsibility which the political system has allocated elsewhere, and should seek to maximize wealth in their judgments, to the extent that they are not restrained from so doing by precedent, by unmistakable statutory direction, or by other authority.

Mercuro and Samuels [25], however, are not easily silenced on the circularity issue, which indeed is central to their attack on Posner's wealth-maximization hypothesis. In uncharacteristic fashion, they rest their case on an empirical assertion, challenging Posner in terms of Chicago methodology:

> The issue remains that of whether courts affect the distribution of rights and of wealth. We affirm that in a slow gradual, incremental manner, the courts, through the precedential and appellate system are making law and that in making law they are determining who will have what rights and that this constitutes determining the distribution of wealth in society. Surely Posner does not think that with respect to rights litigants are indifferent as to what courts decide. The only question then is whether court decisions effect prices through affecting the distributional basis of prices, namely rights. We affirm that they do [26].

Of course, if the Pareto principle in its unconstrained form is applied in place of wealth maximization, without any assistance from Kaldor-Hicks, the circularity issue disappears, except for those relatively rare instances where rights have yet to be defined. For, in such circumstances, the status quo ante prevails, constraining movements to particular segments of the contract locus that depict the efficiency alternatives available. Even in legal cases that involve coercive transfers once the rights are established, by statute, or by precedent, the concept of efficiency appears relatively unambiguous.

Before 1970, scholars like Buchanan, who stressed the primacy of Paretian efficiency in its strictest form as a normative objective, genuinely considered their ideological position to be compatible with libertarian principles. Efficiency was seen to rest entirely upon consent among uncoerced individuals, even under Kaldor-Hicks conditions, as long as actual rather than potential compensation was required. The veto power over policy proposals accorded to all individuals by the Paretian axioms was viewed as a complete safeguard for individual rights, save in such specific exceptions as lunatics, minors, and drug addicts who were more or less explicitly excluded as decisionmakers from the welfare calculus.

Such complacency was disturbed in 1970 when Amartya Sen [27] demonstrated that a condition of minimal liberty was incompatible with the weak Pareto condition, even for a social-decision mechanism that does not require strict transitivity of preferences and independence of irrelevant alternatives, as was required by Kenneth J. Arrow [28] for his social-decision machanism. Although Sen's example is somewhat artificial in that rights are not assigned and thus exchange possibilities are disallowed, the logic of his proof has not been challenged successfully in a large literature of subsequent debate.

Sen's proof involved the specification of a social choice function (F) that must always accommodate the following conditions:

1. Condition U (unrestricted domain): The domain of (F) includes all logically possible n-tuples $\langle R_1 \text{———} R_n \rangle$ of individual preference orderings over X.

2. Condition P (weak Pareto principle): For any x, y from X, if xP_iy for all i, then xPy.

3. Condition L (minimal libertarianism): There is at least one pair of persons decisive both ways over at least one pair of alternatives each, i.e., for each i there is a pair of alternatives in X (x_i, y_i) such that $x_iP_iy_i$ implies x_iPy_i and $y_iP_ix_i$ implies y_iPx_i.

Sen demonstrated that such a social-choice function was impossible even in the most limited case of two individuals (Man 1 and Man 2) and two pairs of alternatives (x, y) and (z, w) respectively, with $x = z$ for further simplification. Assume that Man 1 prefers x to y and y to w, while Man 3 prefers y to w and w to $z = (x)$. Both individuals thus evidence transitive preferences. By Condition V, their preference orderings are in the domain of the social-choice function. By Condition L, x must be preferred to y and w must be preferred to x. However, by Condition P, y must be preferred to w. A choice function for the society, as prescribed by Sen, therefore, does not exist.

The configuration of preferences outlined in Sen's proof turns out, in its real-world context, to reflect meddlesome predilections on the part of individuals in society. It is this meddlesomeness that sets the libertarian and the Paretian conditions in conflict with each other. Sen illustrates by reference to a social choice concerning the book *Lady Chatterley's Lover*, namely, whether it should by read by Mr. Lascivious, by Mr. Prude, or not at all. Although Mr. Lascivious would like to read it, rather than let it go to waste, his first preference is to have Mr. Prude read it. Although Mr. Prude's first preference is for the book to go unread, he prefers to read it himself rather than for Mr. Lascivious to be titillated. Thus, they both agree that the book should by read by Mr. Prude and not by Mr. Lascivious, even though the former does not wish to read the book and the latter does.

Sen's impossibility theorem, weak though its premises are, is perfectly general [29]. Potential incoherence in social choice can be avoided only by limiting the domain of social choice to exclude "private" choices where they run counter to the Pareto criterion, or by modifying the range of the function to override automatically efficiency in favor of liberty or liberty in favor of efficiency wherever incoherent preference configurations are drawn from its domain.

Returning to the book example, once rights are assigned over the book, in the pre-social-choice situation, the particular problem identified by Sen dissolves, albeit at the expense of collective choice [30]. If the right is vested in Mr. Prude, the book will go unread unless Mr. Lascivious evidences willingness to pay in a magnitude sufficient to divert him from his propriety. Given his preferences, Mr. Lascivious, would never offer the larger sum necessary to purchase the book from Mr. Prude for his own enjoyment. If the right is vested in Mr. Lascivious, he will read the book unless Mr. Prude purchases it from him to abort a reading, in which case further exchange may induce Mr. Prude to read the book. Evidently, there is no coercion in any such outcome since there is no social choice in these rights-based solutions.

Even in such a Lockeian world conflict between the conditions of Pareto and of liberty is not entirely averted. All depends on the preference configurations. Suppose there are in society individuals who intensely enjoy coercing others yet none who enjoy being coerced. Coercive contracts may emerge as the sadists purchase the right to coerce. Suppose alternatively that there are individuals who intensely enjoy being coerced, but none who enjoys coercion. Coercive contracts once again are feasible but not certain as the masochists offer to pay others to coerce them. Even if rights are clearly defined, therefore, including rights to minimal liberty, such rights may be freely transferred, with highly illiberal consequences, in societies composed of individuals with meddlesome preferences.

Finally, this section turns to "justice" or "fairness," inevitably focusing upon issues surrounding the primary distribution of income and wealth, the fulcrum on which the willingness to pay criterion is based. Fairness is an exceptionally elusive concept, susceptible to manipulation by self-seeking individuals. The dictionary definition is process- rather than end-state-oriented: "Free from bias, dishonesty or injustice..., legitimately sought, done, etc; proper under the rules."

In this sense, a distribution is fair if it is the result of an honest, just, or legitimate process. In essence, such was the approach attempted by the Harvard philosopher, John Rawls [31], when deriving the famous, if in our view misconceived, difference principle. For Rawls, "justice as fairness" could be determined only by abstracting from the process of political bargaining and the conflicting calculus of competing collective interests which he saw to be incompatible with a "just" society. In an important contribution to moral philosophy, Rawls set out the principles of justice that free and rational persons would accept—and in his view would accept unanimously—if they were able to deliberate in a hypothetical situation corresponding to the state of nature in traditional social contract theory.

In this initial position, individuals do not know their places in society, their class position or social status, their fortunes in the distribution of natural assets and abilities, even their conception of the good. Thus deliberating behind a veil of ignorance, individuals determine their rights and duties in an universally endorsed social contract. Such a contract, for Rawls, is not a contract of entry into a particular society or a contract to establish a particular form of government. Rather, the principles of justice derived are those that govern the basic structure of society. Justice as fairness, therefore, may be viewed as the fundamental rule according to which all issues, including the constitution itself, are to be decided [32].

Rawls suggests that the conditions of the original position are such as to induce all deliberators to use the extremely risk-averse strategy of maxi-min/mini-max when selecting the principles of justice that are to govern the basic structure of society. On this important pivot, he derives two principles of justice and asserts that they would be chosen universally by self-seeking deliberators acting under the conditions of his model.

This first principle so derived is that each person is to have an equal right to the most extensive basic liberty compatible with a similar liberty for others. The basic liberties are political liberty (the right to vote and to be eligible for public office) together with freedom of speech and assembly, liberty of conscience and freedom of thought, freedom of the person along with the right to hold personal property, and freedom from arbitrary arrest and seizure as defined by the concept of the rule of law. This principle takes full precedence over the second principle, i.e., it has lexicographic preference.

The second principle so derived is that social and economic inequalities are to be arranged so that they are both 1) reasonably expected to be to everyone's advantage, and 2) attached to positions and offices open to all. Rawls interprets this principle as equivalent to the "difference principle" whereby the social and economic inequalities of the basic structure are subject to veto by the least advantaged members of society. The higher expectations of those better situated are just if and only if they work as part of a scheme that improves the expectations of the least advantage members of society.

These principles together constitute justice as fairness and are both derived from Rawls' assumption that individuals negotiate in the original position from positions of infinite risk-aversion. This assumption is categorically invalid [33], given a normal range of individual attitudes toward risk in games against a nonalien nature. Without it, the difference principle collapses and universal agreement is unlikely [34].

As Rawls' theory of justice has encountered increasing criticism, so egalitarians have espoused alternative theoretical frameworks. Most recently, William J. Baumol [35] has introduced the concept of "super-fairness" as an end-state objective, derived from the concept of envy. Baumol defines envy as existing wherever one individual prefers someone else's bundle of commodities to his or her own. A "fair" distribution is defined as one in which no person envies another—and this ex post, irrespective of the prior and ongoing labor supply of the respective individuals. Indeed, on Baumol's definition, it is not fair to use effort, human capital, past thrift or any criterion other than tastes to determine a fair distribution.

Super-fairness, as above defined, is nonexistent in any real-world economy, the figment of an ivory-tower intelligence. Unfortunately, such concepts lend themselves to unscrupulous manipulation as relatively opaque instruments for wealth redistribution employed by powerful interest groups in rent-seeking societies [36].

2.3. The Efficiency of the Common Law

The new law and economics has exerted a powerful impact in its positive as well as in its normative dimensions, most especially with respect to understanding the common law and court interpretations of the statute law. Posner [37], in particular, has stressed that common law judgments reflect economic efficiency. Probably, a majority of law and economics scholars worldwide subscribe to this viewpoint. The efficiency hypothesis has been tested repeatedly by Posner and others by means of what

Cento G. Veljanovski [38] has labeled "impact studies" or what Werner Hirsch [39] has called "effect evaluation." Unfortunately, strong transaction cost assumptions are usually necessary to support the economic efficiency interpretation in a field where comparative institutions studies are rarely available.

There are three main branches of common law: property, contract, and tort. Property law deals with ownership and rights, including the alienability of rights, and as such plays a pivotal role in resource allocation. Inefficiencies in the law of property conceivably might impose severe efficiency losses upon society offering an identifiable, though not necessarily a dominant impulse for reform. Contract law also plays an important role, determining how the owners of property engage in mutually advantageous trade. In Posner's view, contract law has three functions. First, it maintains proper incentives for exchange, protecting the parties from nonperformance and fraud. Second, it reduces the complexity associated with trade, by establishing a systematic set of rules. Third, it forewarns individuals of the likely impediments to effective exchange, allowing them to plan exchanges more effectively in the future. Each such function has an efficiency characteristic, though whether or not this dominates other impulses must be established empirically.

With respect to Posner's hypothesis, tort law, however, is even more suspect, since it deals with externalities rather than directly with the exchange relationship [40]. The conventional welfare economics literature, at least, suggests that gains-from-trade impulses not infrequently fail to drive an efficiency solution in such circumstances. If not through markets, then how and why through the courts? Where torts are argued before juries, how are the latter imbued with the efficiency objective? Casting these issues aside, Posner argues that the tort law is efficient, even when third party effects must enter into the calculus of the judicial decision. The developed system of liability, together with the rules governing compensation, are viewed as wealth maximizing for society.

Though Posner is forceful in projecting the efficiency hypothesis, he is less forthright in explaining the mechanism through which common law efficiency emerges, relying instead upon the as-if methodology of the Chicago school. Although judges, in his analysis, are perceived to be independent from the legislature, this does not explain why they should show especial malleability when confronted with arguments of efficiency. In Posner's view [41], three factors lead to efficiency in judge-based law:

(1) Wealth maximization is closely related to utilitarianism, and the formative period of the common law as we know it today, roughly 1800–1950, was a

period when utilitarianism was the dominant political ideology in England and America; (2) judges lack effective tools for enriching an interest group or social class other than by increasing the society's wealth as a whole in which the favored group or class presumably will share, and (3) the process of common law adjudication itself leads to the survival of other rules.

Posner's intuitive explanation, which has some force, has been developed and fortified by other scholars in law and economics. Arthur R. Hogue [42], in an important book on the origins of the common law, emphasized the role of competition between the royal and other courts in medieval England in developing the law, most especially that of property, but also of contracts involving a pledge of faith. By the end of the thirteenth century, the royal courts had absorbed much, though not all, of the judicial business of their competitors and had established the "common law" quite generally throughout England, essentially by means of the writ system. It is arguable that efficiency indeed was an important characteristic of a common law system that established itself through a process of keen market competition, and which reflected the preferences not only of English traders but also of alien merchants and money lenders brought to England by the early development of foreign trade. Only England, among the European nations, was successful in carrying the essential elements of its medieval customary legal system into the modern world. Tort law, as a much later development, was not conditioned by such intercourt competition [43].

Yet, through the centuries, the common law has changed, most especially over the period 1800–1950 as identified by Posner. With the judiciary still something of a black box in the economic analysis of law, and with intercourt competition now almost completely absent, in the United Kingdom and (for federal courts) in the United States, any ongoing efficiency impulse is dependent on the strength of early precedent coupled with any coalescence of underlying interests among litigants. Once again, this impulse is apparently strong in the cases of property and contract law, but weaker or nonexistent in the case of the law of tort.

Posner's concept of the judiciary as an essentially independent body, buttressed from interest group pressures by reason of their tenure and salary conditions itself is a chimera in the U.S. legal system. In the case of federal judges, nominated by the Executive and subject to advise and consent by the Senate, public choice influences run rampant, as the unsuccessful nomination of then Judge Robert Bork to the U.S. Supreme Court clearly demonstrated. Even though appointed judges are free to exercise their independent judgments, once in office, they are selected to serve dominant interest groups as manifest at the time of their appointment. Since they may well remain in office well beyond the incumbency of any government, predictably the appointment process attracts heavy rent-seeking outlays.

In the case of state courts, approximately one-half of all judges are appointed, with implications for rent-seeking through public choice as outlined above. The remaining one-half, who are subject to periodic elections, have limited discretion while in office, unless they are serving a terminal incumbency. They must behave as politicians while running for office, balancing the special interest group markets to maximize the probability of election or reelection to the judgeship.

If history and judicial incentives are inadequate to explain economic efficiency in the law, can the lacunae be explained adequately by reference to the process of litigation? Law and economics scholars have debated this issue at length, as yet without any evident consensus of interpretation [44]. The central issues in this discussion all focus on the efficiency characteristics of an adversary-based judicial process [45].

There is a widespread tendency of parties in dispute to settle out of court. Differing interpretations are available, however, concerning the efficiency implications of this phenomenom. In one view, which draws heavily upon a comparative institutions perspective, if the common law was efficient it should dominate the process of dispute settlements [46]. Evidence of out-of-court settlements thus is viewed as contradictory to the efficiency hypothesis. It can be counterargued, however, that out-of-court settlements reached in the shadow of common law judgments are just one institutional route to efficiency in a multi-institutions system.

Recognizing the difficulty of resolving this dispute by reference to the evidence, Paul H. Rubin [47] has resorted to a priori theory in an attempt to identify the characteristics necessary for efficiency as an evolutionary outcome. Following contractarian economics, he suggests that courts will be used more frequently where the law relevant to the dispute is inefficient than when it is efficient. In this perspective, efficient rules evolve from in-court settlements, by their existence reducing incentives for future litigation, and thereby raising the probability that they will persist through time.

Utility maximization by litigants, rather than efficiency predilections by the judiciary, is seen to drive this process. Rubin's argument depends significantly on the existence of potential litigants with an ongoing interest in a specific common law and without a clear-cut notion ex ante of their likely respective position in potential legal disputes. Expected wealth-maximizing motives exercised behind the veil of uncertainty can then offer strong pressures in favor of efficient laws.

Rubin's theory is dependent on an explicit process, generated by far-sighted self-interest on the part of a significant number of litigants. As such, it is not evolutionary in the strict biological definition which assumes an absence of foresight and a random generation of behavioral options. In this latter definition, the evolution of an efficient common law is similar to the attainment of a Nash equilibrium in a noncooperative game. Peter Terrebonne [48] has established that such an equilibrium will emerge, without Rubin's assumption of foresight, under certain conditions, even when the Coase theorem is rendered inoperative by transaction cost consideration. Terrebonne relies, like Rubin, on the assumption that inefficient rules attract high rates of litigation. He further assumes that litigation costs do not deter the litigation of inefficient rules and that legal rules that are litigated more frequently have a lower probability of survival than those that are litigated less frequently.

By relaxing these assumptions, Robert Cooter and Lewis Kornhauser [49] are able to model legal evolution, not as an efficiency-oriented process but rather as a Markov process. One conclusion thus derived is that blind evolution will not cause the legal system to reach some best state or even continually to improve itself. Instead, the process eventually will settle down to a stable state in which each alternative legal rule prevails over a fixed portion of time. This stable state will approximate closer to efficiency, the higher the frequency of litigation over inefficient laws.

The litigation process alone, therefore, cannot be relied upon categorically to drive efficient rules universally and permanently into the common law. Where other efficiency impulses are strong, as arguably in the case with property law and contract law, litigation may guide the law toward a stable structure that corresponds tolerably closely to the tenets of economic efficiency. Where such impulses are weaker, or indeed are absent, as arguably is the case with the law of tort, there is no presumption in favor of evolutionary efficiency, especially when juries assess the damages through processes that resemble a random walk [50]. Moreover, both the law of property and the law of contract, as well as the law of tort, are susceptible to statutory interventions that reflect pressures of public choice.

2.4. The Relevance of Transaction Costs

Conventional welfare economics long has emphasized the importance of transaction costs as a potential barrier to the attainment of allocative efficiency. Indeed, by grouping information costs, bargaining costs, and other institutional impediments to free exchange under this umbrella term, transaction costs and inefficiency were rendered virtual synonyms by the new welfare economics until Harold Demsetz [51] and others challenged "nirvana economics" from a comparative institutions perspective.

By means of an impressive research program, deployed at Chicago during the 1970s, Posner utilized the new institutional economics to evaluate the efficiency of the common law. In many ways, his research was rigorous, faithful to the scientific method of Popper, and evaluating the efficiency hypothesis circumspectly against evidence drawn from almost every branch of the common law. Yet inevitably he was forced into speculation when contrasting an existing law with alternatives that had no real-world presence within the legal system under consideration. Such speculation, or a priori reasoning, relied heavily upon assertions as to the magnitude of transaction costs in alternative judicial, or indeed, administrative systems.

Chicago [52], with its traditional emphasis on low transaction costs, high factor mobility and efficient information markets, does not find much difficulty in determining "that what is, is efficient" with respect to private market outcomes. That Posner was able to reach a similar conclusion with respect to the public bureaucracy of the courts is more surprising. It is important to note that the common law is not a private market; it is heavily impregnated with the impulses of public choice. Yet, in its judgment, Chicago seems to have been fortified by the contributions of New England scholarship, notably through the scholarship of the new institutional economists researching in the Yale law and economics programs [53].

The transaction costs approach to the analysis of institutional adjustment, developed principally by Oliver Williamson [54] and by Douglass North [55] from important early contributions by Ronald Coase [56], defines institutional arrangements as contracts, or governance contracts, between principals and/or between principal and agents. Utility maximization is viewed as the driving force behind such contract negotiations. The analysis rests on three fundamental assumptions: 1) that individuals behave in their own, rather than in any collective interest; 2) that specifying and enforcing the rules that underpin contracts is costly; and 3) that ideology modifies the nature of maximizing behavior. If there is ideological conformity in society, formal institutional rules will be minimal and enforcement procedures will be unimportant. If ideologies sharply conflict, resources increasingly will be devoted to rules definition and to rules enforcement.

North, in particular, focuses attention on the cost of transaction as a central determinant of the structure of rights. Ideological conflict, and its resolution, is viewed as constraining individual utility maximization over many margins. However, given ideology, transaction cost minimization delivers institutions that reflect constrained social efficiency within any specific society, at least in the long run. Although he does not explicitly link this proposition to the law and the legal process, such an extension is essential for the logical consistency and the generality of his analysis.

Williamson's contribution relates more directly to the common law, especially to the law of property and contract, but also to the law of tort. Private institutional adjustments are viewed as protecting society against efficiency losses in circumstances where classical contracting is nonviable. Specifically, where planning is incomplete because of bounded rationality, where unguarded promise is eroded by changing circumstances that allow for opportunistic behavior, and where the pair-wise identity of the contracting parties matters because of asset specificity, transaction costs exerts a nontrivial influence in determining the institutions of private ordering. This is the world of "governance" whether it emerges through private contracts or through legislative intervention.

Neither North nor Williamson displays the same degree of faith in an efficient legal system as does the Chicago approach, most especially of Posner. Indeed, they are both prepared to incorporate the "value of fairness" as an additional and relevant argument in individuals' utility functions. Nevertheless, if utility rather than wealth is viewed as the relevant "efficiency" objective, transaction cost constrained efficiency is central to the new institutional economics [57]. The problem surrounding the actual measurement of transaction costs is neglected typically in this approach [58].

2.4. The Common Law as a Spontaneous Order

An alternative approach, due to Friedrich A. Hayek [59], is supportive of the common law and critical of the public law from the standpoint of liberty, defined in the negative sense of the absence of coercion of some individuals by others. In the view of scholars such as Hayek [60], individual preferences over alternative social states are not easily divined by potential social decisionmakers. Information is costly, the future is characterized by Knightian uncertainty, resistant even to the probability calculus; and those who believe they have the capacity to plan and mould the future suffer from "synoptic delusion."

In such a society, rules of conduct are required for the successful interaction of a specialized economy. Fundamental to the emergence of such rules of conduct is the establishment of an effective system of property rights. Central to such rules are the criteria defining the processes of contracting and of resolving less direct, noncontractual, and even third party interactions. In essence, the common law of property, contract, and tort emerges to protect individuals from the anarchy of the jungle and to provide a basis for realizable expectations in an environment encompassed in Knightian uncertainty. As Hayek [61] wrote:

> It will be one of our chief contentions that most of the rules of conduct which govern our actions, and most of the institutions which arise out of this regularity, are adaptations to the impossibility of anyone taking conscious account of all the particular facts which enter into the order of society.

Thus is it that rules of conduct regulating the behavior of individuals in terms of contractual commitments precede society, even though they do not initially take the form of property rights formally endorsed by some kind of constitutional contract. These rules of conduct, together with the associated institutions which support them, manifest a regularity of interacton in matching expectations to the extent possible with out-turns. Such an order, which for the most part is self-generating, has been designated by Hayek as a "spontaneous order" capable of encompassing circumstances beyond the comprehension of any single individual mind.

Spontaneous orders do not always protect liberty, as the English feudal system clearly demonstrated. Nevertheless, Hayek has argued that certain characteristics of spontaneous orders, most especially those that encourage the formation of realizable expectations in a decentralized decision-making environment, are conducive to the establishment and maintenance of classical liberalism. In particular, the evolution of the common law has been characterized by a generalized support for principles designated by Hayek as "the rule of law" which he regards as an absolute prerequisite for negative freedom.

The judge at common law, in this perspective, assists the spontaneous order unwittingly by restricting consideration, in his judgments, to the legitimate expectations of the parties in conflict as formed on the basis of established custom, or preexistent legal precedent. As such, he is concerned not at all about any wider, third party implications of the judgment. The rule of law requires that laws should conform to a set of principles. First, they must be prospective and not retrospective in their effect, since the intention always is to influence future choices. Second, laws must be known and certain, to the extent feasible, so that individuals are in a position accurately to predict the decisions of the courts. Third, laws must apply with equal force to all individuals, including those who govern, without exception or discrimination. Such, it is urged, is the reality of common law save where it is distorted by legislative intervention.

This view of the common law, both in its prescriptive and in its descriptive form, is challenged by scholars of the new law and economics. Given the incompatibility between efficiency and liberty in the meddle-some society, those who believe that the common law is (and should be) efficient do not want the rule of law to obstruct the dynamic response of the judges to changing preferences and technologies; they do not want strict adherence to rights to outweigh wealth-enhancing opportunities. Those who espouse critical legal studies, and who despise both liberty and efficiency as the twin enemies of justice, galvanize all their efforts to the smashing of spontaneous orders as a route to socialism. Those who conform to the new welfare economics encourage the substitution of public for common law as a prerequisite for the constructivist rationalist end-state blueprint.

In the meantime, public choice scholars, however enamored they may be concerning the qualities of a spontaneous order, recognize the internal pressures within a society that obstruct such an achievement even within the common law itself and agonize over the constitutional adjustments that might be necessary to rein in constructivist rationalism that might force individuals to be free [62].

3. The Public Choice Research Program

Following early contributions by Anthony Downs [63], Buchanan and Tullock [64], and Mancur Olson [65], a considerable literature has now developed in the field of public choice. At one level, theories of spatial politics center attention upon the equilibrium properties of political markets, in which the motivating assumption is that of self-seeking, with politicians maximizing individual utility functions in which expected votes, expected wealth, and ideology feature and in which "the public interest" does not.

On the assumption that political issue space can be collapsed into a single dimension, that the distribution of votes preferences over that dimension is single-peaked, that all voters vote, that only two political parties compete, that both parties are spatially mobile in response to expected votes, and that the political market as a whole is characterized by efficient information, both parties are predicted to converge at the median of the voters' preference distribution. Such an outcome, though evidently not a Pareto optimum, given heterogeneous preferences, squared well with the principle of majority vote.

However, if the above-mentioned conditions are relaxed—notably the single issue space, the single-peakedness, the universal vote, the two-party competition, the spatial mobility, and the full information assumptions—the median voter outcome is suspect, and the existence, uniqueness, and stability of spatial political equilibrium are each in doubt [66]. Even James Enelow and Melvin J. Hinich [67], who still argue forcefully that centrifugal forces nevertheless dominate in political elections, are hard-stretched to justify this viewpoint as the assumptions of Downs are seen to crumble. Only by allowing political parties to shift the voters' preference distribution can they justify their theory, once spatial immobility is evident in party politics [68].

In any event, elections are only periodic occurrences in the continuous political market process; indeed, they are occurrences which many public choice analysts now play down as unimportant in view of the insignificance of any individual vote and the rational ignorance among the electorate to which such insignificance gives rise. Given memory decay on the part of individual voters, incumbent governments have considerable effective policy discretion. In such circumstances, increasing attention is placed upon the behavior of interest groups, both as demanders and as suppliers of policies. The stylized theory of interest-group politics essentially relegates elected politicians to a brokerage function designed to ensure continuous clearing in political markets.

In his book, *The Logic of Collective Action*, Olson [69] placed existing theories of interest groups into a clearly defined public chocie perspective. The idea that groups would tend to act in support of their respective interests had long been viewed as a logical consequence of rational behavior. Since groups were only aggregations of individuals, collective action was viewed in essence as no different from individual action. In consequence, interest-group activity was seen only as consolidating, and not as transforming, the vote motive in the political marketplace. Olson disposed of this naivety and demonstrated that rational self-interest in individual behavior typically would not lead to effective collective action [70].

Olson [71] demonstrated indeed that "unless the number of individuals in a group is quite small, or unless there is coercion or some other special device to make individuals act in their common interest, rational self-interested individuals will not act to achieve their common or group interests." Indeed, large groups will not even form to further their common goals "in the absence of the coercion or the separate incentives just mentioned."

Olson's proof starts from the premise that individuals have purely personal interests different from other members of the group with whom they share a common interest. Such private interests compete with the common interest at least for the time of those who contemplate collective action. Since each individual makes only a small contribution to the collective action of a small group, the withdrawal of such contribution will not be viewed as important to the expected success of failure of the aggregate venture. If the common goal has publicness characteristics, especially that of nonexcludability, a free-rider problem will seriously obstruct interest groups as they attempt to engage in collective action. Typically this is the case of large interest groups, at least with regard to the indispensable common purposes of their existence.

If large groups predictably fail to provide themselves will public goods, the tendency in small groups is toward a suboptimal rate of provision of such goods. The suboptimality will be the more serious, the smaller the fraction of the commodity demanded by the largest "demander" in the group. Since the largest demander will bear a disproportionate share of the burden of collective action, there is a systematic tendency for "exploitation" of the great by the small. Paradoxically, the greater the size "inequality" within the group, the more likely it is that a group of given size will be effective in collective action.

Large pressure groups, to be effective, must be organized for other purposes, which provide selective benefits to the membership, pursuing the common interest only as a byproduct. The large organizations that can employ such methods are those that 1) have the authority and capacity to be coercive, and/or 2) have a source of positive inducements that they can offer to the individuals in a latent group. Smaller organizations may engage in collective action without recourse either to coercion or to positive inducements, by utilizing their "special interest" advantages. Producer groups typically benefit from special interest advantages; consumer groups do not.

In Olson's view, the byproduct theory explains the lobbying organizations that represent agriculture, labor, and the professions; the special interest theory of small lobbying groups explains the organizations that represent business interests. Available evidence does not refute his theory. Large groups of individuals with evident (but latent) common interests evidently exert zero voice in the political marketplace, even when they suffer seriously adverse consequences of political brokerage.

Olson's theory suggests that interest groups introduce significant bias into political markets that otherwise might respond to the median voters' preferences. In particular, small interest groups advantaged by special interests and large interest groups able to byproduct their common goals on selective benefits predictably will be more successful in political markets than will large groups with general interests. This view contrasts sharply with orthodox interest group theory as outlined above. It contrasts equally sharply with the view of Gary Becker that competition between pressure groups serves to correct market failure by favoring policies that raise efficiency in the political market competition.

Olson's view of interest groups, realistic though it is, incorrectly emphasizes the transfer nature of political markets. In 1967, Tullock [72] corrected this error with his rent-seeking contribution, which destroyed the notion that interest group lobbying is a costless, even a wealth-enhancing exercise. Interest groups thus are defined as rent seekers who expend resources in institutional settings where attempts at wealth transfers generate social waste rather than social surplus, not infrequently through invasion of political markets. Where rents are artificially available from government, organized interest groups will sacrifice scarce resources in competing for them. Unlike the competition for entrepreneurial rents, however, nothing of social value results from this competition. The opportunity cost of resources dedicated to rent-seeking, whether to induce or to take advantage of government constraints, represents social waste.

Rent-seeking, through government, into the property rights of others stimulates a rent-protection reaction from those whose wealth is placed at risk. The more transparent the rent-seeking, the better organized the rent protectors, the more vigorous predictably will be the rent-protection response. Whether or not this competition for rents will under—or over—or exactly dissipate the rents available and whether this will occur up front or in an ongoing manner are presently unresolved issues [73]. It is quite clear, however, that Chicago complacency concerning the efficiency characteristics of pressure group competition cannot survive the combination of Olson's and Tullock's insights.

Among the special interests playing a strong role on the demand side of political markets are to be found the many bureaus that comprise the executive branch of government [74]. Senior bureaucrats, according to William J. Niskanen [75], maximize a utility function that can be reflected in terms of the proxy variable of budget size. Such bureaus engage with

Congress—even with the Executive—in bilateral bargaining, and typically dominate the policy debate as a consequence of information advantage. Thus, the bureaus distort legislation—even electoral platforms—away from median voter preferences and in favor of excessive rates of public provision. Alternative public choice theories of bureaucracy, for example, by Barry Weingast and Mark J. Moran [76] and Charles K. Rowley and Robert Elgin [77], view bureaucrats as agents of their legislator principals, though with variable discretion as the consequence of the latter's truncated property rights in political market residuals.

In either perspective, tension exists between any government and its bureaus, both in the formulation and in the implementation of policies. To weaken the bargaining power of a bureau, or to reduce agent discretion, governments may reduce the tenure of senior bureaucrats, set up competitive bureaus, collapse intransigent bureaus, or reduce appropriations. They are restricted in such exercises, however, by the lobbying, explicit or implicit, of bureaus and of supportive special interests both directly into the legislature and indirectly into the electorate itself.

For all the above-mentioned reasons, public choice theory offers little confidence that unconstrained political markets will reflect the preferences of the median voter, still less that they will satisfy the necessary conditions for liberty, efficiency, or justice. Rather, in the absence of institutional constraints, political markets are seen to respond to rent-seeking and rent-protection outlays [78] mounted by the more effective interests groups (typically small rather than large), often acting from a minority vote position, supported by the maneuvering of self-seeking bureaucrats in areas where inadequate legislative monitoring so allows.

In such circumstances, the question arises whether political markets should be reined in by constitutional constraints designed to protect individuals from the predation on their rights by interest groups that reflect minority interests or even by a transient majority of the electorate. H. Geoffrey Brennan and Buchanan [79] and others working within the framework of the Virginia school have argued persuasively the reason of constitutional rules. The Wicksellian imperative [80] of universal or near-universal consent for rules that constrain in-period majoritorian pressures on all branches of the federal and state governments is an important element of political economy.

Yet, even at the level of the constitution itself, public choice analysis offers a less-than-optimistic prospectus [81]. First, it is by no means self-evident that those very special interest groups which control unconstrained political markets would not also control any constitutional convention (or any Congress in its constitutional role) especially where multiple issues are under consideration, with all the logrolling opportunities so provided. Modern conventions, unlike the Philadelphia convention in 1787, would be the focal point of media and lobbying activity, not dissimilar in character to that evident in Presidential elections.

Second, it is not clear that those called upon to draft Constitutional clauses (especially if it were the Congress) would not seize the opportunity so provided to incorporate loopholes favorable to their respective constituencies—loopholes which, in the aggregate, may return full discretion to the in-period legislature and which may allow bureaus considerable discretionary power to pursue their private objectives.

Third, it is not clear that unforeseen escape routes would offer to various actors in the political marketplace opportunities to evade the spirit, if not the letter, of the Constitution. Such would appear to have been the fate of much of the U.S. Constitution, both in its initial form and as subsequently amended. Even where the "loopholes" exploited in fact infringed the Constitution, enforcement procedures may prove inadequate. If the judiciary refrains from challenging legislative abuses, as typically has been the case, and if the Executive refuses to enforce the delivered judgments of the courts, as is not an unheard-of occurrence, the letter of the Constitution is worthless.

Fourth, constitutional rules are vulnerable to activist judicial interpretation, most especially by the Supreme Court. Interest groups that fail to penetrate the legislature sufficiently to achieve constitutional amendments favorable to their causes may well turn their pressure upon the judiciary. It is surprising that even advocates of the new law and economics such as Posner, who view individual behavior for the most part as being predicated on self-interest, are prepared to make an exception for Supreme Court Justices [82]. In reality, political penetration of the Bench is a long-seated aspect of the U.S. separation of powers, with successive Presidents seizing such opportunities as arise for nominating to the federal courts individuals of a sympathetic political persuasion, and with the Senate reflecting interest group pressures in the process of advise and consent [83].

Finally, in countries like the United Kingdom that do not have a written constitution but which have a lengthy history of parliamentary sovereignty, formal constitutional rules are not feasible. Such constitutional rules as do exist are buried in the common law which is not immune to legislative intervention. It is not surprising, therefore, that *An Economic Theory of Democracy* [84] which concerned itself with the economics of political market competition has been much more influential in Europe than *The Calculus of Consent* [85] which focused attention on the logical foundations of constitutional democracy.

3.1. *Tensions over Normative Methodology*

Although the Virginia school [86] is much more cohesive in its ideology and methodology than the new law and economics, that does not imply an absence of intellectual tension over such important normative issues as efficiency, rights, and justice. Since the Virginia school is unquestionably the dominant force in normative public choice, this section is intended to focus on the areas of major disagreement, and discuss the relationship between the Wicksellian unanimity principle and the choice between competing values.

Virginia political economy in its normative (as in its positive) analysis systematically emphasizes catallactics, or the science of exchanges. Essentially, it reflects a consentaneous vision of nonmarket decisionmaking and stresses the process of exchange, or of agreement to contract, as the area of politics susceptible to normative economic analysis. The perspective imposed upon this approach is one of methodological individualism and of process, and not of some end-state social welfare function. There is a categorical difference between the approach of the Virginia school and that of Kenneth Arrow's social choice research program.

The citation by the Royal Swedish Academy of Sciences, in awarding the Nobel Prize in October 1986, noted the role in the development of Buchanan's thinking played by the writings of Knut Wicksell. For Buchanan, Wicksell indeed "is the primary precursor of modern public choice theory" [87]. *A New Principle of Just Taxation* [88] attacked "the inadequacies of the traditional methods of the science of public finance," suggesting that late nineteenth century texts left the impression "of some sort of philosophy of enlightened and benevolent despotism." He developed instead a voluntary exchange approach to the public finances and argues for a principle of "approximate" unanimity.

Buchanan has made it his lifetime's work, since his 1948 discovery of Wicksell, to pursue the latter's vision, emphasizing in his own many contributions to public choice three crucial components: methodological individualism, *homo economicus*, and politics-as-exchange. The relevant difference between private markets and politics is not to be found in the kinds of values or interests that people pursue but in the conditions (concerning both expected costs and expected rewards) under which they pursue their various interests. The role of the public choice normative analyst is not that of philosopher-king but rather of hypothesis creator and consensus-seeker, at least in Buchanan's view.

Economic efficiency is viewed radically differently in the Virginia perspective than within the perspectives of Chicago and of Yale. Efficiency for Posner, Chicago, indeed for the law and economics program writ at large, is evaluated by reference to specific end-state outcomes, given an initial distribution of rights. Outside observers are deemed to be capable of effecting an objective assessment of the efficiency or otherwise of specific institutional arrangements. Efficiency in Virginia political economy is an entirely different concept, subjective contractarian and process-oriented [89]. If the only relevant valuation is the choice-influencing cost subjectively experienced by the parties to actual or potential change, external observers cannot determine whether observed trades fall short of or exceed some attainable standard.

Indeed, within the institutional setting specific to an exchange relationship, absence of consummated exchange demonstrates that resources are in their most highly valued uses. Efficiency, given the institutions, is ensured as long as all parties are free to engage or not in the exchange mechanism. Yet, the Virginia efficiency concept is not a tautology given opportunities for institutional reform both at the level of the normal political process and at the higher constitutional level [90].

Buchanan does not stop short at such positive analysis. Pursuit of efficiency has played a central role in his moral philosophy. [91] It is in this respect that tension is observable within the Virginia school, especially since the early 1970s. Prior to the Sen impossibility theorem in 1970, it was usual to regard the requirement of universal consent as a sufficient guarantor of the protection of individual rights—of liberty in the negative sense of Hayek [92]. The right of individual veto was seen to protect against coercion in political as well as in private markets. Certainly, this view permeated *The Calculus of Consent* [93] and was retained in *The Limits of Liberty* [94].

Sen demonstrated [95] that the paradox of the impossible Paretian liberal cannot be ignored in a society characterized by individuals with meddlesome preferences unless the range of social choice is restricted to reflect a predetermined initial distribution of rights. Buchanan is not a Lockeian—indeed he berated the book on the minimal state by Robert Nozick [96] precisely because it assumed a Lockeian initial set of rights, and therefore failed to integrate the libertarian position with a consent-based theory of distributive justice [97]. Ultimately, Buchanan wants it all—efficiency, liberty, and justice—enshrined in one universal consent. Others in the Virginia school consider this to be an unattainable objective [98].

In his search for consent, Buchanan has utilized the contributions both of Thomas Hobbes [99] and of Rawls [100], both separately and in combination. From Hobbes he has taken the threat of anarchy, which precludes any concept of rights or entitlements, and in which life is "unpleasant, brutish and short" [101]. Even in anarchy a "natural distribution" emerges dependent on the relative strength, fortunes, and abilities of individuals. This distribution is not a structure of rights and, certainly, is not based upon consent. Yet, this distribution, given the great costs that individuals impose upon each other, provides a basis for mutually advantageous exchange, at least to establish the minimal and perhaps to confirm the productive state.

So far so good for efficiency and for classical liberalism, if not for justice. If rights are to be determined by some social contract, which introduces the minimal state as referee, there are only limited issues of the extent and nature of consent that lie between John Locke and Hobbes—between classical liberals and Buchanan. If the productive state can be restricted only to the provision of commodities with extreme publicness characteristics—and this is an unresolved problem of public choice—classical liberalism and efficiency can live together, albeit uneasily [102]. For Buchanan, however, this is insufficient. The initial "rights" in the minimal state are windfalls, the outcome of jungle politics. They constitute the Lockeian rights that he abhors. Consent is sought, therefore, for the redistributive state, something which Hobbes alone cannot provide. Instead, Buchanan seeks out an alternative metaphor—justice as fairness—derived from Rawls.

Through dubious reliance upon an assumption of universal, infinite risk-aversion characteristic of all individuals behind the veil of ignorance, Rawls had established two consentaneous principles which he designated as justice as fairness, namely, the principle of equal liberty and the principle of distributive justice. The first principle carries lexicographic preference over the second. Uneasy about relying upon such risk aversion as the pivot of consent, Buchanan [103] has applied worst-case scenarios to justify risk-averse behavior by risk-neutral individuals when creating government. Recognizing postconstitutional enforcement problems, he has employed the threat of Hobbesian anarchy in societies characterized by team production to derive consent-based protection against postcontractual renegements [104].

One serious problem remains, however, even with justice as fairness in the sense either of Rawls or of Buchanan [105]. Suppose that the critics are correct; that social justice even determined behind the veil, is destructive of rights; that redistributive politics cannot be chained in by constitutional constraints. In such circumstances, Rawls' second principle must be discarded in favor of the preferred principle of equal liberty. The difference principle, and with it justice as fairness, would be universally rejected by all individuals behind the veil as incompatible with equal access to liberty.

3.2. Tensions in Positive Public Choice

Public choice is a young research program, with many of its theories and hypotheses the subject of ongoing testing. Inevitably, there are important, unresolved controversies. The more important of these in terms of the law and economics program are here reviewed.

The vote motive [106] is clearly relevant to the development of statute law; indeed, the latter forms a central component of public choice research. It cannot be ignored, however, with regard to the common law, given the political pressures evident in the appointment and in the election of judges, and in the ever-present threat of invasive legislation should the common law fail to reflect the preferences of a decisive legislative majority. All law, even constitutional law, ultimately is vulnerable to politics.

The issue of the median voter theorem is one focal point of public choice controversy. Should the theorem hold, political markets will reflect the central tendency among voters' preferences. Majoritarian democracy thus is a politically meaningful concept. If the vote process should fail to satisfy the necessary assumptions, however, significant uncertainty ensues, raising important questions concerning the existence, uniqueness, and stability of political market equilibrium. Is equilibrium, if it exists, at some point of central tendency or is it at some off-center position in issue space? Is such equilibrium unique? Is such equilibrium stable [107]? Does logrolling affect the outcome? If so, does it offer a "minimum winning coalition", as Tullock [108] suggests, or "a coalition of the whole," as others have counterargued? Evidence certainly suggests the presence of significant political stability [109]. Research into why there is so much stability is a much needed in contemporary public choice.

Given the discontinuous nature of elections and the limited reach of the vote motive, the impact of interest groups on both statute and common law cannot be ignored. On this issue, also, there is continuing dispute. As section 3 indicates, the theory of interest groups developed by

Olson suggests that such groups introduce significant bias into political markets. Specifically, small groups endowed with special interests and large groups endowed with coercive powers over membership and/or able to pursue common goals as a byproduct of selective benefits will experience differential success in political markets.

Contrast this view with the Chicago theory of competition among pressure groups for political influence [110]. Closely following the Chicago paradigm of "what is is efficient" with respect to political as well as to private markets, Becker defines a theory of interest groups that runs diametrically counter to that of Olson [111], indeed which views interest groups as a powerful force in favor of political market efficiency in the sense of Paretian welfare economics. In Becker's view, policies that raise efficiency are likely to win out in the competition for influence because they produce gains rather than deadweight losses. Thus competition between interest groups tends to be an efficiency-enhancing process.

In Becker's view, this analysis unifies the view that governments correct market failures with the view that they favor the politically powerful. Competing pressure groups generate efficiency outcomes by effectively controlling political markets. To justify this strong conclusion, Becker allows for a suppression of the vote motive as a consequence of rational ignorance and for the effective control by interest groups over both politicians and their bureaucrats, who are hired to further the interests of the successful lobbyists. He recognizes the possibility of a principal-agent problem in this relationship, but leaves an explanation of its implications for a later (as yet unforthcoming) analysis.

The Chicago approach to public choice, like so much of the Chicago economics program [112], is strong on neoclassical economic theory but weak on institutions. Voters, politicians, interest groups, bureaucrats, and lawyers exercise only shadowy roles in abstract market analytics, and the new institutional economics has made no inroad into this well-established research paradigm. Moreover, Chicago assumptions that resources are highly mobile, information freely available, and transaction costs typically low fuel models that depict political markets typically as efficiency instruments for serving individuals' perferences [113].

Not so with Virginia political economy [114], which attaches importance to institutions as well as to the specific reward-cost structures of particular political markets. Through a blend of spatial political analysis, including logrolling, and interest group theory in the sense of Olson, Virginia political economy offers a much richer institutional insight into the working of democratic political markets. By explicitly recognizing rent-seeking [115], this program confronts not only the predictable allocation inefficiencies associated with political markets but also the potentially serious wealth losses associated with the use of political markets for rent-seeking and rent-protection goals. This approach is applicable to the law and legal institutions to the extent that the agents concerned—judges as well as attorneys—are vulnerable to public choice pressures as outlined above.

The behavior of bureaus, and their precise role in political markets, is yet another focal point of controversy in the public choice research program. Some analysis, like Niskanen [116], employ budget maximization by senior bureaucrats as a generative assumption to predict excessively high rates of bureau outputs and x-efficiency in bureau budgets. By modeling bureaus as supply monopolies with information advantages over their legislative oversight committees, Niskanen emphasizes their distortive impact on the supply side of political markets through differential success in a bilateral bargaining. Oversupply, in this model, is measured in terms of underlying median voter preferences, and not in terms of the Pareto criterion.

Albert Breton and Ronald Wintrobe [117], in contrast to the monolithic bureau model of Niskanen, concentrate on the development of an exchange-based theory of supply, with significant internal trading and competitive characteristics. Since property rights typically do not exist, at least in conventional form, internal trading between superiors and subordinates is facilitated by the existence of trust—confidence in some degree by one bureaucrat that another will effect his promise. Trust networks are the analogues of markets, just as trust is the analogue of law and law enforcement. Selective behavior—the extent to which bureaucrats choose to deviate from efficiency objectives within the limits of their capacity—is viewed as the outcome of bargaining within trust networks. Bureau competition will not eliminate selective behavior, given the vulnerable characteristics of trust. Breton and Wintrobe thus discern an important monitoring role for the legislative sponsors.

Rowley and Elgin [118], in contrast, analyze bureaus in a principal-agent property right theoretical framework. In this perspective, bureaus exert a dual impact on political markets, as a demand influence in the special interest sense of Olson and as a supply influence as agents to their legislator principals [119]. Predictably, both supply and demand impacts result in oversupply in the sense of Niskanen, though for different reasons. The attenuation of property rights in political markets provides opportunities for bureau discretion on both sides of the political market. In consequence, bureau excess supplies and x-efficiency may persist given the opportunity that such discretion provides for bureaus to lobby the voters and the effective special interests.

Distinct though these three theories of bureaucracy are, they are yet much closer to each other than to the public interest model of Max Weber. They each offer important insights into the new law and economics. The judiciary itself, as well as all the agencies of law enforcement—the police, the district attorney's office, the courts, and the jails—are bureaus whose behavior can be modeled in terms of public choice. Considerable importance attaches, therefore, to the precise model utilized, not least when evaluating the independence or otherwise of the judicial and the legislative branches of government.

The new law and economics, for the most part, views the judiciary, if not the law enforcement agencies, as independent of all pressures. As such, the concept of the separation of powers is retained as an integral component of the research program despite the warning of James Madison in *The Federalist Papers*, that the legislative branch would always dominate.

The independent judiciary concept retains credibility if the Niskanen model is accepted, though only as the consequence of the superior bargaining abilities of the bureau over the legislation. In the Breton and Wintrobe model, however, the internal structure of the judiciary bureau is viewed as vulnerable to selective behavior as trust relationships within the judiciary itself give way to self-seeking. In the Rowley and Elgin model, Madison's prediction of legislative supremacy over the other branches is reinforced.

4. Public Choice, Law, and Economics: Lessons and Opportunities

It is now appropriate to visit briefly specific areas of the law and legal institutions—property law, tort law, criminal law, and constitutional law—to indicate possible public choice lessons for the new law and economics, especially in its Posnerian form, and to define major opportunities for additional research.

4.1. The Law of Property

Public choice lessons for the economic analysis of the law of property are here illustrated by reference to an exchange between Richard Epstein [120] and myself [121] in which I critiqued a paper that fell primarily in the wealth-maximization tradition of the Chicago school of law and economics.

Epstein separated his analysis into two broad categories: problems that arise because of events that occurred in the past, and problems that arise because of what might happen in the future. From the backward perspective, Epstein suggested that property rights should be grounded in first possession as a means of moving valuable resources into the hands of private owners expeditiously and efficiently. Epstein recognized the existence of adverse possession—a doctrine that allows the claims of the first possessor to be defeated by a later possessor—and noted that this implied the potential for an involuntary transfer in property rights, as defined by first possession.

He justified adverse possession as a wealth-maximizing doctrine on the ground that rectification costs, as true owners attempt to assert first possession rights, increase with the passage of time. At some point, the error cost of maintaining an ideal system of corrective justice (his liberatarian ideal) is outweighed by efficiency considerations. In Epstein's view, the statutes are tolled correctly from a wealth-maximizing perspective (note that the tolling is based on statute and not on common law):

> The general historical tendency has been to reduce the period of limitation. While periods of 20 years were once commonplace, today one sees statutes in which the basic period is in the range of six to ten years, the shorter number predominating when the adverse possessor pays taxes. Overall, the long period in early times was perhaps a result of high politics and of gaps in civil order that arose from the forced absence of landowners from the land because of plague, crusade or military service. Today the shorter period seems to make better sense because there are fewer obstacles to taking prompt action once adverse possession occurs [122].

From a forward-looking perspective, Epstein is markedly less compromising in support of property rights. Once again his normative thrust is drawn from the expected wealth-maximization directive, though in this case it is much more compatible with classical liberalism. He defends the potentially infinite duration of the fee simple on the ground that a temporally limited system of rights would encounter insuperable problems concerning the allocation of rights to the remainderman and in avoiding distorted incentives on the part of primary owners.

He endorses the vesting of owners with complete freedom to determine the future use and ownership of property, thus striking down all doctrines, such as the rule against perpetuities, that limit such powers of an owner. His justification is the wealth-maximizing goal of "rational" property owners. For the future, though not for the past, pure corrective justice is the endorsed conduit of wealth-maximizing efficiency in the law of property. Where postcontractual opportunities for strategic behavior otherwise threaten the contractarian basis on which the law of property is seen to rest, Epstein, less elegantly than Williamson, but equally forthrightly, views the emergence of appropriate governance structures as a spontaneous wealth-maximizing response.

Epstein's views on the law of property are incompatible, in important respects, with those of Virginia political economy. From the normative perspective, Sen's paradox denies Epstein the opportunity to pursue simultaneously the objectives of liberty and efficiency, despite his efforts to combine them. In all essentials, however, he ranks efficiency ahead of liberty, in conformity with the majority view of the Virginia school, though not all commentators in the 1986 symposium recognized this to be the case.

Consider Part I of Epstein's paper, devoted to the battle between first possession and adverse possession as the basis of property law. Libertarian philosophy would stress the primacy of first possession, irrespective of its distance in the past and the litigation cost in its determination, as an unassailable legal right and an important safeguard of negative freedom. Epstein, while recognizing this case, nevertheless, endorses statutes of limitation by reference to utilitarian cost-benefit analytics. Indeed, he suggests that developments in conveyancing, recordation, zoning, and other land-use controls have also evolved to maximize expected wealth.

In this judgment, Epstein not only breaks faith with liberty but incidentally infringes almost all elements of the Virginia political economy research program:

> He does not rely upon higher-level consensus between the transacting parties as evidence of an efficiency outcome. Statutory interventions via a special-interest-ridden pluralist machine of government do not necessarily reflect a calculus of consent. Transaction-cost differentials, which fuel Epstein's explanation, are asserted without any evidence....Epstein does not rely upon a theoretical structure such as that advanced by Williamson, to predict transaction-cost differentials qualitatively, given the difficulty of quantitative analysis [123].

Epstein overrides libertarian rights and the principle of corrective justice by reference to this utilitarian criteria. In so doing, he lauds as cost effective legislative interventions which may have been parleyed by special interests quite conceivably to endorse the seizure of property by carpet baggers in an application of Tullock's law: "might is might."

Epstein failed to limit his praise to the generalities of limitations statutes. He demonstrated eagerness to fine-tune the system, advocating two-tier statutes to cater for infants and the insane, the "bad faith" and the "good faith" adverse possessor, the tenant in possession and the remainder man. Legislative fine-tuning of this kind is an attractive rent-seeking instrument for attorneys and a source of bureau budget augmentation for the judiciary and its courts. As such, it is a source not of wealth enhancement but of wealth destruction.

Part II of Epstein's paper is directed at time and the future, providing a utilitarian perspective on uncertainty costs, and in so doing, endorsing infinite duration of ownership acquired by first possession while balancing between the rights of owners of limited interests and those of the remainder men on the basis of explicit cost-benefit analysis. This calculus is utilized also to justify the law of private inheritance which allows the owner of property unfettered discretion in choosing his successor in title.

Fortuitously, in these cases, the utilitarian and the libertarian outcomes coincide [124]. Even in these cases, Epstein makes no attempt to explore pressures that might have been exerted upon or have emanated from the courts to forge the modern law of property, nor does he seek an understanding as to why such pressures essentially satisfied the utilitarian calculus. Public choice research into such issues must result in a better understanding of the legal process than the black box explanation of Epstein. Certainly, it would attempt to test empirically the transaction cost assertions of Epstein on which his efficiency conclusions are grounded.

4.2. The Law of Tort

The law of tort, as it is analyzed by Posner [125] and by most other scholars who adhere to the efficiency hypothesis, is a highly idealized concept. Tortious acts are seen to be clearly defined, with issues of evidence, emphasized for example by Tullock [126] as a central issue in the economics of law, relegated to the seventh order of smalls. The liability rule is also viewed as clearly defined ex ante, despite fierce debate over the alternatives available. Judges are viewed as endowed with universal facility in compounding and discounting techniques and with an unusual sensitivity in the selection of appropriate rates of time discount. Damages, therefore, are tolled perfectly to adjust private decisionmaking ex ante to the social optimum.

In such circumstances, the significant issue under debate concerns the comparative efficiency of alternative liability rules: strict liability negligence, contributory negligence, comparative negligence, or no fault. In the absence of transaction costs, Tullock has demonstrated [127], as the Coase theorem would suggest, that the issue of liability does not matter. All liability rules are efficient. Since transaction costs are rarely calculated, especially in a suitable comparative institutions framework, it is not difficult for Posnerian analysts to assert transaction cost configurations that provide efficiency results, especially when third party effects are ignored.

The reality of contemporary U.S. tort law is sharply at odds with Posner's idealized view [128]. Indeed, tort law is regarded by many cognoscenti as being in a state of crisis, with state legislatures invading the common law to cap damage awards and to require private insurance companies to abate premium increases. Physicians and surgeons are warily avoiding high-risk services, or attempting to extract enforceable waiver contracts from desperately ill patient. Even attorneys are hounding each other out of business with legal malpractice suits which seek millions of dollars in damages—and attorneys usually do not carry insurance in the magnitude that is now considered prudent among medical practitioners.

The explanation of the tort law crisis is to be found in five aspects of tort litigation which, in combination, involve a significant departure from the idealized model of Posner: 1) the movement to no-fault liability; 2) the undermining of causation; 3) escalating litigation costs; 4) the explosion in tort suits; and 5) the augmentation of damage awards by tort juries. Arguably, all such features are the outcome of the forces of public choice, not the efficiency calculus.

The movement toward no-fault liability began during the 1960s in the United States and accelerated during the 1980s. Its momentum stemmed from a sociology-based attack on the two historic pillars of the law of tort—deterrence and compensation—undermining fault as a moral and doctrinal element. With its erosion, moral hazard advanced, with individuals seeking remedies for damages to which they exposed themselves. With it also has arisen the attack on "deep-pocket" defendants, however minimal their contribution to the tort under consideration.

The undermining of causation brought with it an attorney-based attack on the concept of proximate cause, which had required a reasonable relationship to be established between casue and effect. Aided by politically motivated judges in some jurisdictions and sympathetic juries (biased selection) [129], this attack has seen an increasing use of joint and several liability to shift the cost of compensation to deep-pocket defendants. In some courts, the burden of proof has been shifted to force defendants to prove lack of causation in order to avoid liability. Rent-seeking has manifested itself in such circumstances in a "junk science" invasion of the courts.

The escalation of litigation costs is a direct consequence of overt rent-seeking by attorneys, utilizing the contingent fee mechanism. A 1985 study by the Institute for Civil Justice of U.S. asbestos litigations established that 62 percent of all damages were lost in attorneys' fees and litigation costs. This did not include court costs. Successful plaintiffs themselves lost 34 percent of their damages to legal fees and an additional 5 percent to legal expenses.

The rents available to the legal profession have induced an explosion of tort litigation in the United States, with the number of product liability cases filed in federal district courts rising from 1,579 in 1974 to 13,554 in 1985 and with the number of claims filed against physician-owned companies rising from 10,568 in 1979 to 23,545 in 1983. Inevitably, the consequence has been a substantial lift in insurance premia or an outright withdrawal of insurance support in high-risk areas.

Finally, there has been an unprecedented growth especially since 1975, in damage awards in tort cases, most notably in cases involving jury verdicts. An entire sociology literature has developed on the techniques of introducing jury bias, especially against deep-pocket defendants. The success of this approach is reflected in damage awards. In 1975, average medical malpractice jury verdicts awarded $220,028. By 1985, this had increased to $1,017,716. Over the same time period, average product liability jury awards climbed from $393,580 to $1,850,452. Large damage awards are composed to a differentially high extent of compensation for pain, suffering, and mental anguish, which are, to say the least, highly subjective notions.

Public choice insights offer much more than the efficiency calculus to an understanding of tort law in a country which increasingly deploys litigation as an individualized reaction to self-induced losses.

4.3. The Criminal Law

Wrongful conduct in the sense of contract breach or common torts typically subject the wrongdoer to the payment of money damages to the victim or to prohibition (on pain of contempt) from continuation of repetition of the wrong (enjoinment). In either case, for penalties to apply, the victim must sue or settle out of court in the shadow of the law. Crimes, in contrast, whether in terms of the common or the statute law, are prosecuted by the state; and the criminal is forced to pay a fine to the state or to undergo a nonpecuniary sanction, notably imprisonment.

Posner [130] distinguishes five principal types of wrongful conduct made criminal in the Anglo-Saxon legal system. The first major category is the intentional tort, representing a pure coercive transfer either of wealth or utility from victim to wrongdoer. Murder, robbery, burglary, larceny, rape, assault and battery, mayhem, and false pretenses, punishable under the English common law, as amended by statute, are instances of such intentional torts. Second are other coerced transfers, such as tax evasion and (in the United States) price-fixing, the wrongfulness of which is not recognized at common law. Third are voluntary, and for Posner, potentially value-maximizing exchanges, incidental to activities that the state has outlawed. Prostitution, the sale of pornography, the sale of babies for adoption, and trafficking in narcotics are instances of such voluntary exchanges. Fourth are certain menacing but nontortious preparatory acts, such as the unsuccessful conspiracy to murder. Fifth is conduct that, if allowed, would complicate other regulations. Examples are leaving the scene of an accident and fraudulently concealing assets from a judgment creditor.

Posner is concerned to justify all such aspects of the criminal law as efficiency-enhancing. To this end, he first must justify the existence of criminal law. Why cannot all five categories be left to the law of tort? Categories three and four pose the greatest difficulty in this regard, since no one is hurt (third party effects ignored). Certainly, if the activities are judged wrongful, there is a detection problem since there is no victim. However, punitive damages could be adjusted upward to reflect this under provision of lawsuits, as also might be the case in category five. In each case, however, the higher the optimal level of punitive damages, the less likely it is that there will be a feasible damages sanction.

Posner is less equivocal with respect to categories one and two, recognizing that the paper sanction for a pure coercive transfer, such as theft, must be greater than the estimate of the victim's loss, to confine transfers to the market. Optimal damages, augmented by the problem of concealment, will often be astronomical, well in excess of bankruptcy constraints for most individuals. Tort-feasors typically would not pay. Three responses are possible, all available in criminal law, namely 1) the imposition of nonmonetary penalties such as imprisonment and death (in some cultures torture and dismemberment), 2) police investigation, and 3) the imposition of fines. In Posner's view, therefore, the criminal law is designed primarily for the nonaffluent, with the affluent capable of being monitored by the law of tort.

The efficiency approach to the criminal law, based on a model by Becker [131], views the criminal as a rational utility maximizer and the criminal law as imposing a cost-effective combination of detection and penalty provisions designed to optimize the rate of criminal activity. Once again, by appropriate transaction cost assertions and with bold delineations of the social cost of crime, Posner has been able to mount an influential case for his efficiency hypotheses.

Yet doubts remain. Tullock's rent-seeking insight, unlike Becker's theory, views expenditures on crime as involving not transfers but social waste [132]. Olson's theory of interest groups, unlike Becker's, suggests that criminals, benefiting from "special interest," will lobby more effectively than noncriminals to abate the severity of the detection/punishment control mechanism. George Stigler [133] has argued cogently that the economics of bureaucracy may focus crime enforcement procedures excessively on activities easy to monitor, where enforcement agencies perceive the greatest budgetary reward for high rates of successful conviction.

The public choice analysis of the judiciary [134] suggests that judges will sentence in response to vote and interest group pressures and not to reflect the efficiency calculus. The sociology of jury selections suggests that jury bias in force of the defendant may impose systematic distribution in favor of excessively high acquittal rates and low penalties. The economics of bureaucracy suggests that discretionary power in the police function will be reflected in discriminating police surveillance detrimental to perceived minority interests. The research agenda is challenging indeed if the new law and economics and public choice are to be reconciled on these important issues.

4.4. The Constitution

It would be surprising indeed if a contribution such as this were not to conclude with some remarks on the debate between the strict constructionists and the advocates of the living Constitution. It is to this central issue that attention is here directed, drawing from the alternative research programs of law and economics and conventional public choice.

For advocates of the efficiency of the law, the U.S. Constitution differs from an ordinary statute both in its subject matter and in its costs of enactment and amendment. The principle that constitutional provisions are to be interpreted more flexibly than statutes reflects the greater costs of changing the Constitution than of changing a statute. Thus flexible interpretation is seen to impact generality to the constitutional language and, hence, durability.

For Posner [135] the distinctive subject matter of the Constitution is found in its provisions allocating the powers of government between the states on the one hand and the federal government on the other, and, within the latter, among the executive, legislative, and judicial branches of government. The nature of such provisions, he argues, requires that it be very costly to change them. Posner suggests that constitutional provisions guaranteeing equal protection of the laws and due process of law do not provide the courts with the authority to invalidate legislation as unreasonable even if such legislation violates the allocation of governmental powers or invades specific personal rights. His judgment in this area rests uneasily upon a calculus of consent view of the legislature that he does not elsewhere endorse.

In essence, Posner views the judicial branch as (deliberately) weak and dependent in the other branches, Congress cannot lower the salaries of federal judges during their incumbency. Yet, the judiciary cannot operate without congressional appropriations, and cannot enforce its judgments without the cooperation of the executive branch. Moreover, the federal courts, whatever their role, cannot make policy except in the context of deciding justiciable cases. For this reason, it is difficult for them, even should they so wish, to establish a coherent agenda for policymaking. Furthermore, judges have some career incentives, save for Supreme Court justices, to adhere to precedent, and this itself limits the pace at which policy changes will be adjudicated.

William Landes and Posner [136] adhere, nevertheless, to the concept of an independent judiciary, constrained though it is by the above-mentioned weaknesses. They interpret the independence thus granted to be the deliberate gift of the legislature, designed to consolidate legislative deals arising within an interest-group-dominated, pluralistic political system. If Congress is to be capable of appropriating the present value of long-term legislative commitments to particular interest groups, the probability of subsequent renegements must be low. The independent judiciary, by upholding congressional contracts, may facilitate wealth maximization within the legislature.

Public choice, however, casts serious doubts on the independence of judges, as on the alleged efficiency motivation that drives them into office. The political market pressures that invade the legislative and executive branches of government without doubt also invade the judicial branch. Evidence of the behavior certainly of the Warren Supreme Court in no sense refutes the notions of public choice. Equally, there is little evidence that activism has taken a pro-efficiency profile.

Yet, this essay will not close with a counsel of despair; will not endorse the current public choice view that political stability reflects a stable equilibrium of rent-seeking, rent-protection pressures; will not deny the force of new ideas and the impact of constitutional thinking. It is appropriate, in this regard, to draw upon the critical words of the leading exponent of constitutional economics James M. Buchanan, in his 1976 response to Landes and Posner:

> I want an independent judiciary to restrict the actions of legislative bodies and administrative agencies to modify these rules when they are not legitimately empowered to do so. This role for the judiciary extends further than the Landes-Posner one of forcing legislative and executive branches to keep past commitments. I want the courts to start once again to take a hard look at the constitutionality of legislative and executive actions, but in terms of the existing rules of the game, and not in terms of the judges' own social or ethical ideals. The tragedy of Earl Warren's court lay not in its activism, but in its avowal of a role for the judiciary that is wholly inconsistent with the structure of constitutional democracy [137].

If the positive lessons of public choice are learned, and rational ignorance does not prevent the political implementation of restorative measures, it is not farfetched to suppose that a reconstructed Supreme Court might return from activism to constitutional interpretation; from the invasion of individual rights embedded in the Constitution to their protection [138]. To do so, a new breed of justices will have to leash themselves by hand and by foot to the mast, as they steer a passage between the sirens of liberty, efficiency, and justice and reaffirm the constitutional intent of the Founding Fathers.

If such a return to constitutionalism occurs, it will be due in no small measure to the interactive influence of law and economics and public choice, both as predictive sciences and as moral philosophies.

References

1. Buchanan, J. M., "What Can Economics Contribute to its Neighbors?," in Krepp S. R. (ed.), *The Structure of Economics Science* (New York: Prentice-Hall, 1986).
2. Coase, R., "The Problem of Social Cost," *Journal of Law and Economics* Vol. III (October 1960), pp. 1–44.

3. Buchanan, J. M., and Tullock, G., *The Calculus of Consent* (Ann Arbor: University of Michigan Press, 1962).
4. Veljanovski, C. G., "The Economic Approach to law: A Critical Introduction," *British Journal of Law and Society*, Vol. 7 (1980).
5. Popper, K.R., *The Logic of Scientific Discovery* (New York: Basic Books, 1959).
6. Friedman, M., *Essays in Positive Economics* (Chicago and London: University of Chicage Press, 1953), pp. 3–47.
7. Lakatos, I., "Falsification and the Methodology of Scientific Research Programs," in Lakatos, I., and Musgrave, A. (eds.), *Criticism and the Growth of Knowledge* (New York: Cambridge University Press, 1970).
8. Knight, F. H., *Risk, Uncertainty and Profit* (Chicago: University of Chicago Press, 1921).
9. Galbraith, J. K., *The New Industrial State* (Boston: Houghton Mifflin, 1967).
10. Rowley, C. K., "Social Sciences and Law: The Relevance of Economic Theories," *Oxford Journal of Legal Studies*, Vol. 1, No. 3 (Winter 1981), pp. 391–405.
11. Posner, R. A., *Economic Analysis of Law* (New York: Little Brown, 1986).
12. Rowley, C. K., and Peacock, A. T. *Welfare Economics: A Liberal Restatement* (Oxford: Martin Robertson, 1975).
13. Buchanan, J. M., "Positive Economics, Welfare Economics and Political Economy," *Journal of Law and Economics*, Vol. 2 (October 1959), pp. 124–138; and Buchanan, J. M., "A Contractarian Paradigm for Applying Economic Theory," *American Economic Review*, Vol. 65 (May 1975), pp. 225–230.
14. But see Mercuro, N., and Ryan, T. P., *Law, Economics and Public Policy* (Greenwich: JAI Press, 1984).
15. Posner, *supra* note 11, p. 13.
16. *Ibid.*, p. 13.
17. *Ibid.*, p. 14.
18. *Ibid.*, pp. 14–15.
19. Posner, R. A., "Some Uses and Abuses of Economics in Law," *University of Chicage Law Review*, Vol. 46 (Winter 1979), pp. 281–306.
20. Mercuro, N., and Samuels, W. J. "Posnerian Law and Economics on the Bench," *International Review of Law and Economics*, Vol. 4, No.2 (December 1984), pp. 107–130.
21. Mercuro, N., and Samuels, W. J. "Wealth Maximization and Judicial Decision-Making: The Issues Further Clarified," *International Review of Law and Economics*, Vol. 6, No. 1 (June 1986), pp. 133–138.
22. Mercuro and Samuels, *supra* note 20, p.108.
23. Posner, R. A., "Wealth Maximization and Judicial Decision-Making," *International Review of Law and Economics*, Vol. 4, No. 2 (December 1984), pp. 131–135.

24. Posner, *supra* note 11, p. 133.
25. Mercuro and Samuels, *supra* note 21.
26. Mercuro and Samuels, *supra* note 21, p. 135.
27. Sen, A., "The Impossibility of a Paretian Liberal," *Journal of Political Economy*, Vol. 78, No. 1 (January 1970), pp. 152–157.
28. Arrow, K. J., "A Difficulty in the Concept of Social Welfare," *Journal of Political Economy*, Vol. 58 (1950), pp. 328–46.
29. Rowley, C. K., "Liberalism and Collective Choice: A Return to Reality?" *Manchester School* (September 1978), pp. 224–251; and Rowley, C. K., "Collective Choice and Individual Liberty," *Ordo Band*, Vol. 30 (March 1979), pp. 107–115.
30. Nozick, R., *Anarchy, State and Utopia* (New York: Basic Books, 1976).
31. Rawls, J., *A Theory of Justice* (Fair Lawn: Oxford University Press, 1973).
32. Rowley, C. K. "Rules versus Discretion in Constitutional Design," in Laidler, E. D. (ed.), *Responses to Economic Change* (Toronto and London: University of Toronto Press, 1986), pp. 75–104.
33. Rowley and Peacock, *supra* note 12.
34. Rowley, *supra* note 32.
35. Baumol, W. L., "Applied Fairness Theory and Rationing Policy," *American Economic Review*, Vol. 72, No. 4 (1982), pp. 639–656.
36. Holcome, R. G., "Applied Fairness Theory: Comment," *American Economic Review*, Vol. 73, No. 5 (December 1983), pp. 1153–1156; and Crew, M. A., and Rowley, C., "Toward a Public Choice Theory of Monopoly Regulation," *Public Choice*, Vol. 56 (forthcoming, 1988).
37. Posner, *supra* note 11.
38. Veljanovski, *supra* note 4.
39. Hirsch, W., *Law and Economics: An Introductory Analysis* (New York: Academic Press, 1979).
40. Rowley, C. K., and Brough, W., "The Efficiency of the Common Law; A New Institutional Economics Perspective," in Pethig, R., and Schlieper, U. (eds.), *Efficiency, Institutions and Economic Policy* (Berlin: Springer-Verlag, 1987).
41. Posner, *supra* note 19.
42. Hogue, A. R., *Origins of the Common Law* (New York: Liberty Press, 1985).
43. Rowley and Brough, *supra* note 40.
44. Goodman J. C., "An Economic Theory of the Evolution of Common Law," *Journal of Legal Studies*, Vol. 7 (June 1978); Higgins, R. S., and Rubin, P. H., "Judicial Discretion," *Journal of Legal Studies*, Vol. 9 (January 1986), pp. 129–139; and Rowley and Brough, *supra* note 40.
45. For an alternative view see Tullock, G., *Trials on Trial* (New York: Columbia University Press, 1980).
46. Rowley and Brough, *supra* note 40.
47. Rubin, P. H., "Why is the Common Law Efficient?" *Journal of Legal Studies*, Vol. 6 (January 1977), pp. 51–63.

48. Terrebonne, P. A., "A Strictly Evolutionary Model of Common Law," *Journal of Legal Studies*, Vol. 10 (June 1981), pp. 397–407.
49. Cooter, R., and Kornhauser, L. "Can Litigation Improve the Law Without the Help of Judges?" *Journal of Legal Studies*, Vol. 9 (January 1980), pp. 139–163.
50. Rowley and Brough, *supra* note 40.
51. Demsetz, H., "The Exchange and Enforcement of Property Rights," *Journal of Law and Economics*, Vol. 3 (October 1964), pp. 11–26; and Demsetz, H., "Information and Efficiency: Another Viewpoint," *Journal of Law and Economics*, Vol. 3, No. 1 (1969), pp. 1–22.
52. Becker, G., "A Theory of Competition Among Pressure Groups for Political Influence," *Quarterly Journal of Economics* Vol. 98 (1983), pp. 371–400, and Stigler, G. J., "The Economic Theory of Regulation," *Bell Journal of Economics*, Vol. 2, No. 1 (1971), pp. 3–21, and Stigler, G. J., "Xistence of X-efficiency," *American Economic Review*, Vol. 66, No. 1 (1976), pp. 213–216.
53. North, D. C., "Transaction Costs Institutions and Economics History," *Journal of Institutional and Theoretical Economics* (March 1986), pp. 7–17, and North, D. C., "New Institutional Analysis," *Journal of Institutional and Theoretical Economics* (March 1986), pp. 230–237.
54. Williamson, O. E., *Markets and Hierarchies* (New York: Free Press, 1975); and Williamson, O. E., "Franchise Bidding for Natural Monopoly—In General and with Respect to CATV," *Bell Journal of Economics*, Vol. 7 (1976), pp. 73–104; and Williamson, O. E., "Transaction Cost Economics: The Governance of Contractual Relations," *Journal of Law and Economics*, Vol. 22 (1979), pp. 233–261.
55. North, *supra* note 53.
56. Coase, *supra* note 2.
57. Crew and Rowley, *supra* note 36.
58. Cooter, R. "The Cost of Coase," *Journal of Legal Studies*, Vol. 9 (January 1982), pp. 1–34.
59. Hayek, F. A., *Law, Legislation and Liberty Vol. 1 Rules and Order* (London: Routledge and Kegan Paul, 1973); and Hayek, F. A., *Law, Legislation and Liberty Vol. 2 The Mirage of Social Justice* (Chicago and London: University of Chicago Press, 1976); and Hayek, F. A., *Law Legislation and Liberty Vol. 3 The Political Order of a Free People* (Chicago and London: University of Chicago Press, 1979).
60. Hayek, F. A., *The Constitution of Liberty* (London: Routledge and Kegan Paul, 1960).
61. Hayek (1973), *supra* note 59, ch. 13, p. 13.
62. Rowley, C. K., "The Failure of Government to Perform Its Paper Task," *Ordo Band*, Vol. 34 (March 1983), pp. 39–58.
63. Downs, A., *The Economic Theory of Democracy* (New York: Harper and Row, 1957).
64. Buchanan and Tullock, *supra* note 3.

65. Olson, M., *The Logic of Collective Action* (Cambridge: Harvard University Press, 1965).

66. Rowley, C. K., "The Relevance of the Median Voter Theorem," *Journal of Institutional and Theoretical Economics* (March 1984), pp. 104–135.

67. Enelow, J. and Hinich, M. J., *The Spatial Theory of Voting* (New York: Cambridge University Press, 1984).

68. Rowley, C. K., "The Spatial Theory of Voting: A Review Article," *Public Choice*, Vol. 48, No. 1 (1986), pp. 93–99.

69. Olson, *supra* note 65.

70. Olson, M., *The Rise and Decline of Nations* (New Haven and London: Yale University Press, 1982).

71. Olson, *supra* note 65, p. 2.

72. Tullock, G., "The Welfare Costs of Tariffs, Monopolies, and Theft," *Western Economic Journal*, Vol. 5 (June 1987), pp. 224–234.

73. Tullock, G., "Back to the Bog," *Public Choice* Vol. 46 (1985), pp. 259–263.

74. Rowley, C. K., and Elgin, R., "Toward a Theory of Bureaucratic Behavior," in Greenaway, D., and Shaw, G. K. (eds.), *Public Choice, Public Finance and Public Policy* (Oxford: Basil blackwell, 1985); and Rowley, C. K., and Elgin, R., "Government and Its Bureaucracy: A bilateral Bargaining versus a Principal-Agent Approach," in Rowley, C. K., Tollison, R. D., and Tullock, G. (eds.), *The Political Economy of Rent-seeking* (Boston: Kluwer Academic Press, 1988).

75. Niskanen, W. A., *Bureaucracy and Representative Government* (New York: Aldine-Atherton, 1971).

76. Weingast, B., and Moran, M., "Bureaucratic Discretion or Congressional Cartel?," *Journal of Political Economy*, Vol. 91 (1983), pp. 765–800.

77. Rowley and Elgin, *supra* note 74.

78. Peltzman, S., "Toward a More General Theory of Regulation," *Journal of Law and Economics*, Vol. 19 (1979), pp. 211–240.

79. Brennan, H., and Buchanan, J. M., *The Reason of Rules* (New York: Cambridge University Press, 1985).

80. Wicksell, K., "A New Principle of Just Taxation," reprinted in Musgrave, R. A., and Peacock, A. T. (eds.), *Classics in the Theory of Public Finance* (New York: MacMillan, 1958).

81. Rowley, C. K., "Rent Seeking in Constitutional Perspective," in Rowley, C. K., Tollison, R. D., and Tullock, G. (eds.), *The Political Economy of Rent Seeking* (Boston: Kluwer Academic Press, 1987).

82. Kimenyi, M., and Shughart, W. F. II, "What do Judges Maximize?" *Economica Delle Scelte Publiche* (1985), pp. 181–185.

83. Rowley, C. K., "A Public Choice Perspective on Judicial Pragmactivism," in Dorn, J., and Manne, H. (eds.), *Economic Liberties and the Judiciary* (Fairfax: George Mason University Press, 1987), pp. 219–224.

84. Downs, *supra* note 63.

85. Buchanan and Tullock, *supra* note 3.
86. Breit, W., *Creating the "Virginia School": Charlottesville as an Academic Environment in the 1960's* (Center for Study of Public Choice, George Mason University, 1986); and Rowley, C. K., and Seldon, A., *A Primer on Public Choice* (Oxford: Basil Blackwell), forthcoming; and Mueller, D. C., *The "Virginia School" and Public Choice* (Center for Study of Public Choice, George Mason University, 1985).
87. Buchanan, J. M., "The Constitution of Economic Policy," *The American Economic Review*, Vol. 77, No. 3 (June 1987), pp. 243–250.
88. Wicksell, *supra* note 80.
89. Buchanan, J. M., "Rights, Efficiency and Exchange: The Irrelevance of Transaction Costs," *Arbeitstagung des Vereins fur socialpolitik* (Baul 1983), pp. 9–24; and Buchanan, J. M., "Rights, Efficiency and Exchange," *Anspruche, Eigentums und Verfugungs-rechte* (Berlin: Dunker and Humblot, 1984), pp. 9–24; and Buchanan, J. M., *Cost and Choice* (New York: Markham, 1969).
90. Rowley, C. K., "The Law of Property in Virginia School Perspective," *Washington University Law Quarterly*, Vol. 64 (Fall 1986), pp. 759–774.
91. Rowley, C. K., "The Economic Philosophy of James M. Buchanan," *Economic Inquiry* (forthcoming, 1988).
92. Hayek, *supra* note 60.
93. Buchanan and Tullock, *supra* note 3.
94. Buchanan, J. M., *The Limits of Liberty: Between Anarchy and Leviathan* (Chicago: University of Chicago Press, 1975).
95. Sen, *supra* note 27.
96. Nozick, *supra* note 30.
97. Buchanan, J. M., "The Libertarian Legitimacy of the State," in Buchanan, J. M. (ed.), *Freedom in Constitutional Contract* (College Station: Texas A & M Press, 1977), pp. 50–63; and Buchanan, J. M., "Utopia, The Minimal State and Entitlement," *Public Choice*, Vol. 23 (Fall 1975), pp. 121–126.
98. Rowley, *supra* note 91.
99. Hobbes, T., *Leviathan*, Everyman's Library No. 691 (London: J. M. Dent, 1651).
100. Rawls, *supra* note 31.
101. Buchanan, J. M., "A Hobbesian Interpretation of the Rawlsian Difference Principle," *Kyklos* (1976), pp. 5–25.
102. Rowley, *supra* note 91.
103. Buchanan, J. M., and Faith, R., "Subjective Elements in Rawlsian Agreement on Distributional Rules," *Economic Inquiry* (January 1980), pp. 23–28; and Brennan, H. G., and Buchanan, J. M., "Predictive Power and the Choice Among Regimes," *Economic Journal*, Vol. 93, No. 369 (March 1983), pp. 89–105.
104. Rowley, *supra* note 91.
105. Buchanan, J. M., "The Justice of Natural Liberty," *Journal of Legal*

Studies, Vol. 5 (January 1976), pp. 1–16; and Buchanan, J. M., and Lomasky, L., "The Motive of Contractarian Justice," *Social Philosophy and Policy* (Autumn 1986), pp. 12–32.

106. Tullock, G., *The Vote Motive* (London: Institute of Economic Affairs, 1976).
107. Rowley, *supra* note 66.
108. Tullock, G., "Why So Much Stability?," *Public Choice*, Vol. 37, No. 2 (1981), pp. 189–202.
109. Tullock, G., "Why So Much Stability Revisited?," *Public Choice* (forthcoming, 1988).
110. Becker, Stigler, *supra* note 52.
111. Olson, *supra* notes 65 and 70.
112. Crew and Rowley, *supra* note 36.
113. Cooter, *supra* note 58.
114. Rowley, C. K., "The Relationship Between Economics, Politics and the Law in the Formation of Public Policy," in Matthews, R. C. O. (ed.), *Economy and Law* (London: McMillan, 1985).
115. Tullock, *supra* note 72.
116. Niskanen, *supra* note 75.
117. Breton, A., and Wintrobe, R., *The Logic of Bureaucratic Conduct* (New York: Cambridge University Press, 1982).
118. Rowley and Elgin, *supra* note 74.
119. Weingast and Moran, *supra* note 76.
120. Epstein, R. A., "Past and Future: The Temporal Dimension in the Law of Property," *Washington University Law Quarterly*, Vol. 64, No. 3 (1986)), pp. 667–722.
121. Rowley, *supra* note 90.
122. Epstein, *supra* note 120, pp. 681–682.
123. Rowley, *supra* note 90, p. 771.
124. Anderson, G., and Brown, P., "Heir Pollution: A Note on Buchanan's Law of Succession and Tullock's Blind Spot," *International Review of Law and Economics*, Vol. 5, No. 1 (June 1985), pp. 15–24.
125. Posner, *supra* note 11.
126. Tullock, G., "On the Efficient Organization of Trials," *Kyklos*, Vol. 28, (1975), pp. 745–762.
127. Tullock, G., "Negligence Again," *International Review of Law and Economics*, Vol. 1, No. 1 (June 1981), pp. 51–62.
128. Rowley and Brough, *supra* note 40.
129. Fukurai, H., Butler, E. W., and Huebner-Dimitrius, J. "Spatial and Racial Imbalances in Voter Registration and Jury Selection," *Sociology and Social Research*, Vol. 72, No. 1 (October 1987), pp. 33–38.
130. Posner, *supra* note 11.
131. Becker, G., "Crime and Punishment," *Journal of Political Economy*, Vol. 76, No. 2 (March/April 1968), pp. 169–217.

132. Tullock, G., "Does Punishment Deter Crime?" *The Public Interest*, Vol. 36 (Summer 1976), pp. 103–111.
133. Stigler, G. J., "The Optimum Enforcement of Laws," *Journal of Political Economy*, Vol. 78, No. 3 (May/June 1970), pp. 526–537.
134. Kimenyi and Shughart, *supra* note 82.
135. Posner, *supra* note 11.
136. Landes, W. M., and Posner, R. A., "The Independent Judiciary in an Interest Group Perspective," *Journal of Law and Economics*, Vol. 18, No. 3 (December 1975), pp. 875–902.
137. Buchanan, J. M., "Comment on-The Independent Judiciary in an Interest Group Perspective," *Journal of Law and Economics*, Vol. 18, No. 3 (December 1975). pp. 903–906.
138. Buchanan, J. M., "Good Economics—Bad Law," *Virginia Law Review*, Vol. 60 (1974), pp. 483–492.

6 PROPERTY RIGHTS AND CHOICE

Louis De Alessi
Robert J. Staaf

1. Introduction

The economics of property rights, also known as the new or the neoinstitutional economics, began modestly in the late 1950s with work by Armen A. Alchian [1]. Abetted by seminal articles on transaction and information costs by Ronald H. Coase and George J. Stigler [2], this line of inquiry attracted other scholars and, by the mid 1970s, had generated a substantial and growing body of theoretical and empirical research [3].

Taking account of the constraints imposed by alternative institutions and by transaction costs has allowed some major extensions of economic theory. Economists, political scientists, and legal scholars are casting new light on the nature, evolution, and choice of business organizations, the behavior of government-regulated and government-owned business firms, the behavior of government itself, and the evolution and consequences of alternative laws [4].

The authors gratefully acknowledge comments by Terry L. Anderson, Roger E. Meiners, and Bruce Yandle, Jr.

Current research spans the full range of economic and legal issues. To keep matters within acceptable bounds, this chapter provides a brief review of the literature explicitly concerned with property rights and of related work on transaction costs [5]; it then addresses the issue of subjective versus objective costs. This distinction has important analytical implications; for example, it helps to explain the existence of self-enforcing contracts.

2. Development

The fundamental insight of economics, that individuals respond predictably to changes in their opportunities for gain, was first clearly articulated by Adam Smith [6]. In analyzing the choices of consumers and producers, Smith explicitly considered the effect of institutions.

Subsequent economists gradually abstracted from the complexities of reality by focusing on the behavior of idealized variables under highly purified conditions. In addition to such simplifications as characterizing both inputs and outputs as homogeneous and perfectly divisible, economists implicitly or explicitly took all rights to the use of resources to be fully allocated, privately held, assigned to productive purposes purely in response to pecuniary incentives, and exchanged at zero transaction costs, broadly defined as the costs of obtaining information and of negotiating, policing, and enforcing contracts. In time, neoclassical theory, defined as the conjunction of the utility-maximization theory of consumer choice and the profit-maximization theory of the firm, emerged as a tight mathematical construct honed by the careful application of Occam's razor and stripped of all institutional content [7].

Such abstractions are necessary if a scientific theory is to be sufficiently general to deal with the phenomena within its field of inquiry. When the theory is applied, however, the variables reflecting the particular circumstances of time and place must be identified and related to their empirical counterparts, either directly or by way of other hypotheses specifying the nature of the relationship. Unfortunately, economists seldom observed this requirement. The reason may have been a failure to distinguish between the assumptions (antecedent conditions) that specify the set of circumstances in which the theory is applicable, and thus must be identified empirically, and the assumptions (axioms) that are the theory's initial hypotheses, and whose usefulness typically is established less directly by testing the theory's implications [8].

By the 1950s, neoclassical economics was under intense attack on both theoretical and empirical grounds [9]. In particular, there was growing evidence that the theory of the firm, even after its restatement in terms of wealth rather than profit maximization, did not predict consistently and accurately the production and pricing choices of business firms. Moreover, it did not apply to the increasingly important sector of the economy encompassing business firms regulated or owned by government, nonprofits, and other nonproprietary forms. Indeed, it did not even adequately explain why business firms exist, let alone why particular organizational structures evolve and survive [10].

The perceived limitations of neoclassical theory gave rise to a spate of ad hoc models. Subject to a profit constraint, managers were hypothesized to maximize such alternative goals as sales [11], the rate of growth of sales [12], the size of the firm [13], and the rate of growth of the firm [14]. A related approach, generally associated with the Carnegie school, rejected maximizing behavior and focused on the process of decisionmaking within the firm; central concepts included satisficing, multiple goals, organizational slack, resistance to change, and other "behavioral" characteristics [15]. These approaches did not yield a coherent theory; among other weaknesses, they failed to provide the criteria for determining a priori such things as the level of the profit constraint or which of the conflicting objectives was supposed to apply. Nevertheless, they helped to focus attention on specific limitations of neoclassical theory and to stimulate its revision.

Many of the apparent shortcomings of neoclassical theory arose because economists simply ignored the appropriate antecedent conditions. Thus, taking property rights to be fully defined and allocated, privately held, and exchangeable at zero costs did not reflect conditions in the real world and inevitably led to at least some implications inconsistent with the evidence.

A logical and fruitful line of reform sought to generalize the neoclassical framework by extending the utility-maximization hypothesis to all choices under constraints, including institutional constraints (the system of property rights) and transaction costs [16]. Thus, Gary S. Becker expanded the utility function to include nonpecuniary variables [17], Alchian explored the economic consequences of alternative structures of property rights [18], and Oliver E. Williamson sought to reconcile various strands of the Carnegie school with orthodox theory by introducing a utility function in which managers explicitly sought discretionary emoluments [19]. This work, together with subsequent contributions by Harold Demsetz [20] and others [21], showed that different institutions typically embody different structures of rights to the use of resources, providing decisionmakers with different opportunities for gain and affecting their choices systematically.

Concurrently, Coase [22] and Stigler [23] showed that transaction costs affect not only the extent to which resources are realigned in response to a change in circumstances but also exert a powerful influence on the evolution and survival of institutional arrangements designed to facilitate the flow of resources to their highest valued use [24].

The work on property rights and transaction costs had obvious relevance to the law beyond the traditional limits of antitrust and the regulation of public utilities. Rapidly growing research in law and economics quickly extended the application of economics (the so-called new law and economics) to the entire spectrum of legal issues, from the common law fields of contract, negligence, and property to criminal law, family law, legal judicial administration, and even the evolution of law itself [25].

Reformulating neoclassical theory to take account of the system of property rights and transaction costs has obvious methodological advantages. First, deriving business choices explicitly from the hypothesis that individual decisionmakers within the firm maximize their own utility has ended the apparent dichotomy of the theory between consumption and production choices. Second, taking the appropriate institutional constraints into account has allowed the theory to cover many of the events addressed by earlier ad hoc models, and is receiving growing empirical support [26]. This simplification has been encouraged by the introduction of the household production function [27] and the continuing generalization of the individual utility function [28]. Reducing the theory to a simpler form has increased its generality and, therefore, its range of application, while focusing on the individual has called attention to the characteristics of the institutions used to arrive at group decisions, thus encouraging the analysis of a broader range of organizational forms and legal rules.

3. Current State

The choice of property rights affects and is affected by transaction costs. Accordingly, it is useful to examine both.

3.1. Property Rights

Individuals respond to a change in relative prices by consuming more of those pecuniary and nonpecuniary sources of utility that have become relatively cheaper and to an increase in income by consuming more of all sources of utility. How prices, including incomes, are set is determined by the system of property rights.

Property rights are the rights of individuals to the use of resources. These rights are established and enforced not only by formal legal rules and the power of the state but also by social conventions. Thus, the choices that individuals make regarding what to wear and how to talk are constrained by custom and enforced by social ostracism.

The system of property rights adopted within a society provides a mechanism for assigning to specific individuals the authority to decide how specific resources may be used. It does that by specifying the nature of the rights that individuals may hold to the use, income, and transferability of resources. For example, under some usufruct arrangements (e.g., ejido land tenure in Mexico) an individual may hold the exclusive right to the use of a resource and the resulting income while other individuals, perhaps government employees, have the authority to assign and transfer the right. Under some common ownership rules (e.g., various fishing arrangements with open access), on the other hand, individuals may have exclusive right to the income that they extract from a resource while the right to the use of the resource may be held in common and be nontransferable. Similarly, an entrepreneur may have the right to harm (reduce the wealth) of competitors by introducing a superior product but not by shooting them, while the same entrepreneur may be allowed to shoot an intruder but not to sell goods below a fixed price. Accordingly, the system of property rights determines, through explicit or implicit prices, how the benefits and the harms resulting from a decision are allocated between the decisionmaker and other individuals; thus, it helps to define the structure of costs and rewards and establish the expectations that individuals may hold in their dealings with others.

In practice, the bundle of rights to the use of a resource typically is partitioned so that different individuals concurrently hold different rights to the use of a particular resource. For example, the lease of a plot of land assigns different rights to the lessor and the lessee; owners of adjacent plots may have the right to walk across the land, and all individuals in the community may share in common the right to fly over the land or dump smoke on it. Contract law deals with the assignment of rights among the parties to a contract, whereas tort and nuisance laws deal with conflicts arising when the exercise of rights by one or more individuals imposes harms on owners of other rights.

Private property means that an owner's rights to the use and income of a resource are exclusive and voluntarily transferable. The lower are transaction costs or the higher the benefits of privatization, other things being the same, the greater is the extent to which private property rights are defined, allocated, and enforced; consequently, the closer is the relationship between the welfare of the owners and the economic consequences of their decisions, and the greater is the owners' incentive to take such consequences into account. Indeed, if transaction costs are zero, there are no external effects: individuals capitalize and take account of all the harms and benefits resulting from their decisions. Under these idealized conditions, resources are priced at their opportunity cost and flow to their highest valued use, regardless of their initial assignment [29].

In reality, of course, transaction costs are positive and rise at the margin, introducing a new constraint and yielding new, efficient solutions. For example, some rights will not be fully defined, assigned (e.g., some rights will be held in common), enforced (e.g., some cattle will be allowed to stray), and priced (e.g., some rights will be assigned on a first-come, first-served basis), thereby reducing the incentive of owners to take full account of the harms and benefits flowing from their decisions.

Other systems of property rights provide different structures of incentives. For example, under common ownership with open entry, individuals lack exclusive, transferable rights to the use of resources [30]. Relative to a system of private ownership, this arrangement implies that individuals make smaller and shorter lived investments in the resources held in common. It also implies increased entry to capture rents and earlier exhaustion of the resources held in common. To mitigate these consequences, institutional arrangements (e.g., limits on catches) arise to act as surrogates for at least some of the constraints that would have existed under private property.

The choice of institutions within a society, of course, is not guided by Pareto efficiency criteria. Seemingly "inefficient" institutions may be established and survive because they are preferred (and individuals are willing to forego other commodities to maintain them) because they work to the advantage of groups with a comparative advantage in the use of political power or because they suit other constraints.

3.2. Transaction Costs and the Organization of Production

Differences in transaction costs explain differences in the choice and evolution of contractual arrangements, including alternative ways of organizing production. Thus, current work suggests that business firms exist to reduce postcontractual opportunistic behavior by lowering the cost of monitoring exchange (including effort) and directing the allocation of jointly cooperating units [31].

Individuals working together as a team frequently can produce an output greater than the sum of the outputs that each could have produced separately. In such cases, they have the incentive to work together. If the output of the individual members of the team is costly to measure, however, each individual has the incentive to shirk. The problem, therefore, is how to structure production and rewards to discourage shirking, including shirking by the monitors.

On this view, the privately owned firm is a set of contracts formed by resource owners to capture the gains of joint production. The problem of shirking by the monitors is reduced by assigning to the owners of the assets that are specialized to the firm both the authority to monitor inputs *and* the residual claim to the net earnings of the coalition [32]. Employees may also own firm-specific assets (e.g., human capital) that, at least in some cases, may act as a performance bond [33].

Shirking includes negligent behavior by members of the team. Thus, the trend in products liability law from caveat emptor to caveat venditor has expanded the concept of jointness among inputs and provided increased incentive to integrate activities within the firm [34].

The possibility of postcontractual opportunistic behavior by agents outside the firm provides the incentive to integrate some activities within the firm, to own (rather than rent or lease) firm-specific assets, and to accept seemingly unfair contracts [35].

Competition further inhibits shirking. Competition from other enterprises provides a check on performance, fosters the evolution and adoption of internal control devices, and eventually eliminates higher cost producers. Competition among actual and prospective shareholders transfers ownership of the specialized assets to coalitions better able to use them, while competition for managerial positions by candidates within and outside the firm discourages shirking by employees [36].

The success in choosing the members of the team and the institutions that bind them together helps to explain the success of the firm or coalition, as well as the heterogeneity of firms' activities and sizes within an industry [37].

Transaction costs also help to explain the evolution and choice of alternative forms of business organization. Thus, if monitoring costs are relatively high and team production yields more output than separate operation, then profit-sharing arrangements are more likely to evolve. Examples include partnerships in professional and intellectual work [38] as well as share contracts in agriculture and mining [39]. If monitoring costs are relatively low, on the other hand, then employer-employee contracts are more likely to evolve (e.g., sole proprietorship, corporation).

When team size can be relatively large, the problem of raising large sums of specific capital encouraged the development of the modern corporation with transferable shares and limited liability as a device for economizing on transaction costs [40]. The low cost of transferring shares makes it easier for actual and prospective shareholders to revise their portfolios, facilitating the realignment of ownership to replace inefficient management. Limited liability further lowers transaction costs by reducing the demand by creditors and shareholders for information about the wealth and other characteristics of current and prospective shareholders.

Within the corporation, individuals specialize. Shareholders hold ultimate control and own the assets that are specific to the firm, bearing the value consequences of exogenous event as well as of decisions made within the firm. Debtholders specialize in the ownership of nonspecific assets and in monitoring the firm's compliance with the loan agreements. Managers specialize in day-to-day monitoring and decisionmaking within the firm, acting as agents for stockholders. Dividends to shareholders and interest payments to bondholders are paid at frequent, regular intervals to lower monitoring costs [41].

Incidentally, corporations and other firms presumably take out property and liability insurance to reduce the shirking-information problem of joint production. Insurance encourages specialization in ownership, increasing the returns to monitoring and lowering shareholders' demand for a more diversified portfolio; it also enhances the credibility of specific assets as a performance bond, and lowers the cost to shareholders of compensating other members of the coalition (e.g., managers) for investing in firm-specific assets [42].

Nonproprietary organizations (e.g., nonprofits, country clubs) evolve if individuals wish to encourage certain kinds of nonwealth-maximizing behavior (e.g., more research, more congenial members). These organizations inhibit the capitalization of future consequences into current transfer prices, thus reducing the ability of any group within the coalition to capture the benefits of improved management as judged by market standards.

3.3. Government Regulation and Ownership

Government regulation of business firms reduces the bundle of rights held by their owners (for example, it may restrict the right to set prices), attenuating owners' private property rights and thereby reducing their ability to capture the benefits of improved management and their incentive to monitor managers [43]. Although the consequences of government regulation depend in part upon the institutions used (e.g., independent commission or government bureau) and their effect on the incentives of regulators [44], it is clear that managers have more opportunities to increase their welfare at the expense of owners and consumers. The supporting evidence is extensive [45].

Government ownership may occur for a variety of reasons, including the desire to solve the shirking-information problem of joint production [46]. Government, of course, can always contract with private firms for the production of goods and services. As the cost of monitoring whether purchased commodities meet contract specifications increases, however, the opportunities for shirking by contractors also increase. At some point, it may become more economical to monitor inputs and integrate the activity vertically within government.

Regardless of the reasons it comes about, government ownership alters the cost-reward structure confronting decisionmakers within the firm, and affects their production and pricing choices. The crucial difference between private and political (government-owned) firms is that property rights in the latter effectively are not transferable [47]. This situation rules out specialization in their ownership, inhibiting the capitalization of future consequences into current transfer prices and reducing the incentive of those who bear such consequences to monitor managerial behavior. As a result, the managers of political firms typically have greater opportunity for discretionary behavior, as judged by market standards, than the managers of privately owned firms. Among other things, this analysis implies that private firms are more likely than comparable political firms to introduce cost-reducing innovations, adopt cost-minimizing input combinations, cater to consumer wants, and respond more quickly and fully to changes in economic circumstances [48].

3.4. Efficiency

Although much of the theoretical and empirical work to date has focused on the economic consequences of alternative institutions, growing attention is being paid to the latter's evolution and adoption taking explicit account of the role of government [49]. Within the broadly conceived field of law and economics, however, this research at times has been confused by the failure to distinguish between positive and normative considerations and to appreciate fully the notion of efficiency [50].

Efficiency may be defined as the solution to a constrained maximization problem. Thus, given a set of institutions, the resulting solution of the economic problem is efficient. Institutions with different legal structures typically yield different efficient solutions, and which institution is adopted depends on the rules for choosing institutions. Economics is a powerful tool for analyzing the consequences of alternative institutions and, given an understanding of the effective constraints, for explaining (predicting) the evolution and adoption of competing institutions. Which institutions ought to be adopted, and whether or not they are more efficient in some sense, ultimately is a normative issue, and economics cannot provide the answer.

4. Subjective Costs

The consequences of alternative systems of property rights depend on the cost-reward structures presented to individual decisionmakers. In deriving testable implications and, for those so inclined, policy recommendations, it is crucial to identify the opportunity costs that decisionmakers perceive, and these are necessarily subjective. Unfortunately, the literature suggests some confusion between objective and subjective costs.

Coase's analysis of private and social costs focused attention on the role of transaction costs [51] and helped to lay the foundation for much of the current research in the economics of property rights, particularly in law and economics. The equally important role of subjective costs, however, has been largely neglected [52]. Depending upon the size of the external effects, if any, "social" costs are partially if not fully reflected in market prices. *Subjective costs, on the other hand, are purely private and are seldom reflected in market prices except at the margin.* The resulting divergence between subjective and objective costs creates a problem for a legal system that relies on market prices to measure damages and other costs.

4.1. Transaction and Subjective Costs: Tensions at the Margin

When transaction costs are zero, the Coase theorem holds that private property rights flow to their highest valued use through voluntary exchanges. In a world in which all property rights are privately held, there are no external effects, and social costs equal private costs.

When transaction costs are positive, however, trade is inhibited. In these circumstances, even though voluntary exchange may be possible, the theorem has been used to justify the adoption of "efficient" legal rules (e.g., tort, nuisance, remedies, breach of contract) that would allocate the disputed rights to their highest valued use (or assign liability to the least cost avoider) in order to reduce transaction costs [53].

This efficiency argument, however, is very similar to the Pigovian position that Coase severely criticized in the second half of his article. Pigou's distinction between social and private net costs is based on the premise that costs are externally observable and objective [54]. Indeed, a rule of law that assigns property rights and thus liability is similar to a tax in modifying individual behavior. The principal difference is whether the levy is described as a *damage* (individual compensation) or as a *tax* (government compensation). Thus, compensatory tort damages are similar to the external observer's calculation of the proper Pigovian tax that would eliminate the divergence between social and private costs. For example, a smoke nuisance (externality) may be internalized by liability for the payment of compensation to those individuals or firms held to have been damaged (private nuisance) or by liability for the payment of taxes to the Environmental Protection Agency (statutory nuisance) [55]. As Coase emphasized, the assignment of a disputed right necessarily entails the imposition of a reciprocal cost on the person who does not receive it [56].

Economists generally agree that the cost of an event is the highest valued opportunity foregone. Because cost arises from the act of choice, it depends on the alternatives perceived by the individual [57]. It follows, as James M. Buchanan has argued, that cost is subjective and based on the anticipations of the decisionmaker, who bears it exclusively [58].

It should be stressed that, in equilibrium, the subjective (or personal use) value that an individual attaches to an *additional* unit of a commodity is equal to the market price. For each individual, this market price reflects the opportunity foregone at the margin. The same market price, however, is smaller than the subjective value that the individual attaches to the inframarginal units. Indeed, this difference represents the gains from trade (consumer's surplus) and provides the individual with the incentive to trade. Thus, expenditures generally underestimate cost because they exclude the gains from trade on the (inframarginal) units purchased whereas cost includes the gains from trade on the opportunity foregone.

In the case of a voluntary exchange, of course, the *relative* magnitude of costs or values is revealed. For example, a person who purchases an easement from another must value it more than the seller. In the case of

an involuntary exchange, on the other hand, an external observer, such as
a judge or jury, cannot possibly make a true determination of the costs
(damages) claimed by the participants to the legal dispute. Accordingly,
"efficiency" arguments in tort law (i.e., involuntary transactions) used
to favor various rules for internalizing externalities are suspect on
grounds similar to those that Coase used to undermine Pigovian taxes or
subsidies [59].

4.2. Breach of Contract

Subjective cost considerations are also relevant, but more subtle, in
contract law. When a contract is formed, each of the contracting parties
does not and cannot know the costs of entering the contract (a choice)
that the other party incurs. The promisee receives a right from the
promisor, and for every legal right there is a legal duty and a corresponding remedy for the breach of that duty. Whether the remedy is fully
compensatory depends on how costs are defined. As a result, the nature
of the remedy affects the decision whether to enter the contract and,
having entered it, whether to breach. In most cases, the remedy for a
breach of contract is the damages suffered. But these damages are calculated using market information that, except in certain circumstances, fails
to include subjective costs.

A landmark case, *Jacob & Youngs, Inc.,* v. *Kent,* illustrates the issue
[60]. Jacob & Youngs, a contractor, built a home for Kent. Although the
contract specified that a brand of pipe known as "Reading Manufacture"
was to be used for plumbing, the contractor used a different brand, of
supposedly equal quality and value, in part of the construction. Kent
refused to pay the balance owed on the house until the nonspecified pipe
was replaced by "Reading" pipe or he received the cost of reconstruction.
To install Reading pipe would have required tearing out and rebuilding
walls, a considerable expense. The contractor refused and sued Kent.

Judge J. Cardozo ruled that the homeowner was entitled to an allow-
ance for defects of *trivial* and *inappreciable importance,* but *not* to the
cost of reconstruction. According to Cardozo:

> Those who think more of symmetry and logic in the development of legal rules
> than of practical adaptation to the attainment of a just result will be troubled
> by a classification where the lines of division are so wavering and blurred [61].

Judge J.J. McLaughlin dissented, stating:

> What his reason was for requiring this kind of pipe is of no importance.... It
> may have been a mere whim on his (homeowner's) part, but even so, he had a

right to this kind of pipe, regardless of whether some other kind, according to the opinion of the contractor or experts, would have been "just as good, better, or done just as well" [62].

Cardozo's reference to a lack of symmetry is a refusal to define Kent's rights in terms of Jacob & Youngs' duty and the latter's rights in terms of Kent's duty. In Cardozo's view, symmetry is replaced by an external observer's notion of a just result, whereas in McLaughlin's view the subjective nature of cost is emphasized. To Cardozo, the objective cost to the homeowner of not having Reading pipe is a suitable substitute. To McLaughlin, a suitable substitute, if one exists, is known only to the chooser.

Cardozo's decision might be interpreted as enhancing efficiency because the (objective) value to the homeowner of the right to complete (specific) performance (installing Reading pipe in place of the substitute) is less than the (objective) costs that would be incurred by the contractor [63]. Accordingly, the remedy of specific performance seems to result in a private and social waste of resources.

The inference, however, is incorrect. Suppose that the remedy in this case is specific performance. If the subjective (dollar) value to the homeowner of the right to specific performance is less than its subjective (dollar) cost to the contractor, then, as implied by the Coase theorem, the homeowner has the incentive to give up the right to specific performance in exchange for a payment (settlement) smaller than the contractor's cost of replacing the pipe. Of course, if the homeowner values Reading pipe more than the cost of specific performance, then there is no exchange or settlement. In either case, however, resources are allocated to their highest valued use and there is no economic waste [64].

In any given suit the right to specific performance, relative to the nominal damages granted under the doctrine of substantial performance, benefits the homeowner relative to the contractor. The right to substantial performance, on the other hand, benefits the contractor relative to the homeowner. Who gains and who loses, however, is a distributional issue inherent to any definition of rights whereby someone must always bear a cost.

Cardozo's decision could also be defended on the "efficiency" ground that it economizes on transaction costs. Thus, it might be argued that the value to homeowners of the right to specific performance typically is less than its cost to contractors, so that denying a remedy of specific performance in the first instance avoids additional transactions (homeowners selling their rights). Alternatively, it might be argued that the transaction costs of negotiating a settlement are too high and thereby lead to an inefficient (wasteful) outcome. Both arguments, however, presume incorrectly that costs can be observed objectively by an external party such as a judge or jury.

Moreover, even if in 999 out of 1,000 cases individuals were to contract around a particular assignment of a property right, it does not follow that an alternative assignment of the right would be desirable. The value placed on the right by the one-thousandth individual may well exceed the sum of the values assigned by the other 999 individuals.

If transaction costs are negligible, the right of specific performance always guarantees that subjective costs are taken into consideration. Accordingly, the transaction cost and the subjective cost perspectives can be taken to represent conflicting arguments about the assignment of rights.

Buchanan and Gordon Tullock address this issue in a different context [65]. In examining different collective decisionmaking rules at the constitutional level, they consider the tradeoff between external costs and transaction costs. The higher are external costs, the greater is the incentive to tolerate the higher transaction costs associated with higher majority (e.g., two-thirds or three-quarters) or unanimity rules. Within this framework, contract law, which deals with *private* decisions, embodies the principle of unanimity.

There is no reason, however, to expect that a particular legal rule would be favored by *all* members of a society. Thus, common law—just like statutory and constitutional law—may be expected to generate some external costs. Unanimity in this instance can be interpreted as the *right to contract around* the rule. If there is any meaning to the notion of common law efficiency, it is not that the rules per se are necessarily efficient in some global sense (clearly a normative judgment), but rather that the parties generally are free to contract around such rules [66].

Specific performance, which is discussed below, may be interpreted as a proxy for satisfying a requirement of unanimity. Damages based on market prices, which are a collective measure of costs determined at the margin, do not provide compensation for private costs.

4.3. Subjective and Objective Legal Doctrines of Contract

The legal process necessarily entails an external observer in the form of a judge or jury. At the turn of the twentieth century, legal scholars debated the relative merits of an objective versus a subjective doctrine of contract; the latter was embodied in such concepts as the "meeting of the minds," a metaphysical state in which offer and acceptance were perceived as mirror images in the minds of the offeror and offeree. This subjective view of contracts is clearly inconsistent with the economist's concept of subjective cost, which implies that each party to a contract cannot know the other's cost: each is an external observer of the other's choice.

Justice Learned Hand's classic statement best illustrates the distinction between a subjective and an objective doctrine of contracts:

> A contract has, strictly speaking, nothing to do with the personal or individual intent of the parties. A contract is an obligation attached by mere force of law to certain acts of the parties, usually words, which ordinarily accompany and represent a known intent. If, however, it were proved by twenty bishops that either party, when he used the words, intended something else than the usual meaning which the law imposes upon them, he would still be held, unless there were some mutual mistake or something else of that sort [67].

As Edward J. Murphy and Richard E. Speidel suggest, "[T]he 'objective' test affords the courts an opportunity to control or regulate individual exchange behavior through use of that great 'collectivist' the 'reasonable' person" [68]. James W. Hurst has argued that the objective test is consistent with a market institution "...to create and maintain a framework of reasonably well defined and assured expectations as to the likely official and nonofficial consequences of private venture and decision" [69]. Hurst generally is correct if the good is not unique (e.g., wheat or lumber of a certain grade) and available in the market; then subjective and objective costs typically are the same. Trademark goods (e.g., Reading pipe), on the other hand, provide customers with unique expectations of quality or performance; thus, what constitutes an acceptable substitute can only be determined subjectively. Decisions such as *Jacob & Youngs Inc., v. Kent* ignore these market differences.

Damages at law are allowed only to the extent that they are compensatory. They cannot be used to penalize a breaching party because that would take away (or increase the cost of) the right to breach. This prohibition of penalty clauses rests on the objective doctrine of contract and the notion of objective costs. Hence, participants to an exchange may not be able to enter mutually beneficial agreements that would compensate a nonbreaching party for subjective costs: such a clause may be interpreted as a penalty and thus held to be unenforceable [70].

If the parties to a contract perceive that legal damages for a breach are inadequate and if damage clauses to compensate for subjective costs are not enforceable, then individuals have the incentive to seek other institutional arrangements. Possibilities include internalizing the activity within the firm and adopting self-enforcing contracts.

4.4. Self-Enforcing Contracts

The problem of subjective costs has some important implications regarding the organization of economic activity. Thus, inadequate compensation associated with objective measures of damages helps to explain the evolution and adoption of a broad range of self-enforcing contracts.

Recent literature on opportunistic behavior has shown that the market, as distinct from formal legal channels, may be used to enforce contracts, including warranties and promises of quality [71]. The quality characteristics of most products (and services) cannot be determined costlessly before or even after purchase, and the enforcement of sellers' representations (including advertisements) about them is also costly. As transaction costs increase relative to the value of performance if a firm's representations were held to be deceptive, firms would have increased incentive and opportunity to represent their products as being of higher quality than they really were. The resulting increase in uncertainty regarding the quality of any product would raise transaction (including information) costs to consumers.

Under these circumstances, some firms would have the incentive to provide assurances of quality to consumers by charging a price premium and investing in firm-specific assets, including brand-name (trademark) capital (e.g., Reading pipe). Specific capital has negligible or zero value outside the firm. If a firm's representations regarding its warranties and the quality of its products then become less informative or more deceptive, future sales will fall and the reduction in the firm's reputation is reflected in a lower market value of its trademark capital. The price premium presumably is larger the less frequently a good is purchased, the more durable it is, and the higher is the cost of enforcing legal contracts.

Specific capital investments by firms selling trademark products can be interpreted as a performance bond that is partially or wholly forfeited if the represented level of quality is allowed to deteriorate. Thus, specific capital assures market performance of quality representations, an assurance that would not be necessary in a world of zero transaction costs. Specific capital may include not only brand-name advertising and specialized equipment used in production, but also such things as expensive storefronts, displays, and signs indicating a commitment of capital to the enterprise [72]. In competitive equilibrium, investment in the firm-specific bond would be equal to the present value of the income stream from the price premium.

Damages at law are based on objective costs and penalty clauses are unenforceable. If the subjective costs of a breach of contract are expected to exceed the damages based on objective costs, then a self-enforcing contract may benefit both parties. The loss of specific capital resulting from a breach has the same deterrent effect as a penalty clause. Moreover, it avoids the problem, associated with penalty clauses, of inducing a breach.

Taking account of the specific capital at stake with trademark goods further suggests that the "efficiency" case for strict product liability may be flawed. According to that argument, a rule of negligence is inefficient because the resulting market prices do not include all (objective) costs, thereby creating overconsumption of some products or an externality; a rule of strict liability, on the other hand, is efficient because the resulting market prices incorporate all costs, including damages arising from non-negligent behavior, such as an accident [73]. This line of reasoning, however, fails to consider trademark products with specific capital at risk. The price premium used to fund specific capital already raises the market price and may exceed the price premium associated with a change in the liability standard from negligence to strict liability. Thus, the efficiency argument for the strict liability standard becomes irrelevant at the margin for trademark goods. This conclusion is supported by empirical studies of the fall in stock prices after defects were discovered in drugs and automobiles: shareholders bear losses well in excess of the direct costs (e.g., destroying or repairing defective products) involved, reflecting a reduction in the firm's specific capital [74].

4.5. Transaction Costs, Subjective Costs, and Quality Assurance

Investment in specific assets as a bond to assure quality is explained by the existence of positive transaction costs. The nature of the transaction costs at issue, however, must be clarified.

The standard argument for the use of self-enforcing contracts is that they are less expensive to enforce than formal legal contracts. Firms with an interest in assuring quality, however, could insure legal enforcement by stipulating that they would pay all legal enforcement costs. Or, as many firms in fact do, they could provide their products on approval or accept payment at a later date, thereby absorbing the enforcement costs [75].

A more general explanation for a firm's specific investment in trademarks is that such investments in effect provide a bond assuring specific performance, protecting consumers from the subjective costs associated with nonperformance. Because the transaction (mainly information) costs of accurately measuring the difference between subjective and objective costs are prohibitive, legal remedies are limited to objective costs. Thus, even if the costs of meandering through the legal process were zero, the legal remedy would not be relied upon because it is not compensatory (e.g., *Jacob & Youngs, Inc.,* v. *Kent*). Accordingly, specific capital investments may be undertaken simply to bond performance, protecting consumers from bearing subjective costs, without reference to such traditional factors as frequency of purchase, durability, or legal costs of enforcement.

Specific performance and specific capital have comparable significance. Both are important when the market alternative (e.g., damages) is considerably less valuable. The hypothesis is that performance-assuring specific investment in trademarks and other assets is related to the subjective costs associated with performance and the existence of a legal rule that prohibits penalties. If damages are adequate (e.g., the difference between subjective and objective costs is negligible) or the legal system permits penalties, then there will be fewer trademarks.

5. Summary and Conclusions

Alternative institutional arrangements typically embody different structures of property rights and thus present decisionmakers with different constraints. The resulting differences in cost and rewards affect choices systematically and predictably.

The existence of positive transaction costs affects consumption and production choices, including the evolution and choice of contractual arrangements. For example, it explains the existence of firms and the choice of particular organizational forms.

Taking property rights and transaction costs into account has permitted some major extensions of economic theory. Moreover, a variety of implications have received strong empirical support.

The analysis, however, has also been used to defend certain legal rules, even in cases where the exchange is involuntary, on the ground that they lower transaction costs. Such arguments fail to recognize that "efficient" legal rules face the same criticism that Coase advanced for "efficient" Pigovian taxes. The subjective nature of costs, often ignored, analytically can be just as important as transactions costs.

In general, if the purpose of a legal remedy is to provide full compensation, then specific performance is required to cover subjective costs.

This remedy eliminates an inquiry into the costs of nonperformance. Obviously, specific performance is not possible for many tort transactions. In many cases where specific performance is possible, however, substantial performance is allowed. Thus, for example, a party may have the right to breach and pay damages based on market prices that do not reflect subjective costs. Moreover, clauses designed to compensate for unobservable subjective costs may be interpreted as penalty clauses and held to be unenforceable.

In resolving disputes, the law necessarily requires an external observer, and a judge or jury has little option but to use objective costs in awarding damages. Subjective and objective costs as they relate to damages, however, are the same only if specific performance can be obtained indirectly through the market. Only then is a breach unequivocally efficient by Pareto criteria. If performance involves an element of uniqueness, then objective damages may not be adequate. In these circumstances, the parties have an incentive to adopt other institutional arrangements, such as integrating the activity within the economic unit (firm or household) and forming self-enforcing contracts.

Self-enforcing contracts, initially understood as a means of assuring quality, can be interpreted more broadly as a means of assuring contractual performance in general and of taking account of subjective costs. Subjective costs represent an interesting issue because they are not fully reflected in market prices, which provide the legal basis for awarding damages. Thus, in certain circumstances, self-enforcing contracts offer a powerful alternative for coping with the problem of subjective costs.

References

1. Alchian, Armen A., "Private Property and the Relative Cost of Tenure," in Bradley, Philip D. (ed.), *The Public Stake in Union Power* (Charlottesville: University of Virginia Press, 1959), pp. 350–371; and *Some Economics of Property* (Santa Monica: Rand Corporation, 1961).

2. Coase, Ronald H., "The Problem of Social Cost," *Journal of Law & Economics*, Vol. 3 (October 1960), pp. 1–44; and Stigler, George J., "The Economics of Information," *Journal of Political Economy*, Vol. 69, No. 3 (June 1961), pp. 213–225.

3. De Alessi, Louis, "The Economics of Property Rights: A Review of the Evidence," *Research in Law and Economics*, Vol. 2 (1980), pp. 1–47.

4. For a comprehensive review of the literature to date, see Eggertsson, Thrainn, *Economic Behavior and Institutions: Property Rights, Transaction*

Costs and Agency—A Survey (London: Cambridge University Press, forthcoming).

5. The review of the literature (sections 2–3) draws on previous publications by De Alessi, including "Nature and Methodological Foundations of Some Recent Extensions of Economic Theory," pp. 51–76 in Radnitzky, Gerard, and Bernholz, Peter (eds.), *Economic Imperialism: The Economic Method Applied Outside the Field of Economics* (New York: Paragon House, 1987).

6. Smith, Adam, *The Wealth of Nations*, Cannan edition (New York: Random House, 1937).

7. For a more detailed discussion of neoclassical conditions, see Bator, Francis M., "The Simple Analytics of Welfare Maximization," *American Economic Review*, Vol. 47, No. 1 (March 1957), pp. 22–59.

8. See Nagel, Ernest, "Assumptions in Economic Theory," *American Economic Review, Proceedings*, Vol. 53, No. 2 (May 1963), pp. 211–219. The methodological issues are discussed in Blaug, Mark, *The Methodology of Economics* (Cambridge, England: Cambridge University Press, 1980); and Caldwell, Bruce, *Beyond Positivism* (London: George Allen & Unwin, 1982).

9. Early criticisms and some of their more recent reincarnations are noted in De Alessi, Louis, "Property Rights, Transaction Costs, and X-Efficiency: An Essay in Economic Theory," *American Economic Review*, Vol. 73, No. 1 (March 1983), pp. 64–81.

10. The first explanations were offered by Knight, Frank H., *Risk, Uncertainty and Profit* (New York: Hart, Schaffner & Marx, 1921); and Coase, Ronald H., "The Nature of the Firm," *Economica*, N.S., Vol. 4 (November 1937), pp. 386–405.

11. Baumol, William J., *Business Behavior, Value and Growth* (New York: Harcourt Brace & World, 1959).

12. Baumol, William J., "On the Theory of Expansion of the Firm," *American Economic Review*, Vol. 52, No. 5 (December 1962), pp. 1078–1087.

13. Marris, Robin, *The Economics of 'Managerial' Capitalism* (New York: Free Press of Glencoe, 1964).

14. Penrose, Edith T., *The Theory of the Growth of the Firm* (New York: John Wiley & Sons, 1959).

15. Simon, Herbert A., "New Developments in the Theory of the Firm," *American Economic Review, Proceedings*, Vol. 52, No. 2 (May 1962), pp. 1–15; Cyert, Richard M., and March, James, *A Behavioral Theory of the Firm* (Englewood Cliffs: Prentice Hall, 1963); and Day, Richard H., "Review of *A Behavioral Theory of the Firm* by Cyert and March," *Econometrica*, Vol. 32, No. 3 (July 1964), pp. 461–465.

16. The literature is reviewed by Furubotn, Eirik G., and Pejovich, Svetozar, "Property Rights and Economic Theory: A Survey of Recent Literature," *Journal of Economic Literature*, Vol. 10, No. 4 (December 1972), pp. 1137–1162; De Alessi, *supra* note 3; and Eggertsson, *supra* note 4.

17. Becker, Gary S., *The Economics of Discrimination* (Chicago: University of Chicago Press, 1957).
18. Alchian, Armen A., "Some Economics of Property Rights," *Il Politico*, Vol. 30, No. 4 (December 1965), pp. 816–829; "How Should Prices Be Set?" *Il Politico*, Vol. 32, No. 2 (June 1967), pp. 369–382; and with Kessel, Reuben A., "Competition, Monopoly, and the Pursuit of Money," in *Aspects of Labor Economics* (Princeton: Princeton University Press, 1962), pp. 157–175.
19. Williamson, Oliver E., "Managerial Discretion and Business Behavior," *American Economic Review*, Vol. 53, No. 5 (December 1963), pp. 1032–1057; and *The Economics of Discretionary Behavior: Managerial Objectives in a Theory of the Firm* (Englewood Cliffs: Prentice Hall, 1964).
20. Demsetz, Harold, "The Exchange and Enforcement of Property Rights," *Journal of Law & Economics*, Vol. 7 (October 1964), pp. 11–26; and "Toward a Theory of Property Rights," *American Economic Review, Proceedings*, Vol. 57, No. 2 (May 1967), pp. 347–359.
21. For example, De Alessi, Louis, "Implications of Property Rights for Government Investment Choices," *American Economic Review*, Vol. 59, No. 1 (March 1969), pp. 13–24.
22. Coase, *supra* note 2.
23. Stigler, *supra* note 2.
24. See also Williamson, Oliver E., "Hierarchical Control and Optimum Firm Size." *Journal of Political Economy*, Vol. 75, No. 2 (April 1967), pp. 123–138; and Demsetz, Harold, "Information and Efficiency: Another Viewpoint," *Journal of Law & Economics*, Vol. 12, No. 1 (April 1969), pp. 1–22.
25. For example, see Posner, Richard A., *Economic Analysis of Law*, 3rd ed., (Boston: Little, Brown, 1986), and Manne, Henry G. (ed), *The Economics of Legal Relationships: Readings in the Theory of Property Rights* (St. Paul: West Publishing, 1975).
26. De Alessi, *supra* note 3.
27. Lancaster, Kelvin, "A New Approach to Consumer Theory," *Journal of Political Economy*, Vol. 74, No. 2 (April 1966), pp. 132–157.
28. Ehrlic, Isaac, and Chuma, Hiroyuki, "The Demand for Life: Theory and Applications," pp. 243–268 in Radnitzky and Bernholz (eds.), *supra* note 5.
29. The initial assignment of property rights affects the distribution of wealth and thus may indirectly affect the final allocation of resources. Coase, *supra* note 2.
30. Political scientists are currently doing some excellent research on alternative systems of common ownership. See Schlager, Edella, and Ostrom, Elinor, "Common Property, Communal Property, and Natural Resources: Some Conceptual Clarifications" (Unpublished manuscript, Workshop in Political Theory and Policy Analysis, Indiana University, 1987); and McKean, Margaret, "Success on the Commons: A Comparative Examination of In-

stitutions for Common Property Resource Management" (Unpublished manuscript, Duke University, 1987).

31.   Alchian, Armen A., and Demsetz, Harold, "Production, Information Costs, and Economic Organization," *American Economic Review*, Vol. 12, No. 5 (December 1972), pp. 777–795; Williamson, Oliver E., *Markets and Hierarchies: Analysis and Antitrust Implications* (New York: Free Press, 1975); and Klein, Benjamin, Crawford, Robert G., and Alchian, Armen A., "Vertical Integration, Appropriable Rents, and the Competitive Contracting Process," *Journal of Law & Economics*, Vol. 21, No. 2 (October 1978), pp. 297–326.

32.   The effect of moral hazard on the organization of the firm is discussed in Barzel, Yoram, "The Entrepreneur's Reward for Self-Policing," *Economic Inquiry*, Vol. 25, No. 1 (January 1987), pp. 103–116; and in Alchian, Armen A., and Woodward, Susan E., "Reflections on the Theory of the Firm," *Journal of Institutional and Theoretical Economics*, Vol. 143, No. 1 (March 1987), pp. 110–136.

33.   Klein, Benjamin, and Leffler, Keith B., "The Role of Market Forces in Assuring Contractual Performance," *Journal of Political Economy*, Vol. 89, No. 4 (August 1981), pp. 615–641.

34.   De Alessi, Louis, and Staaf, Robert J., "Liability, Control, and the Organization of Economic Activity," *International Review of Law and Economics*, Vol. 7, No. 1 (June 1987), pp. 5–20.

35.   Such contractual provisions as termination at will and exclusive dealing may simply be designed to reduce transaction costs and facilitate mutually beneficial exchanges. Klein, Benjamin, "Transaction Cost Determinants of 'Unfair' Contractual Arrangements," *American Economic Review, Proceedings*, Vol. 50, No. 2 (May 1960), pp. 356–362.

36.   Manne, Henry G., "Mergers and the Market for Corporate Control," *Journal of Political Economy*, Vol. 73, No. 2 (April 1965), pp. 753–761; Williamson, Oliver E., *Corporate Control and Business Behavior* (Englewood Cliffs: Prentice Hall, 1970); Jensen, Michael C., and Meckling, William H., "Theory of the Firm: Managerial Behavior, Agency Costs and Ownership Structure," *Journal of Financial Economics*, Vol. 3, No. 4 (October 1976), pp. 305–360; Fama, Eugene F., "Agency Problems and the Theory of the Firm," *Journal of Political Economy*, Vol. 88, No. 2 (April 1980), pp. 288–307; and De Alessi, Louis, "Private Property and Dispersion of Ownership in Large Corporations," *Journal of Finance*, Vol. 28, No. 4 (September 1973), pp. 839–851.

37.   For example, see Oi, Walter Y., "Heterogeneous Firms and the Organization of Production," *Economic Inquiry*, Vol. 21, No. 2 (April 1983), pp. 147–171.

38.   See Alchian and Demsetz, *supra* note 31. See also McChesney, Fred S., "Team Production, Monitoring, and Profit Sharing in Law Firms: An Alternative Hypothesis," *Journal of Legal Studies*, Vol. 11, No. 2 (June 1982), pp. 379–393.

39. Cheung, Steven N. S., "Transaction Costs, Risk Aversion, and the Choice of Contractual Arrangements," *Journal of Law & Economics*, Vol. 12, No. 1 (April 1969), pp. 23–42; and Hallagan, William, "Self-Selection by Contractual Choice and the Theory of Sharecropping," *Bell Journal of Economics*, Vol. 9, No. 2 (Autumn 1978), pp. 344–354.

40. Ekelund, Robert B., Jr., and Tollison, Robert D., "Mercantile Origins of the Corporation," *Bell Journal of Economics*, Vol. 11, No. 2 (Autumn 1980), pp. 715–720; Williamson, Oliver E., "The Modern Corporation: Origin, Evolution, Attributes," *Journal of Economic Literature*, Vol. 19, No. 4 (December 1981), pp. 1537–1568; and Woodward, Susan E., "On the Economics of Limited Liability" (Unpublished manuscript, University of California, Los Angeles, 1985)

41. De Alessi, Louis, and Fishe, Raymond P.H., "Why Do Corporations Distribute Assets? An Analysis of Dividends and Capital Structure," *Journal of Institutional and Theoretical Economics*, Vol. 143, No. 1 (March 1987), pp. 34–51.

42. De Alessi, Louis, "Why Corporations Insure," *Economic Inquiry*, Vol. 25, No. 3 (July 1987), pp. 429–438. Tax and other factors may further encourage individual firms to insure. Mayers, David, and Smith, Clifford W., Jr., "On the Corporate Demand for Insurance," *Journal of Business*, Vol. 55, No. 2 (April 1982), pp. 181–196.

43. De Alessi, *supra* note 3.

44. Eckert, Ross D., "On the Incentives of Regulators: The Case of Taxicabs," *Public Choice*, Vol. 14 (Spring 1973), pp. 83–100.

45. De Alessi, *supra* note 3.

46. De Alessi, Louis, "On the Nature and Consequences of Private and Public Enterprises," *Minnesota Law Review*, Vol. 67, No. 1 (October 1982), pp. 191–209.

47. Alchian, *supra* note 18.

48. De Alessi, *supra* note 3.

49. For example, see the continuing work on institutions and economic growth by North, Douglass C., "Institutions, Economic Growth and Freedom: An Historical Introduction" (Unpublished manuscript, Washington University, 1986), and the recent work on solutions to the common property problem by Libecap, Gary, "Contracting for Property Rights" (Unpublished manuscript, University of Arizona, Tucson, 1987); much of the literature is summarized in Feeny, David, "The Supply of Institutional Change" (Unpublished manuscript, McMaster University, 1987). See also the hypotheses regarding the evolution of the common law proposed by Rubin, Paul A., "Why is the Common Law Efficient?" *Journal of Legal Studies*, Vol. 6, No. 1 (January 1977), pp. 51–63, and by Priest, George L., "The Common Law Process and the Selection of Efficient Rules," *Journal of Legal Studies*, Vol. 6, No. 1 (January 1977), pp. 65–82, and the criticism of these and related arguments by Aranson, Peter, "Economic Efficiency and the Common Law: A Critical Survey," in Schulenburg, J-Matthias G., and Skogh, Goran

(eds.), *Law and Economics and the Economics of Legal Regulations* (Boston: Kluwer Academic Publishers, 1986), pp. 51–84. Political scientists are currently exploring the rules for changing the system of property rights. For example, see Ostrom, Vincent, *The Political Theory of a Compound Republic*, 2nd ed. (Lincoln and London: University of Nebraska Press, 1987).

50. The literature in the new law and economics concerned with efficiency is massive. For example, see the "Symposium on Efficiency as a Legal Concern," *Hofstra Law Review*, Vol. 8, No. 3 (Spring 1980), pp. 485–770; and "A Response to the Efficiency Symposium," *Hofstra Law Review*, Vol. 8, No. 4 (Summer 1980), pp. 811–972.

51. For example, see Zerbe, Richard O., "The Problem of Social Cost in Retrospect," *Research in Law and Economics*, Vol. 2 (1980), pp. 83–102.

52. Notable exceptions are Muris, Timothy J., "Cost of Completion or Diminution in Market Value: The Relevance of Subjective Value," *Journal of Legal Studies*, Vol. 12, No. 2 (June 1983), pp. 379–400; and Schwartz, Alan, "The Case for Specific Performance," *Yale Law Journal*, Vol. 89, No. 2 (December 1979), pp. 271–306.

53. As Richard A. Epstein has suggested, much of Posner's work can be interpreted as constructing pseudo-exchanges. See Epstein, Richard A., "A Theory of Strict Liability," *Journal of Legal Studies*, Vol. 2, No. 1 (January 1973), pp. 151–204; and "Defenses and Subsequent Pleas in a System of Strict Liability," *Journal of Legal Studies*, Vol. 3, No. 1 (January 1974), pp. 165–215, both reprinted as *A Theory of Strict Liability* (San Francisco: Cato Institute, 1980); see also Epstein's "Causation and Corrective Justice: A Reply to Two Critics," *Journal of Legal Studies*, Vol. 8, No. 3 (June 1979), pp. 477–504.

54. Coase, *supra* note 2, pp. 28ff, Pigou, A. C., *The Economics of Welfare*, 4th ed. (London: Macmillan, 1932).

55. There are differences that are not important for our purposes. See Polinsky, A. Mitchell, "Controlling Externalities and Protecting Entitlements: Property Rights, Liability Rule, and Tax-Subsidy Approaches," *Journal of Legal Studies*, Vol. 8, No. 1 (January 1979), pp. 1–35; Rose-Ackerman, Susan, "Effluent Charges: A Critique," *Canadian Journal of Economics*, Vol. 6, No. 4 (November 1973), pp. 512–546; and White, Michelle J., and Wittman, Donald, "A Comparison of Taxes, Regulations, and Liability Rules under Imperfect Information," *Journal of Legal Studies*, Vol. 12, No. 2 (June 1983), pp. 413–425.

56. Coase, *supra* note 2.

57. For an excellent discussion of subjective cost and its tradition in economics, see Buchanan, James M., *Cost and Choice* (Chicago: Markham, 1969). See also Alchian, Armen A., "Cost," in Alchian, Armen A., *Economic Forces at Work* (Indianapolis: Liberty Press, 1977), pp. 301–333.

58. Buchanan, *Ibid.*, at p. 43.

59. Involuntary transactions in tort give rise to the same problems associated with the taking of property with "just" compensation under the power of

eminent domain. See Epstein, Richard A., *Takings: Private Property and the Power of Eminent Domain* (Cambridge: Harvard University Press, 1985).

60. 203 N.Y. 239, 129 N.R. 889 (1921).

61. *Ibid.* at p. 891.

62. *Ibid.* at p. 893.

63. A more recent case, *Plante* v. *Jacobs*, 103 N. W. 2d 296 (1960), deals with a contractor who, among other things, had misplaced the wall between the living room and kitchen by over one foot. The court held the contractor to substantial rather than to specific performance, stating that "The cost to rectify the defect may greatly exceed the value of the structure as corrected."

64. Buchanan and Faith have argued that a liability rule (damages) presents entrepreneurs with lower costs relative to a property rule and thus encourages growth; see Buchanan, James M., and Faith, Roger, "Entrepreneurship and the Internalization of Externalities," *Journal of Law & Economics*, Vol. 24, No. 1 (April 1980), pp. 95–111. Their argument presumes incorrectly that ex post legal damages are equal to the subjective costs borne by the individuals affected.

65. Buchanan, James M., and Tullock, Gordon, *The Calculus of Consent* (Ann Arbor: University of Michigan Press, 1962).

66. This position is fundamentally different from the arguments for the efficiency of the common law advanced by Posner, *supra* note 25, Rubin, *supra* note 49, and Priest, *supra* note 49.

67. *Hothkiss* v. *National City Bank of New York*, 200 F. 287, 293 (S.D.N.Y., 1911).

68. Murphy, Edward J., and Speidel, Richard E., *Studies in Contract Law* (New York: Foundation Press, 1977), p. 98.

69. Hurst, James W., *Law and the Conditions of Freedom in Nineteenth Century America* (Madison: University of Wisconsin Press, 1956), pp. 21–22.

70. See Clarkson, Kenneth, Miller, Roger L., and Muris, Timothy "Liquidated Damages v. Penalties: Sense or Nonsense?," *Wisconsin Law Review*, Vol. 1978, No. 2 (1978), pp. 351–390, for the argument that penalties would induce breach; and Goetz, Charles, and Scott, Robert E., "Liquidated Damages, Penalties and the Just Compensation Principle: Some Notes on an Enforcement Model and a Theory of Efficient Breach," *Columbia Law Review*, Vol. 77, No. 4 (May 1977), pp. 554–590, for a subjective view of liquidated damage clauses.

71. See Klein and Leffler, *supra* note 33.

72. For example, the frequent use of noted personalities in commercials may be attributed in part to consumers' perception of the high cost of these endorsements. Pepsi made no secret of the fee paid for the Michael Jackson commercials, and local promotions often refer to expensive advertisements elsewhere (e.g., "As advertised on the 'Tonight' show"). See Klein and Leffler, *Ibid*, at p. 625.

73. Shavell, Steven, "Strict Liability versus Negligence," *Journal of Legal Stu-*

dies, Vol. 9, No. 1 (January 1980), pp. 1–25. The literature on quality assurance casts doubt on Shavell's assumption that consumers are not informed.

74. See Jarrell, Gregg, and Peltzman, Sam, "The Impact of Product Recalls on the Wealth of Sellers," *Journal of Political Economy*, Vol. 93, No. 3 (June 1985), pp. 512–536. See also Benjamin, Dan, and Mitchell, Mark, "Commitment and Consumer Sovereignty: Classic Evidence from the Real Things" (Unpublished manuscript, Clemson University, 1987).

75. See Laband, David N., and Maloney, Michael, "Why Do Sellers Finance?" (Unpublished manuscript, Clemson University, 1987).

7 LAW AND ECONOMICS: SETTLED ISSUES AND OPEN QUESTIONS

Thomas S. Ulen

1. Introduction

One of the truly remarkable stories of academic scholarship of the late twentieth century is the rise of the field of law and economics. First of the several notable characteristics of this field is its very rapid growth. There were early harbingers of the field's subject matter [1]—the use of microeconomic analysis to evaluate the economic efficiency of the common law rules of property, contract, and tort and various topics in civil and criminal procedure, substantive criminal law, the law of corporations, and so on—and isolated but seminal articles by Ronald Coase and others in the 1950s and 1960s. But I think that it is fair to say that law and economics was born and brought to adolescence in the course of a single decade, the 1970s. Very few innovations in economic or legal scholarship of the recent past have grown so rapidly.

Second, the field of law and economics has had a profound impact on legal scholarship. Several leading legal scholars, notably Bruce Ackerman, have remarked that law and economics is the most important change in the field of law since the rise and fall of legal realism. A compendium of the legal issues upon which economics has thrown new light would include such fundamental matters as the choice of legal remedy in property and contractual disputes, the delineation of which promises should be enforceable at law, and which accidents should be controlled by a negligence standard and which by strict liability, and whether the rules selected by the common law process are efficient.

Third, the field has begun to have a marked impact on the law as handed down by federal and state courts. Several distinguished practitioners of law and economics have ascended to the bench and have used the tools of analysis from the field to decide cases before them. This development has, naturally, caused attorneys to pay closer attention to the field and that, in turn, has led to such novel developments as economists being named partners in law firms and to a boom in litigation support provided by economic consultants.

None of this is to say that law and economics has run its course. As stated above, the field had grown to adolescence in the 1970s, stressing the word "adolescence" rather than, say, "maturity" or "senility," because there is still much more growing to be done. At the end of my comments on the articles in this book, I intend to take stock of where we are in law and economics and to suggest how the field will develop in the near future.

It is a testament to the vitality and continuing growth of the field of law and economics that Nicholas Mercuro has been able to assemble the work of a group of distinguished authors who approach the field from vastly different perspectives. I believe that these perspectives, while distinct and, in some cases, apparently warring, can most profitably be viewed as complementary. They each contribute a valuable insight to the subject matters of law and economics. To ignore any of these would repeat the errors of the blind men who independently examined the various parts of an elephant and, not putting their reports together, drew erroneous conclusions about the remainder of the beast by extrapolating from the part each had examined.

2. The Institutionalist Perspective

A. Allan Schmid summarizes the field of law and economics as seen from the institutionalist perspective. While I am not consciously a member of this camp, nor familiar with all of the literature produced by its adherents, I would like to describe briefly what I take to be the gist of the institutionalist perspective and then evaluate what this perspective can contribute to law and economics.

Institutionalist theory has a distinguished past. It traces its origins to the work of John R. Commons, Thorstein Veblen, and their students in the first half of this century. Since then, there have always been a few economists who called themselves institutionalists, and today there are even those who call themselves neoinstitutionalists.

The institutionalist perspective has never been fully articulated, and for that reason it is difficult to convey precisely what the concerns and accomplishments of the perspective are. Nonetheless, I discern a common theme in the institutionalist literature, and that is a dissatisfaction with the formalism of modern microeconomic theory, especially as it applies to public policy issues. But I also discern two separate camps in this dissatisfaction, with an important difference between them.

One group of institutionalists appears to center its dissatisfaction on the fact that the mathematicization of microeconomic theory has obscured at least as much as it has illuminated so that, on balance, there is little explanatory power from modern theory. The claim is not, I think, that formal theory is per se bad. Rather, the objection is to the particular kind of formalism that has become conventional in modern economics, a formalism that abstracts from the important institutional details of the economy. These institutionalists believe that the particular time and place and institutional setting of economic decisions are at least as important to the explanation of economic phenomena as are the preferences, production technology, market structure, and relative prices of the conventional explanation.

To see the difference between the conventional economic and the institutionalist explanations of an economic event, consider an example. Suppose that the phenomenon to be explained is the development of the open-hearth furnace for the production of steel. The starting point for a conventional economic analysis would be an estimation of the prevailing production function in the iron and steel industry, and an investigation of the relative prices of the inputs into the process. The maintained hypothesis would be that the development of the new techology and its diffusion could be largely explained by changes in the relative prices of the inputs, by a sustained increase in the demand for steel, and, possibly, by an exogenous increase in the supply of inventive activity. The explanation could be translated to different cultures, to different regions within the same culture, or even across time in the same culture by the appropriate adjustment in the relative prices of inputs, in the parameters of the production function, and in various supply-and-demand schedules. On the other hand, the institutionalists would find this explanation to be, at best, incomplete. The crucial variables in the development of the open-hearth furnace would be the institutional setting in which the producer and inventor found themselves: such issues as whether society was well- or ill-disposed toward change; what groups in society would win and which would lose as a result of the change; and whether the society had found a means of protecting the inventor's intellectual property [2].

There is a second group of institutional economists whose dissatisfaction with modern economic theory focuses not on the failure to invoke institutions as important explanatory variables but rather on modern microeconomic theory's failure to offer economic explanations of the existence and form of those institutions themselves [3]. For example, modern microeconomic theory has not been very much interested in the development of the corporate form of business organization, nor in the evolution of the administrative agency form of regulation. Conventional analysis typically takes these sorts of institutional details as given or, like consumer preferences, as exogenously determined. By contrast, this second strand of institutional economics is interested in explaining why the corporate form of business appeared when and where and in the form it did. Moreover, these institutionalists attempt to explain the appearance and character of institutions using the traditional sorts of microeconomic variables that more conventional analysis uses. In short, this group believes that institutions are endogenous. An important example of this sort of institutionalist economics is, I believe, the new political economy.

To summarize, we have two different but related strands in the institutionalist camp. One group is dissatisfied with the highly formal, mathematical character of modern microeconomics and sees this formalism as causing modern economists to pay insufficient attention to the influence of the particular time and place and institutional setting in which economic decisions are made. A second group does not object so much to the formalism of modern microeconomics as they do to the fact that institutions are typically considered to be exogenous variables when they are, in fact, endogenous.

In this dichotomy of institutional economics Schmid's sympathies lie with the first group. He identifies several themes of institutional analysis, most of which are evidence of his dissatisfaction with the prevailing paradigm in microeconomic theory. Some of the reasons he gives for this dissatisfaction are more cogent than others. Let me concentrate on several themes that Schmid implies are more central than the others. First, he says that institutional economics recognizes conflict and issues of power as central. We learn in the discussion of this theme that "[g]overnment is an arena of power play and an object of legal control" and that "[l]aw is the result of the resolution of social conflicts and not some deduction from universal principles which all rational people accept."[1] Second, "people matter, the specific goods and their situation matter, and the detail of the law matters." This is, I think, a straightforward statement of the main theme of the first kind of institutionalist economics outlined above. But the discussion of the manner in which people, specific goods, and legal details matter is not clear, and illustrates a problem that institutional law and economics must clear up in order to have a wider impact on scholarly activity in law and economics.

The problem is that the points made are not adequately finished off. Schmid makes a criticism of conventional microeconomic theory and then contends that he prefers some alternative. The reader is never shown examples of the shortcoming of the conventional assumption nor of the advantage of the alternative. In this regard, Schmid's piece seems polemical rather than balanced. Because I find myself in sympathy with many of the criticisms he makes, I am dismayed and wish that he could make them more clearly and extensively. For example, Schmid characterizes the conventional assumption that consumers are utility maximizers as unhelpful because it is not a precise enough predictor of human behavior. As an illustration, he says that conventional theory argues that it is necessarily utility-maximizing to free-ride on public goods. But, he says, there may well be consumers who derive utility from *not* free-riding but instead from bearing what they take to be their fair share of the costs of providing a collective good. Because it is impossible to distinguish ex ante between those who do and do not derive utility from free-riding, Schmid says that utility maximization "does not help predict [consumer] behavior unless the content of their utility is known." Included in this content are the concept of bounded rationality and of the difficulty of determining the utility today of actions and goods in the future.

The point about there being those who derive utility from participating in the provision of a public good, contrary to the assumption of conventional theory, is well taken. So, too, are the points about bounded rationality and difficulties in determining the worth of future goods and actions [4]. But important though these points are, I do not see that they add up to a convincing case for scrapping the assumption that consumers maximize utility. Rather, they make the careful scholar alert to the possibility that tastes differ and that there may be situations in which the assumption of unbounded rationality is inappropriate. Many noninsitutionalist scholars are well aware of these pitfalls.

Schmid's chapter contains numerous other criticisms of conventional work in microeconomics and in law and economics with which I sympathize—e.g., his call for adequate description of legal settings and institutions rather than abstract formalism, and his call for an investigation of the special characteristics of group, as opposed to individual, decisionmaking. But the institutional perspective will unfortunately remain a diffuse collection of criticisms—the intellectual equivalent of Monday-morning quarterbacking—until the advocates of this perception of law and economics engage in a more accessible statement of what they take to be the shortcomings of the conventional approach, of what they propose as an alternative, and why.

3.   The Critical Legal Studies Perspective

Gary Minda of the Brooklyn Law School has performed two extremely valuable services in his chapter: first, he has made the general concerns of the critical legal studies (CLS) movement intelligible; second, he has shown the similarities and differences between the CLS and law and economics movements, and placed them in the intellectual history of twentieth century American legal scholarship. This is a laudable exercise in communication, understanding, and synthesis. Despite some profound differences, the CLS and law and economics movements share a similar view of what constitutes valuable legal scholarship. This particular agreement, about which I was unaware prior to Minda's work, raises the possibility of a partnership or synthesis of these two schools at some time in the future (see section 7 below).

Those from outside the CLS camp who have tried to learn what the field is about have not had an easy time. Until Mark Kelman's recent work [5], the practitioners of CLS have seemed to be talking only to each other, speaking in tongues, as it were, intelligible only to the true believers [6]. I suspect that the most common reaction of those outside CLS to their work is befuddlement. Clear writing and speaking have not been the long suit of this movement.

In this regard, if in no other, the CLS movement and professionally trained economists should make common cause. Both groups are proficient in bad prose. Anyone who has been through a Ph.D. program in economics and who regularly reads the leading economics journals knows a great deal about graceless, mind-numbing, and obscurantist writing. (By contrast, it is exhilarating to read the wonderfully lucid prose of our mainstream legal academic brethren.) My suspicion is that because much of the CLS literature reads as if it had been written by economists, it has not been taken seriously by the legal community, whose standards for cogent argument are higher than those of economists. This has, I would guess, unnecessarily exacerbated the more substantive disagreements that exist between CLS and the rest of the legal academic community.

Minda's presentation makes the CLS claims clear enough so that their strengths and weaknesses can be discussed much like those of any other serious scholarship. The members of the CLS movement perceive their role in legal scholarship to be deconstructionist; that is, they wish to "unmask" the law, to show the relationship between legal rules and the prevailing social ideology, power structure, and economic basis of that power. The colloquialism used to describe this process is "trashing." This criticism of law and its culture is all-consuming, so much so that one of the repeated criticisms of CLS is that it is too negative [7], that it offers no affirmative theory of what the law ought to be. Martha Minow has described the following four activities as the core beliefs of the CLS movement:

1. [t]he critical scholar seeks to demonstrate the indeterminacy of legal doctrine; any given set of legal principles can be used to yield competing or contradictory results.
2. [t]he critical scholar engages in historical, socioeconomic analysis to identify how particular interest groups, social classes, or entrenched economic institutions benefit from legal decisions despite the indeterminacy of the legal doctrines.
3. the critical scholar tries to expose how legal analysis and legal culture mystifies outsiders and legitimates its results.
4. the critical scholar may elucidate new or previously disfavored social visions and argue for their realization in legal or political practice in part by making them part of legal discourse [8].

As clear and important as his clarification of CLS is, I find that Minda's demonstration of the common intellectual origins of CLS and law and economics is even more important and interesting. The rise to importance in legal scholarship of CLS and law and economics is part of a broader and older trend in legal scholarship that, to borrow a phrase from Richard A. Posner, reflects the decline of the law as an autonomous discipline [9]. Minda stresses that this decline has a long heritage. The outlines of the story are reasonably clear. In the decades between the Civil War and the Great Depression the central matter that occupied the U.S. Supreme Court (and may, therefore, be taken as an indicator of a central concern in legal scholarship of that time) was the appropriate scope of governmental regulation of private economic affairs. In deciding several cases dealing with regulation shortly after the Civil War, the Court may be said to have held that state regulation designed to protect public health or to control businesses affected with a broad public interest passed Constitutional muster. Consider as examples the *Slaughterhouse Cases* (in which the Court narrowly approved of Louisiana's having given, ostensibly for health reasons, a 25-year monopoly right to slaughter animals to a single slaughterhouse in New Orleans) [10] and *Munn* v. *Illinois* (in which the Court approved Illinois' regulation of the business practices of grain elevators on the grounds that the elevators were "affected with a public interest") [11]. Then around the turn of the century, the Court seemed to step back from this broad interpretation.[2] In several famous cases—e.g., *Lochner* v. *New York* (in which the Court invalidated a New York statute that limited to 60 per week the number of hours that employees in certain occupations, such as, in this instance, commercial baking, could be required to work) [12]—the Court held that regulation could not legitimately interfere with individuals' right to contract. Much of the work of the Supreme Court from that point until the Second World War consisted of attempts to fine-tune the line between governmental regulation that was and that was not constitutional [13].

Legal scholarship of the early and mid-twentieth century developed against this background. Decisions like *Lochner* were justified by the formalism of the liberty-of-contract jurisprudence, a view that held, roughly, that free individuals competing freely would maximize their own and social welfare. The legal realist movement that appeared during and after World War I was a reaction to the liberty-of-contract school. Legal realism was a broad movement with many different areas of emphasis.[3] There were, however, common themes in these diverse strands: that legal rules had and ought to have social consequences [14], that law could not pretend to objectivity,[4] that legal rules could not be justified solely by formal legal reasoning but must also seek justification from outside the law, and that law could not be separated from the broader political trends in society.

The ferment in legal scholarship as legal formalism and legal realism contended throughout the 1930s and 1940s gave way in the 1950s to a synthesis of the two schools, a synthesis known as the "legal process" school. This new view held that law was to provide a rational process, a process of "reasoned elaboration," for resolving the competing views of public policy.[5] The focus of the legal process school was turned to the manner in which judges should attempt to resolve policy disputes, specifically on the development of neutral principles (as opposed to idiosyncratic preferences) of judicial decisionmaking [15].

The legal process school, still the reigning paradigm in legal education, hoped to achieve a consensus by focusing on reasoned elaboration as the basis for judicial decisions. But this hope has proved chimerical for the simple reason that there is often no single reasoned way to decide a case. Instead, reasonable people, including judges, differ and for perfectly plausible reasons. And when they do, the legal process school offers no method for choosing among the competing views [16].

Minda says that "it is the intellectual oposition to the legal process school which unites the law and economics and the CLS movements." Each school perceives its origin in legal realism. Law and economics derives from the scientific/technocratic aspect of that earlier jurisprudence, and CLS, from the legal realists' perception of a close relationship between the prevailing political ideology and the law.

From this point of common origin, Minda perceives important differences between the CLS and law and economics movements. I am not familiar enough with the CLS literature to say whether Minda's description of that school's differences and aspirations are accurate. But I do take issue with some of the generalities that he makes about law and economics. First, consider his contention that "[m]embers of each movement assert that the judicial process, as it works in practice, is far too inconsistent and unstable to support the claims of liberal scholars who advocate principled, consistent approaches." I am not aware that law and economics scholars are united in this assertion. Indeed, quite to the contrary, I take it as one of the canons of the law and economics faith that the (common law) judicial process is reasonably efficient. Intense study of the efficiency characteristics of common law rules of property, tort, contract, and procedure have generally concluded that common law judges created incentives for efficient behavior.[6] Indeed, one of the central contentions of Frank Easterbrook's article, which Minda cites in support of his assertion that law and economics finds the judicial process inconsistent, is precisely the opposite point: that the Supreme Court's constitutional interpretation has become increasingly consistent as it has adopted the law and economics view of legal rules as implicit prices on different types of behavior instead of inherently subjective notions of fairness or justice [17].

Second, I want to take Minda to task very briefly for leaving out of his intellectual history a third important school that also claims legal realism as its forebear and that also offers an alternative vision to that of the legal process school: the law and society movement. Beginning in the early 1960s with the work of Stewart Macaulay, Willard Hurst, and others, the adherents of this school have pursued the same interdisciplinary view of the law as did the legal realists and the law and economics and CLS movements. My reading of the law and society movement is that while it shares with those alternatives to the legal process school a deep concern for the social consequences and determinants of law, it is more eclectic than law and economics (there is, for example, no unifying paradigm for law and society that is analogous to the role of microeconomic theory in law and economics) and not nearly so iconoclastic and critical of the prevailing legal order as the CLS movement.

Third, consider Minda's contention that "[l]aw and economics scholars take issue with the traditional wisdom of liberal scholars who argue that the legal process should be concerned with *moral* and *distributive* goals; [rather than] the legal process values of 'harmony,' 'stability' and 'shared values,' law and economics scholars argue that in the 'real world' what counts is 'scarcity,' 'choice' and 'self-interested conduct.'" This contention is only partially correct. Economists focus on scarcity and rationally self-interested choice because those are the fundamental tools of their trade. But that certainly does not mean that economists have not found room in their analyses for shared values, a sense of community, and morality [18].

It is true that there is a strong *normative* strain in the law and economics literature that claims that efficiency *should* be the prevailing norm in the law [19] and that there is a wholly distinct *positive* claim that efficiency is the prevailing norm in common law adjudication [20]. But there are also many practitioners of law and economics, including myself, who are agnostic on both of this normative and this particular positive claim. My intuition is that the only claim that would win widespread acceptance among law and economics scholars is the positive claim that the consequences of a given legal rule can be fruitfully examined using microeconomic theory. Indeed, I would venture to say that this assertion would win widespread acceptance among *any* legal scholar, adherent of law and economics or not. There is nothing value-laden in this assertion. It is simply a positive *style of analysis*. It does not say that legal rules should be rejected or affirmed depending on what the microeconomically demonstrated consequences of those rules are. While that may be important information, it is not dispositive. Consider the extensive literature on the death penalty [21]. Even if the deterrent effect of executions were solidly established, no one who is to be taken seriously as a law and economics scholar would contend that this showing constitutes an end to the debate on whether the death penalty is good or bad public policy.

I think that what Minda has had to say about the common intellectual origins of law and economics and CLS is extraordinarily valuable. There is a sort of humbling comfort in discovering that one's work fits into a larger story. But there is more than that to be had from this intellectual history of law and economics and of critical legal studies. In understanding and evaluating the claims of the adherents of these positions, it helps very much to see whence these intellectual trends came.

4. Legal Rules as Incentives

Several years ago Lewis Kornhauser wrote an article that summarized the central premises of the law and economics field as viewed by mainstream microeconomic theory [22]. In this chapter he elaborates on the themes of that earlier article and attempts the tremendously important task of reconciling the economic theory of the law with the view of the law as a public ideal. He does this by focusing on this question: "to what extent do legal rules provide reasons or motives for action?"

Kornhauser sees the distinctive characteristic of the economist's notion of law and economics to be its investigation of the incentive effects of legal rules. Legal rules create implicit prices for different kinds of behavior and the responses to those implicit prices can be examined in the same way that economists examine the response of consumers to explicit prices of goods and services: the rule that gift promises are generally unenforceable raises the implicit price to those who truly wish to make such a promise and also raises the price of taking action in reliance on such a promise's being fulfilled; the rule that grants an exclusive property right, good against the world, to the person who authors an original novel lowers the costs to the author of defending her work against expropriation and thereby induces her to expend additional resources in writing; the rule that imposes liability on someone who fails to take a reasonable amount of precaution raises the price of being careless and thereby increases the amount of precaution consumed.

Kornhauser distinguishes a naive theory of the law from the economic theory of the law. Under the naive theory, which is a highly stylized version of what Minda characterizes as the legal process school, individuals conform their behavior *perfectly* to the legal rule. Their reason for doing so is that the law provides what Kornhauser calls a directive force. Under the economic theory, individuals conform their behavior *imperfectly* to legal rules; a legal rule in and of itself provides no insurmountable directive force. The law's impact on behavior arises from its impact, if any, on the actor's rationally, self-interested calculations of cost and benefit.

This fundamental distinction is well worth making. It points out important and illuminating parallels and differences between the economic theory of law and the legal process or naive theory. For example, both theories share a directive view of the law; that is, both believe that the goal of the law is to guide human behavior. But the two theories seem to direct behavior toward very different goals. The economic theory of law holds, as we have just seen, that legal rules direct behavior by creating implicit prices on behavior. Presumably, these implicit prices are to be set so as to guide behavior toward the more efficient use of resources. (This, of course, need *not* be the end toward which the prices are set. We shall return to this point in section 7 below.) By contrast, the naive theory directs behavior toward some goal other than efficiency. But Kornhauser is not explicit about what that other goal is.[7] One possibility is what some writers have called the "public ideal" conception of the law [23]. This conception perceives part of the function of law to be a statement of the goals to which the community aspires. By devising a law that holds up that goal as an achievable standard, the law is enlisted to serve the ideal of making society a better place. On this argument, the law does not merely codify currently acceptable practice; rather, it charts a course toward a *better* practice. Thus, a conception of the law as a public ideal argues in favor of laws against racial and sexual discrimination on the grounds that we aspire to be a society in which people do not discriminate on the basis of race and sex, even though they may do so now.

Another distinction that Kornhauser draws between the naive and economic theories of the law has to do with their primary research material. The legal process scholar uses legal texts, such as judicial opinions, as her primary research material. The law and economics (and law and society) scholar relies less on legal texts and more on direct observation of behavior. I find this distinction between the two theories on the basis of their view of the value of legal texts misleading. The reason that conventional legal scholars focus on texts is not that they necessarily view the policy consequences of the law as less important than other aspects but rather that that is the best place to learn how judges justify their holdings and, therefore, the best material from which to teach aspiring lawyers the most effective types of arguments to make before judges [24]. Moreover, there is no reason to believe that the types of justifications for holdings made in these legal texts will be congenial only to the naive theory of the law. In point of fact, the justifications that are contained in these opinions can be from many camps: law and economics, law and society, neutral principles, and so on. Indeed, an increasingly common justification in judicial opinions is that a particular rule is inefficient [25].

Of the many interesting questions posed by Kornhauser, the most interesting to me is whether there is any normative force in the economic theory of law, as there clearly is in the law-as-public-ideal version of the naive theory. His answer is that there is none, but in the course of reaching this unsurprising conclusion, he sets up an interesting way of looking at the problem. He suggests that the investigation into a normative force in the economic theory of the law may take one of two different tacks. First, it might imagine that there are two types of agents, those who are generally good, law-abiding citizens, and those who are "bad men," who always act according to their perception of their own self-interest (i.e., according to what many believe, wrongly, in my opinion, to be the quintessential economic model). Kornhauser calls the alternative model a "preferences model." Each person is assumed to have the usual utility function defined, in relevant part, over compliance with legal norms and with the consequences of compliance. He implies that these preferences define the usual convex utility function for most people so that they perceive a diminishing rate of marginal substitution between being law-abiding and getting away with violating the law. Just as people have different preferences for different goods and services, they also have different preferences for complying with and violating the law.[8] To push this still further, there may additionally be situations in which people with different preferences face different relative prices for compliance versus violation.

These really are the same theory. The preferences model is the more general one in that it subsumes the bad-men model. The fuller statement would be along these lines. Suppose that citizens have convex preference sets over compliance with the law and breaking the law. For most people, compliance is a "good," that is, a commodity for which more is preferred to less, but law-breaking is a "bad," a commodity for which less is preferred to more. These people can be induced to "consume" law-breaking only by paying them to do so. They will never pay a portion of their own income to consume episodes of law-breaking. For other people, both compliance and law-breaking may be goods, so that there is a tradeoff between those activities depending on their relative prices. These people may not be characterizable as "bad persons," but they are amenable to control through the law's alteration of the relative prices of legitimate and illegitimate activities. For instance, if the price of law-breaking is raised relative to compliance, they will tend to consume less law-breaking and more compliance. If the relative price of compliance increases, then they will tend to break more laws and comply less. Finally, there are the truly bad people who, at the extreme, consider compliance with the law's norms to be a bad and breaking the law to be a good. These sociopaths, as they probably are, must be paid to comply with the law. Left to their own devices, they will pay a portion of their own resources to consume law-breaking episodes.

This more complex preferences model may allow a fuller investigation into the presence of a normative force in the economic theory of law. However, one thing that the theory will never be able to provide is a theory of how legal norms influence preferences themselves, as they no doubt do, nor of whether they may be some configurations of the utility function over compliance and violation that are socially preferable to others. These things cannot be explained for conventional goods and services in standard microeconomic theory, so it is not surprising that an economic theory of the law cannot answer these vital questions about the origins and worth of different preferences for compliance with the law and breaking the law. Still, the preferences model strikes me as the place to begin this inquiry into the normative force of the law.

There is a larger context in which the issue is usually raised of whether there should be a normative component of the economic theory of law, but Kornhauser does not follow that convention. I suspect that those who ask this important question expect the answer to be "No, there is no normative content in law and economics," or "Yes, there is, but it consists of the narrow normative end of fostering efficiency" [26]. And either of these answers confirms a preexisting disdain for the economic analysis of law. But this disdain presupposes that the *only* appropriate way to look at the law is as a normative force. I do not believe that there is only one way to look at the law; nor do I believe that one way is necessarily better than any of the others. This seems to me an obvious, even trivial point. But it is, nonetheless, one upon which much ink has been spilled. I shall return to a consideration of the normativity of the economic theory of law in section 7 below.

Finally, one of the distinctions that Kornhauser drew between the naive theory and the economic theory of the law was that the economic theory offers a richer framework for explaining why there is imperfect compliance with the law. Recall that the naive theory holds that people comply with the law simply because it is the law. By implication, the naive theory suggests that if people do not comply with the law, that must be because they are uninformed about its requirements. In contrast, the economic theory offers a much fuller list of possibilities for noncompliance with the law, e.g., lack of information, lack of information-processing capability [27], and uncertainty about apprehension and conviction or about how the fact-finder will evaluate one's behavior [28]. I find these possibilities the most productive point from which to begin to construct an explanation of how and why people respond to legal rules. I shall return to this important issue below.

5. The Public Choice Perspective

Charles Rowley has written a discussion of law and economics from the public choice perspective that ranges widely. He begins by drawing a distinction between the positive methodologies of law and of economics. Economists have generally embraced deduction and the positivist theory of Karl Popper.[9] By contrast, the law relies almost exclusively on induction. Additionally, there are tensions between law and economics over normative methodology. Economists take efficiency to be a legal norm; lawyers take justice, fairness, or the philosophical norm of liberty or self-actualization to be the legal norm. Rowley then gives an able summary of some of the most important recent theories of social welfare— John Rawls' theory of justice (which he purports to refute because he believes that Rawls' theory rest on an inappropriate assumption of infinite risk-aversion by those choosing social rules behind the veil of ignorance); wealth maximization; Amartya Sen's demonstration of the impossibility of a Paretian liberal; and William Baumol's notion of "super-fairness" (a state in which no one is envious of another's bundle of goods).

The bulk of the article summarizes the core of public choice economics. For those who are not specialists in the area, this is extremely valuable. Public choice has principally been concerned with issues of why people vote (the median voter theorem, for example) and under what circumstances and how voters and bureaucrats apportion the gains from governmental action. The questions of law upon which public choice has focused have been statutory for the perfectly obvious reason that voters generally vote for legislators, who make statute law.

This would seem to exclude the common or judge-made law from the research agenda of public choice economics because judges are not generally answerable to the electorate. But Rowley claims that public choice techniques also describe the common law for two reasons: one, political pressures apply to the appointment and election of many judges; and two, legislators can step in and accomplish constituents' ends by statute if the common law fails to do so. Later he contends that the rent-seeking expenditures on judicial positions are huge, making the notion of an independent judiciary mythical. If the judiciary is not independent, then Rowley believes that one of the main pillars of the argument for a tendency toward an efficient common law is weakened. But this notion of the judiciary as just another group of politicians subject to the desires of voters goes much too far. There are procedural and other safeguards that are designed specifically to insulate the judiciary from being just another group of politicians and thus to relieve judges from rent-seeking responsibilities to "constituents." For instance, federal judges have life tenure and protection from having their salaries reduced while in office. And the common law's devotion to the notion of *stare decisis* also minimizes the rent-seeking opportunities for judges.

When he tries to be specific about the usefulness of a public choice perspective in explaining specific areas of the common law, Rowley does not succeed. Consider his discussion of tort law.[10] He supports Gordon Tullock's contention that in the absence of transaction costs, any liability rule is efficient. But that is a truism. Indeed, in the absence of transaction costs there is no separate branch of the law called tort. Tort exists to deal with accidents between strangers, people who must allocate responsibility for losses arising from a chance contact outside of the usual rules of contract [29]. Moreover, the economics of choosing among tort liability standards has advanced a great deal beyond the point with which Rowley is familiar. Very briefly, one recent version of the economic theory of tort liability is that negligence rules are superior in inducing precaution to minimize accident costs when precaution is bilateral (both victim and injurer can take action to reduce the probability and severity of an accident) and when it is relatively easy for the court to determine the socially optimal level of precaution. Strict liability is superior when precaution is unilateral (only the injurer can realistically be expected to take precaution to reduce the probability and severity of an accident) and when compensatory damages can be measured perfectly (and they can be more easily measured than the socially optimal level of precaution can be determined) [30].

Rowley offers a public choice explanation for the recent tort liability crisis. He sees the crisis as due to five factors, all of which are the outcome of public-choice determined forces: "(i) the [expansion of] no-fault liability; (ii) the undermining of causation; (iii) escalating litigation costs; (iv) the explosion in tort suits; and (v) the augmentation of damage awards by tort juries." On the first of these points he is factually wrong. The move to no-fault was a short, sharp episode of the 1970s and has been confined almost exclusively to automobile accidents. The trend has not escalated in the 1980s, as he claims. In fact, no-fault is retreating: several states have dropped no-fault in favor of a return to more traditional standards of tort liability.[11] Moreover, even if Rowley were correct about the trend toward no-fault, it would take a tremendously deft theory to explain how this trend, explicitly designed to *substitute* for tort litigation, had led to the increased litigation of the tort liability crisis. Rowley's explanation (that with no-fault "moral hazard advanced, with individuals seeking remedies for damages to which they exposed themselves") is unpersuasive. No-fault applies almost exclusively to automobile accidents, while the heart of the tort liability crisis has been in products liability.

His contention that causation has been eroded is not supported either, but there is a seed of a better explanation for the tort liability crisis in his observation. I doubt that the notion of legal cause has been significantly weakened in the last decade. But there is no question that the defenses available to injurers, especially in cases of product-related harms, have been greatly circumscribed. Courts are increasingly reluctant to allow defendants to bring in the victim's contributory negligence, assumption of the risk, or product misuse. As a result, the products liability system is moving toward a standard of absolute liability, under which there is almost nothing that the manufacturer can do to avoid responsibility for any injuries resulting from the use of his product. Because this greatly increases the probability that the victims of product-related injuries can recover in a tort action, it should come as no surprise to learn that the amount of tort litigation has increased.

With regard to lawyers (typically the villains in this story), Rowley posits without adequate explanation that the rents available to the legal profession have risen considerably and that this has induced lots of litigation.[12] The causal mechanism at work here is not clear. Simple economic intuition would suggest that if litigation costs have risen so dramatically, demand for litigation would decrease and the supply of litigators would increase. This might lead to an increase in litigation, depending on the relative shifts in the supply-and-demand curves, but it will certainly lead eventually to a lowering of the price of litigation. Perhaps what we are observing now is that the heightened litigation costs have caused the minimum amount in controversy in litigated torts to rise, leading to an increase in the size of judgments.

Finally, Rowley applies public choice techniques to the criminal and constitutional law and makes assertions that strike me as far-fetched. He alleges that Mancur Olson's theory of collective choice has something to say about criminal law because criminals are a smaller and, therefore, more effective lobbying group than are noncriminals. Moreover, Rowley alleges that judges sentence criminals in response not to an efficiency calculus but rather in response to votes and interest-group pressure. In the field of constitutional law, he suggests, following William Landes and

Posner, that the role of the independent judiciary is to validate legislative commitments made to interest groups [31]. They facilitate wealth-
maximizing deals done in the legislature with their constituents. He closes
with some highly critical words for the Supreme Court, urging them to
abandon judicial activism in favor of a return to the intent of the founders
of the Constitution. It is not at all clear what this cry is about.

While I am interested in the work of the public choice school in
explaining the dynamics of statutory law and the behavior of legislators, I
am not convinced yet that there is similar insight to be gained from the
public choice perspective on the common law.

6. The Property Rights Perspective

Louis De Alessi and Robert Staaf have provided a useful summary of the
law and economics style that traces its origins to the seminal work on
social cost by Coase. The hallmark of that style is its focus on transaction
costs as the principal explanatory variable for a wide-ranging set of
economic problems. As an example of this style, consider how this
perspective explains the existence of the corporate form of business
organization as a response to the transaction costs of monitoring team
production. Following Armen Alchian and Harold Demsetz, assume that
it is most efficient to produce output by means of team production but
that it is difficult to distinguish the effort of individual members of the
team. This latter condition makes it difficult for the team to reward
individual members according to their productivity. As a result, rewards
must be geared to the average productivity of the team, but this under-
compensates those who work harder than average and overcompensates
those who work less hard than average. Because team members get paid
an average amount whether they work hard or hardly at all, this creates
an incentive to shirk, which reduces the productivity of the team. Thus,
the inherent efficiency of team production can be realized only if the costs
of monitoring the team can be minimized. Alchian and Demsetz posit
that these problems are solved by organizing a "firm." The firm consists
of the production team and a "residual claimant" (an entrepreneur). The
residual claimant hires and monitors and compensates the team, trying to
pay each member the value of his marginal product. His own compensation comes in the form of the residual that remains after the output of the
team is sold to consumers. The greater the difference between the dollar
amount for which the output can be sold and the dollar amount for which
it can be produced, the greater the residual and the greater the residual

claimant's compensation. The residual, in plain terms, is economic profit, and the residual claimant can maximize that profit by more efficiently monitoring the team. This highly stylized explanation seems to fit the division of responsibility in the classical corporation, and has more recently served as the basis for explaining why different levels of transaction costs and different types of productive technologies give rise to different forms of business organizations [32]. The bulk of this chapter is an able and valuable survey of how transaction costs can be employed to explain certain institutional forms. Most of the topics covered and the conclusions reached will not be new to those familiar with the law and economics literature, although the articles and books cited in the notes will be valuable to those new to the subject.

One of the important points that De Alessi and Staaf make is that while the property rights or new institutional economics has made much of the notion of transaction costs, it has not made enough of the parallel notion of *subjective costs*. The authors note that the second half of Coase's "Problem of Social Cost" was a criticism of Pigovian taxes, based on the point that because costs are inherently subjective, correcting market imperfections by policies predicated on the existence of *objective* costs is futile. This notion of subjective cost can be subtle and elusive; I shall postpone a discussion of it until after I make a point about the term "transaction cost."

One of the shortcomings of the chapter is that the authors do not explain what transaction costs are. But, curiously enough, they are not alone in this shortcoming: one can search the voluminous literature cited in the notes in vain for a convincing definition. The words transaction costs have passed into the economists' and lawyers' vocabulary without anyone's being quite sure what they are. This is not a mere quibble; the definition one chooses for this important term is crucial in analyzing legal issues and in prescribing corrective policies.

Toward the end of the chapter the authors leave the survey of property rights in order to make a more substantive point. De Alessi and Staaf consider whether transaction and subjective costs recommend specific performance as the routine contract remedy. Their conclusion is that it does. While this conclusion is not new, I find it entirely welcome [33]. Their analysis is not complete enough to persuade the skeptical,[13] and it contains several errors, such as their belief that a punitive element in a liquidation clause will always induce breach of contract. In fact, the efficiency gains from allowing parties to insert such a clause are substantial. The risk of such clauses is not that they will induce breach but rather that if circumstances change substantially between contract formation and performance, the clause creates an incentive for one party to induce the other party to breach [34].

7. Where Are We in Law and Economics?

As stated above, law and economics has grown very rapidly and is now in its scholarly adolescence. This section suggests where the field might be headed: that is, in what way will the field mature? My focus is biased toward the microeconomic view of the subject, which may cause me to believe that certain issues and ways of approaching them are more pressing than others and that certain questions are settled. Others, working from different paradigms, might take my pressing issues to be secondary and my settled questions to be open. Still, I believe I have learned enough from the authors in this book to be keenly aware and appreciative of alternative ways of thinking about law and economics. While I cannot presume to guess which topics the CLS scholars or public choice scholars working in law and economics should tackle next, I *can* suggest what those and other paradigms might contribute to the scholarship on the topics at the top of the agenda.

Generally, I would suggest that progress will be faster in law and economics in direct proportion to the extent to which we put greater educational requirements on those entering the field. One of the curses of interdisciplinary scholarship is that it makes double work for its practitioners. They must master two fields. Sad to say, many of the current practitioners in the field have not taken the time—and it does require an extraordinarily large commitment of time—to learn the complementary tools of the trade. This seems to me to be true of both lawyers and economists. The clear prescription is for those whose formal training is in the law to learn some graduate-level microeconomics and econometrics and for those whose formal training is in economics to learn at least the equivalent of the first-year curriculum in law school.

Why is this investment worth the effort? I see two salient reasons. First, lawyers and economists think differently, and unless one is aware of and sensitive to how those in the complementary field think, a large potential exists for miscommunication. Consider the area of contract law. How would an economist begin a discussion of that area? He/she would no doubt start with one of the fundamental tenets of modern welfare economics: "voluntary exchange is mutually beneficial." When they hear this phrase, economists typically envision an Edgeworth box and the contract locus along which all the gains from trade have been exhausted.

They also probably recall being apprised of the fact that this tenet is one of the great advances in modern thinking, that it replaces the notion that exchange is inherently exploitative in the sense that one person can benefit only at another's expense. Now, how would a lawyer begin a discussion of contract? His/her categories of analysis are to distinguish enforceable from unenforceable promises; to look for offer, acceptance, and consideration; to investigate whether any of the formation defenses or performance excuses is relevant; and so on.

These are two very different ways of talking, and unless the speakers make a genuine effort to overcome their different vocabularies, there will be suspicion and misunderstanding. Someone might undertake to translate between the paradigms (for instance, a lexicon could indicate that when an economist says "gains from trade" or "mutual benefit," the lawyer should understand him to mean "benefit of the bargain"), or the parties might learn to speak each other's language. Of these alternatives, the one that will allow the most productive communication is for lawyers to learn, formally, microeconomics and econometrics, and for economists to learn, again formally, the law.[14]

A second reason for making the investment in formally learning the complementary field is that there is a great deal of economics to be learned from studying the law and there is a great deal of law to be learned from studying economics. Consider again the area of contract law as an example of what economists might learn from the law. That voluntary exchange is mutually beneficial is a truism among economists, but very few economists whom I know have bothered to think closely about what constitutes a truly voluntary exchange or about how a third party might judge that there was, in fact, mutual benefit. Lawyers are, among other things, experts in these practical details of exchange. The common law of contract has considered the notion of voluntariness for centuries and can provide economists with much valuable insight on the conditions in which exchange is truly voluntary.[15] There are, of course, equally valuable insights on the law of contract that a knowledge of economics can provide a lawyer [35].

Let me now turn to more specific issues in law and economics. What issues are settled in law and economics, and what questions remain open, and how might we approach them? These are extremely broad questions, and so the answers must be broad.

My feeling is that the broad outlines of the economic analysis of the core common law areas—property, contract, and tort—are becoming reasonably clear. The benefit of investigating those rules using economic tools is now beyond doubt, although specific conclusions may remain controversial. Indeed, I will even suggest that I discern the possibility in the near future of a unified economic theory of these core common law areas. By "unified," I mean a general theory of the law with property, contract, and tort (and, perhaps, other areas) considered as special cases. This general theory might focus on the ability of legal rules to induce optimal risk-allocation and information exchange and internalization of external costs [36].

There are, of course, some particular topics in these core areas about which there is not yet general consensus. For example, it is astonishing at this late date in the law, never mind in law and economics, that there is not yet a coherent theory of tort liability [37]. When to use a form of the negligence standard and what form; when to use a form of strict liability and what form (with or without contributory negligence, assumption of the risk, and product misuse); when to use ex ante administrative agency regulation instead of or in addition to tort liability—these are all open questions. And they are also *vital* questions. They concern the most fundamental policy issues in tort law.

With regard to all the core areas of the common law, there is a topic that is receiving increasing attention: uncertainty. As Kornhauser suggests in his chapter of this book, the naive theory of the law assumes that the law is perfectly enforced and obeyed. One of the virtues of the economic theory of the law is that it allows for imperfect compliance with the law. Our economic analysis of legal rules has, with only a few exceptions, assumed that the law is known and obeyed with certainty. That assumption is clearly unrealistic and must be replaced with alternatives that take account of the great amount of uncertainty that pervades the legal system and the behavior of economic agents. Doing so can cause our understanding of legal rules to be changed dramatically. For instance, an analysis of the incentive effects of negligence demonstrates that *all* forms of the negligence rule (simple negligence, negligence with contributory negligence, and the three varieties of comparative negligence) create efficient incentives when the legal standards of care are known and applied with certainty. On efficiency grounds, there is no difference among the various forms of the negligence rule in a world of certainty. However, when we introduce uncertainty (for instance, in the sense that no one can be sure to what legal standard of care he/she will be held or how a fact-finder will evaluate his/her precaution against the legal standard), these results change. Some negligence rules become more efficient than others; for example, comparative negligence, which lawyers and policymakers had long championed as more fair than other forms of the negligence rule but which economists had invariably found to be inefficient, becomes the most efficient negligence rule under some kinds of uncertainty [38]. There are, I am sure, other conclusions about the efficiency of tort, contract, and property rules that will be dramatically amended when we introduce more realistic assumptions about uncertainty.

One topic in law and economics about which we should suspend debate and simply agree to disagree is the controversy about whether the law is or should be concerned principally with economic efficiency or with justice. The law, like many of us, can serve two functions simultaneously and well: it can promote the efficient use of resources while at the same time serving to do justice. There is no necessary mutual exclusivity between these goals. And, happily, efficiency and justice frequently argue for the same legal rule. For example, I believe that specific performance is not only the fairest remedy for breach of contract but is also the most efficient. Similarly, comparative negligence is not only fair; it is also efficient. I am not suggesting the Pollyana-ish conclusion that there are no real conflicts between efficiency and fairness. In fact, there are: to take an example, consider products liability. There, I believe, an attempt to be fair to the victims of product-related harms has led to a great deal of inefficiency (in the sense that several valuable and safe products are in short supply, unavailable, or excessively expensive). In that area, as well as others in which efficiency and fairness are at odds, a tradeoff is called for. The most an economist can do in that situation is point out the *efficiency* and, where economic analysis allows, the *equity* consequences of different legal rules, and then let political pressures and judgments decide what to do. (How those tradeoffs are resolved is part political science, part public choice economics, and part critical legal studies.)

Despite my feeling that there is not a great deal more of profit to be said on the matter of efficiency versus justice, I am certain that this debate will continue. That is because it is part of a larger political debate that will be with us forever. To repeat, I do not believe that there is only one way to look at the law, nor is one way necessarily better than any of the others. Law is both a repository of public ideals of fairness and justice, a battleground for personal and group advantage, and an important tool for encouraging efficiency and its benefits.

Another category of research in law and economics that has previously been slighted but that would be extremely valuable is historical studies of change in legal rules. For example, what objective economic factors, if any, explain why in the last quarter of a century four-fifths of the states have replaced negligence with contributory negligence as the prevailing tort liability standard with comparative negligence? Why did strict liability give way to negligence in the early nineteenth century [39]? Why has products liability law changed so dramatically in the last 80 years [40]? To answer these questions will require, I suspect, cross-fertilization between the public choice, CLS, and institutionalist perspectives in law and economics.

Related to these studies of change are what I think is the great frontier of law and economics: empirical work. What we are doing at the moment in law and economics is elaborating a system of logically consistent hypotheses about the causes and consequences of legal rules. Whether these theories accurately describe or predict real-world events is an entirely different matter. We assume, for example, that decisionmakers respond differently to a negligence rule than they do to strict liability. But do they? (There is some experimental evidence that suggests that they do not [41].) These and other questions about the effect of legal rules must be answered, regardless of the perspective from which one approaches law and economics.

Standing in the way of acceptable empirical work in law and economics is the fact that there are very little usable data in the area, and that there are severe difficulties in using the data we do have. Consider, for example, the problems of using data from jury verdicts. Let us assume that we are interested in learning what those verdicts tell us about the incentive effects of tort liability standards and money judgments. An overarching problem is that we are not even sure how representative the jury verdict data are. Do they represent a biased or unbiased sample of the sorts of tort disputes that arise? That is, do they tell us anything interesting about the sorts of accidents that are *not* litigated? (Incidentally, all is not lost if information generated by court reports or jury verdicts is not representative. There are other sources of relevant information, such as insurance companies, and there are other methods to generate that information, such as laboratory experiments [42].) These and other difficulties can and will be surmounted in order to allow law and economics to proceed to its next great task, testing our theories of the efficiency of various common law rules.[16]

8. Conclusion

Law and economics is still young and growing. Only a few issues in law and economics are so truly settled that there is wide consensus in favor of a single theory or description of an important legal phenomenon. Most law and economics questions are still open and likely to remain so for a long time. The chapters of this work suggest a very important lesson about the manner in which we may best be able to convert these open questions into settled issues: the field must be willing to look to widely different styles of analysis. Just as there is no single view of the law that is either all-encompassing or inherently better or more insightful than another, there is no one approach to the field of law and economics that is inherently better than another. What I said in my introductory remarks bears repeating: to slight any of these methods of looking at law and economics would be to risk not learning something important about the law. There are many paths up the mountain, and, regardless of which path was taken, we should be mindful that along the way each path offers beautiful views.

Notes

1.   Professor Schmid correctly notes that these sentiments are shared by the legal realists and the critical legal studies movement.

2.   I say "seemed" because the Court moved in fits and starts. For example, in *Allgeyer* v. *Louisiana*, 165 U.S. 578 (1897), the Court found a regulation of work hours to be invalid and, in so doing, gave a ringing endorsement of liberty of contract. But one year later, in *Holden* v. *Hardy*, 169 U.S. 366 (1898), the same Court sustained a Utah statute limiting the number of hours that an employee could be required to spend working in an underground mine or in a smelter.

3.   Minda identifies two principal schools of legal realist thought: one school who thought justification for legal rules could not come simply from the law but had to come also from outside the law, and a second school who favored applying scientific and technocratic reasoning to legal problems.

4.   In a famous graphic phrase, it was held that how a judge decided a case depended crucially on what he had for breakfast that morning.

5.   The reason this school stressed the rationality or objectivity of the legal process was in order to draw a sharp contrast to the legal realists' view that judges were essentially unconstrained. As a result, the realists held, *subjective* values and conditions of the judiciary determined legal outcomes.

6.   I am, of course, *not* saying that common law judges reached these conclusions *wittingly*, nor, I suppose, "with malice aforethought."

7.   While he does not speculate about a normative goal for the naive theory's direction of human behavior, Kornhauser suggests that there are two ways to describe the manner in which the naive theory directs behavior. First, the law may attempt to influence behavior by providing information or a *signal* about what is acceptable. As an example, Kornhauser suggests traffic rules: keep to the right, do not pass on hills, yield to oncoming traffic. Second, the law may attempt to influence behavior by *altering tastes and preferences*. As instances of this type of directive force of the law, he suggests laws establishing community norms of safety in activities where others might be hurt and laws defining communal norms of cleanliness. (One intriguing aspect of this latter type of law is that if the law requires

people to do X, then people come to believe that X is desirable and *right*. This is an interesting point, and I suspect that the well-known psychological theory of cognitive dissonance could be helpful in investigating how people come to believe that the law's proscriptions and requirements are desirable.) This distinction between law as signal and law as taste-creator reminds me very much of what the literature asserts to be the two functions of advertising. This unflattering comparison may bear the germ of some interesting future work, but my suspicion is that these categories of the law are excessively artificial.

8. Presumably this could include those who consider breaking the law to be a "bad," something that reduces one's well-being the more of it one has.

9. Dean Rowley also notes that more recently a part of political science has adopted economic methodology and, with it, a more deductive and positivistic view of how to establish acceptable propositions.

10. Earlier he had suggested that while the common law process may well have created efficient rules of property and contract, it could not as effectively do so for tort law. Rowley claims that the interests of litigants in bringing tort cases when the prevailing rule is inefficient are not as strong in the tort area as they are in other areas of the common law.

11. The dominant trend in tort law has been toward comparative negligence, but no one has suggested that comparative negligence has fostered increased litigation or any of the other dire consequences associated with the tort liability crisis.

12. His evidence on rents is the percentage of the total awards in asbestos litigation that goes to attorneys' fees (approximately 62 percent).

13. For example, the authors do not discuss such topics as whether the contract is executory, whether the good to be handed over or the service to be performed is fungible or unique, and what economic sense to make of the usual defenses to a specific performance claim.

14. As an example of what can happen from this failure to communicate, let me draw attention to the manner in which scholars have become familiar with the subject matter of law and economics. Most lawyers learned law and economics from Judge Posner's *Economic Analysis of Law*. That work, a magnificent and classic work of scholarship, treats the topics of law and economics in a manner that is different from the way in which economists were teaching it to their students and differently from the way in which economists were pursuing their own research interests. As a result, throughout the late 1970s and early 1980s, law and economics was proceeding along two separate paths, within hailing distance of each other but nonetheless separate. One path was being blazed by lawyers familiar with economics (through the good offices of Posner's work), and the other, by economists, whose knowledge of the law was largely gleaned from Posner's book. The subject matter of the two inquiries may have been nominally the same, but their research methods and their common knowledge of each other's fields were very different. In large part this difference went unremarked in the enthusiasm of the lawyers and economists for the development of the new field. But the difference was evident to any lawyer who attempted to teach himself/ herself economics or to teach the law to economists and to any economist who attempted to learn the law or to teach economics to lawyers. There were two different world views, two different scholarly methodologies in collision.

15. As an experiment, I suggest that one ask a Ph.D. economist whether an exchange elicited by coercion is voluntary and whether it should be enforced and, if not, why not? Similarly, ask these economists whether an exchange elicited by a fraudulent statement is voluntary and whether it should be enforced and, if not, why not? Consider the following situation. Jack Benny is confronted by an armed robber on a lonely and dark street. The robber says, "Your money or your life!" There is a tense, long pause. Benny finally says, "I'm thinking, I'm thinking."

16. I cannot conclude this section without taking issue with the following contention from Owen Fiss' "The Death of the Law?" supra note 7, at p. 10, where he stated: "[a]ny requirement establishing that legal change can be implemented after empirical proof would be a paralyzing standard which few, if any, reformist projects could satisfy." I would be much more comfortable if the presumption were that a legal change could occur *only* after there was reasonable evidence about the efficiency and equity effects of the change. To do otherwise is to champion change for the sake of change or to court dire, unintended consequences. Many years ago, I was observing a suit against the Indianapolis School Board by the Department of Justice for the Board's allegedly having failed to correct de facto segregation of blacks and whites in the public schools. A witness was describing the details of bussing schemes in other cities: how many children were involved, what the annual cost had been to the school districts, and so on. The judge asked the witness what the effects of bussing had been on the children involved: were their test scores higher or lower?; were they happier or not?; was there increased delinquency and truancy? The witness said that he did not know the answers to those questions, and that, to his knowledge, no one knew. The judge was incredulous, as I was then and still am, that such a policy had been instituted in other school districts and that the Department of Justice was asking for it to be instituted in Indianapolis without any knowledge, however rudimentary, of its effects on some important indicators of the well-being of the school children involved.

References

1. For example, see the parts of Bentham, Jeremy, *A Theory of Legislation* (Ogden ed., 1789, Hildreth trans., 1931) on the incentive effects of punishment for criminal violations, and Blackstone's discussion of the incentive effects of insecure property rights in Blackstone, William, *Commentaries on the Laws of England* (Chicago: University of Chicago Press, 1976).
2. One of the very best essays in this vein, one that illustrates the important proviso I made that this view does not reject formalism as per se undesirable, is the introductory essay in David, Paul A., *Technical Change and Economic Growth* (Cambridge: Cambridge University Press, 1977).
3. For example, see North, Douglass C., and Davis, Lance, *Institutional Change and American Economic Growth* (Cambridge: Cambridge University Press, 1971). See also the discussion below of the chapter by Professors De Alessi and Staaf on the property rights perspective on law and economics. The property rights school is sometimes referred to as the new (or neo-) institutionalist school.
4. For the influence of these latter two effects on the economic analysis of law, see Ulen, Thomas S., "Cognitive Imperfections and the Efficiency of the Law" (Working paper, Institute of Government and Public Affairs, University of Illinois, May, 1988).
5. Kelman, Mark. *A Guide to Critical Legal Studies* (Cambridge: Harvard University Press, 1987).
6. The footnotes in Minda's chapter contain a valuable set of references to the literature of the CLS movement. As an example of the difficulty outsiders are likely to experience in learning about CLS by reading the work of CLS

scholars, consider Unger, Roberto, *The Critical Legal Studies Movement* (Cambridge: Harvard University Press, 1986).

7. See, for example, Fiss, Owen M., "The Death of the Law?," *Cornell Law Review*, Vol. 72, No. 1 (November 1986), pp. 1–16.

8. Minow, Martha L., "The Law Turning Outward," *Telos*, Vol. 73 (Fall 1987).

9. See Posner, Richard A., "The Decline of Law as an Autonomous Discipline: 1962–1987," *Harvard Law Review*, Vol. 100, No. 4 (February 1987), pp. 761–780. Judge Posner views this decline favorably, holding that the study of the law is far richer as a result of the end of its isolation from other fields of scholarship. A contrary view is that of Professor Fiss, who laments the changes that law and economics and CLS in particular have made in the study of the law. See Fiss, *supra* note 7.

10. 16 Wallace 36 (1873).

11. 94 U.S. 113 (1876). See the discussion of the effects of this state regulation in Ulen, Thomas S., "The Regulation of Grain Warehousing and its Economic Effects: The Competitive Position of Chicago in the 1870s and 1880s," *Agricultural History*, Vol. 56, No. 1 (January 1982), pp. 194–210.

12. 198 U.S. 45 (1905).

13. The matter was more or less resolved in favor of a more expansive definition of legitimate governmental regulation. The culmination of this episode was the conflict between the Supreme Court and the Roosevelt Administration over the latter's "Court-packing" proposal of 1937. See Rehnquist, William H., *The Supreme Court: How It Was, How It Is* (New York: William Morrow and Co., Inc., 1987), pp. 215–230.

14. Consider the "Brandeis brief." This style of legal argument, popularized early in the century by Louis Brandeis, then a prominent private attorney and later an Associate Justice of the U.S. Supreme Court, buttressed traditional, formal legal analysis with statistics to demonstrate the effect of certain legal rules. For example, in arguing in favor of a regulation limiting the hours of work for children, such a brief might give statistics on the adverse effects of unlimited hours on the health and mental development of children. (See Llewellyn, Karl, "A Realistic Jurisprudence—The Next Step," *Columbia Law Review*, Vol. 30, No. 4 (April 1930).) There is a clear line of intellectual heritage stretching from the Brandeis brief to the law and economics movement's concern with efficiency. In the penultimate section of this chapter, I urge the increased use of empirical techniques to check the efficiency contentions about the law.

15. The most influential works of this period are Wechsler, Herbert, "Toward Neutral Principles of Constitutional Law," *Harvard Law Review*, Vol. 73, No. 1 (November 1959), pp. 1–35; and Hart, Henry, and Sacks, Albert, *The Legal Process: Basic Problems in the Making and Application of Law*, tent. ed. (Unpublished manuscript, Harvard Law School, 1958).

16. There have, of course, been additional developments in the legal process school. One important such development is "interpretivism," an example of

which is the work of Ronald Dworkin. Interpetivism is explained and criticized in Moore, Michael S., "The Interpretive Turn in Modern Theory: A Turn for the Worse?," Legal Theory Workshop, Faculty of Law, University of Toronto (April 1988). For additional criticism of the interpretivist jurisprudence, see Weinrib, Lloyd, *Natural Law and Justice* (Cambridge: Harvard University Press, 1987).

17. Easterbrook, Frank, "Foreword: The Court and the Economic System," *Harvard Law Review*, Vol. 98, No. 1 (November 1984), pp. 4–60. See also, in the same volume of the *Harvard Law Review*, Laurence Tribe's criticism of Easterbrook's thesis and the reply by Judge Easterbrook.

18. The argument that Robert Cooter and I made in favor of comparative negligence was based, in part, on a Rawlsian notion of what liability rule people might have chosen from "behind the veil." See Cooter, Robert D., and Ulen, Thomas S., "An Economic Case for Comparative Negligence," *New York University Law Review*, Vol. 61, No. 6 (December 1986), pp. 1067–1110.

19. See Posner, Richard A., "The Ethical and Political Basis of the Efficiency Norm in Common Law Adjudication," *Hofstra Law Review*, Vol. 8, No. 3 (Spring 1980), pp. 487–508.

20. This is one of the themes in Posner, Richard A., *Economic Analysis of Law*, 3rd ed. (Boston: Little, Brown, and Co., 1986).

21. This literature and some noneconomic arguments about the death penalty are reviewed in Cooter, Robert D., and Ulen, Thomas S., *Law and Economics* (Glenview, IL: Scott, Foresman, and Co., 1988), ch. 12.

22. Kornhauser, Lewis, "The Great Image of Authority," *Stanford Law Review*, Vol. 36, No. 1 (January 1984), pp. 349–382.

23. See, for example, Fiss, *supra* note 7, and Dworkin, Ronald, *Law's Empire* (Cambridge: Harvard University Press, 1987).

24. See Steiner, Henry, *Moral Argument and Social Vision in the Courts: A Study in Tort Accident Law* (Madison: University of Wisconsin, 1987).

25. See Easterbrook, *supra* note 17.

26. Posner, *supra* note 19. There he has attempted to provide an ethical or normative basis for examining the efficiency consequences of legal rules. The remainder of that issue of the *Hofstra Law Review* and the following issue consist of articles very highly critical of Judge Posner's hypothesis.

27. Ulen, *supra* note 4.

28. See, for example, Kolstad, Charles, Johnson, Gary V., and Ulen, Thomas S., "Uncertainty in Tort Law" (Working paper, Institute of Government and Public Affairs, University of Illinois, June, 1988); and Johnson, Gary V., Kolstad, Charles, and Ulen, Thomas S., "*Ex Ante* Administrative Agency Regulation and *Ex Post* Tort Liability: Complements or Substitutes?" (Working paper, Illinois Seminar in Political Economy, University of Illinois, February 1988).

29. See Cooter and Ulen, *supra* note 21, ch. 8.

30. *Ibid.*

31. Landes, William, and Posner, Richard A., "The Independent Judiciary in an Interest Group Perspective," *Journal of Law and Economics*, Vol. XVII (December 1975), pp. 875–902.
32. Alchian, Armen, and Demsetz, Harold, "Production, Information Costs, and Economic Organization," *American Economic Review*, Vol. 62, No. 8 (December 1972), pp. 777–795. There are, of course, other theories of the existence of the corporate firm and other transaction costs besides those arising from team production that have attracted scholarly attention. For a useful introduction to this literature, see Posner, Richard A., and Scott, Kenneth, *The Economics of Corporation Law and Securities Regulation* (Boston: Little, Brown & Co., 1980).
33. See Ulen, Thomas S., "The Efficiency of Specific Performance: Towards a Unified Theory of Contract Remedies," *Michigan Law Review*, Vol. 83, No. 8 (November 1984), pp. 341–403.
34. On De Alessi and Staaf's point that punitive clauses will induce breach, the literature has always worried more about the exact opposite problem: that punitive elements in a liquidation clause might induce someone to *perform* a contract when it was more efficient to breach. Goetz, Charles J., and Scott, Robert E., "Liquidated Damages, Penalties, and the Just Compensation Principle: Some Notes on an Enforcement Model of Efficient Breach," *Columbia Law Review*, Vol. 77, No. 2 (March 1977), pp. 554–607) showed that this was not the case. See also, Cooter and Ulen, *supra* note 21, pp. 293–296.
35. In chapter 6 of Cooter and Ulen, *supra* note 21, we attempted to develop an economic theory of contract that made use of familiar economic categories to describe familiar categories in contract law.
36. See Cooter, Robert D., "Unity in Tort, Contract, and Property: The Model of Precaution," *California Law Review*, Vol. 73, No. 3 (September 1985), pp. 1–32.
37. Naturally, I quite modestly exempt from this statement the unified theory of tort liability in chapters 8 and 9 of Cooter and Ulen, *supra* note 21. See also the magnificent work in Shavell Steven, *An Economic Analysis of Accident Law* (Cambridge: Harvard University Press, 1987), and Landes, William, and Posner, Richard A., *The Economic Structure of Tort Law* (Cambridge: Harvard University Press, 1987).
38. For a demonstration and discussion of these results, see Cooter, Robert D., and Ulen, Thomas S., "An Economic Case for Comparative Negligence," *New York University Law Review*, Vol. 61, No. 6 (December 1986), pp. 1067–1110.
39. See Horwitz, Morton, *The Transformation of American Law: 1780–1860* (Cambridge: Harvard University Press, 1977). But also see Schwartz, Gary, "Tort Law and the Economy in Nineteenth-Century America: A Reinterpretation," *Yale Law Journal*, Vol. 90, No. 8 (July 1981), pp. 1717–1775.
40. See Landes, William, and Posner, Richard A., "A Positive Economic Analysis of Products Liability," *Journal of Legal Studies*, Vol. 14, No. 3

(December 1985), pp. 535–568; and Priest, George, "The Invention of Enterprise Liability: A Critical History of the Intellectual Foundations of Modern Tort Law," *Journal of Legal Studies*, Vol. 14, No. 3 (December 1985), pp. 461–528.

41. Kornhauser, Lewis, and Schotter, Andrew, "An Experimental Study of Single-Actor Accidents" (Working paper, C.V. Starr Center for Applied Economics, New York University October 1987).

42. For a survey, see Hoffman, Elizabeth, and Spitzer, Matthew, "Experimental Law and Economics," *Columbia Law Review*, Vol. 85, No. 5 (June 1985), pp. 991–1036. See also, Barnes, David, *Statistics As Proof* (Boston: Little, Brown, and Co., 1983), and Rubinfeld, Daniel, "Econometrics in theCourt-room," *Columbia Law Review*, Vol. 85, No. 5 (June 1985), pp. 1048–1097.

8 LAW AND ECONOMICS: PARADIGM, POLITICS, OR PHILOSOPHY

Susan Rose-Ackerman

1. Introduction

Where does theory begin: in a disinterested attempt to understand the world; in an attempt to justify a political program, or in a set of beliefs about how the world ought to be evaluated? Is the ultimate aim scientific, political, or philosophical? Much of the controversy concerning the place of economics in law and the place of law in economics reduces to a debate over the basic goals of those who attempt interdisciplinary work. Are they social scientists seeking to use the tools of economic theory to understand legal phenomena? Are they representatives of the political right (or left) seeking justifications for laissez-faire capitalism and the minimal state (or the welfare state and public regulation)? Are they philosophical utilitarians, Kantians, liberals, or whatever, seeking to buttress their normative arguments through the use of economic theory? Law and economics can never be simply abstract social science. Its subject is "the law," and the law is inevitably linked to both politics and philosophy [1]. Thus since all three goals are present in varying mixtures in most law and economics scholarship, the debate about the value of the work is complicated by the tendency of both critics and practitioners to slide between categories.

233

My aim in this chapter is to articulate two contrasting ways to think about the relationship between law and economics: the Chicago school and what I shall call the reformist school [2].[1] Both schools have pretensions to explain and critically evaluate a very broad range of legal issues, but because of their different philosophical orientations, each has focused on a different class of issues. I will provide rather stark characterizations of each approach that ignore many subtleties and cross-cutting themes in order to emphasize methodological and philosophical differences [3].[2] I hope to show that the Chicago school's appropriation of the law and economics label distorts the profession's perception of the role of economic analysis in the law. An alternative interdisciplinary reformist endeavor is possible and promises a political economy of law that does not have the conservative bias of much Chicago school work.

While Chicago school scholars have written on topics as diverse and broadranging as antitrust, family law, taxation, corporations, and racial discrimination [4], the central core of their research is the economic analysis of the common law fields of tort, contract, and property. For these scholars the most interesting legal questions arise in small-numbers bargaining situations. Lawyer-economists should study transactions because markets will, in general, take care of themselves. These scholars' faith in the market paradoxically implies that it should not be the predominant area for law and economics study. Markets, if they exist, do not often fail in ways that the law can remedy. The real problem is that they do not always exist. When markets are unavailable, legal rules govern disputes between individuals such as parties to a contract, neighboring landowners, or accident victims and injurers. It is here, where market tests are unavailable, that the Chicagoans propose to use economic analysis.

Their model of the economy is the neoclassical synthesis in microeconomics which presupposes an unproblematic assignment of property rights before production and trade take place. The actual assignment of property rights is a central area for study and can have important implications for the efficiency of the economic system [5]. The Chicagoans' political philosophy combines a utilitarian or wealth-maximization ethic with a belief in the independent value of individualism and free choice [6]. The political program is based on support of laissez-faire capitalism and a belief that the state should do little more than define and uphold private property rights, enforce private contracts, and preserve external and internal order.

There are two central tensions in the Chicago school approach. The first is between a faith in the efficiency of the market and a research agenda that focuses on nonmarket interactions. The more pervasive the market, the less important law is as a means of promoting efficiency. The closer the world approaches the Coasian world of zero transactions costs [7], the closer law comes to playing a purely distributive function. A second tension is between the reformist notion that changes in property relations can be used to further efficiency goals and the conservative, status quo orientation of much writing with its heavy emphasis on the preservation of existing rights to property [8].

The Chicago school also comes in an evolutionary-institutional variant. This approach rejects static equilibrium analysis, but continues to hold that the assignment and definition of property rights is the central law and economics issue. Property rights systems, however, evolve over time in response to changes in technology and in society generally. Many scholars working in this tradition emphasize organizational form as well as property assignments and study the way organizations evolve in response to socioeconomic changes [9]. Nevertheless, much of this evolutionary work shares the political orientation and underlying philosophy of the more static work on property rights. In fact, the historical-empirical claims of some scholars in the evolutionary tradition help to resolve one of the tensions in the Chicago school. Property rights are seen as evolving in a way that is consistent with efficient resource allocation. Policy activism may then prove unnecessary.

The contrasting, reformist, approach is oriented toward public statutory law, and legislative and bureaucratic actions. At present it is less well represented on law faculties than is the Chicago school but its potential is, I believe, substantial. Drawing on two largely separate bodies of research, the reformist approach attempts to merge economic work on public policy with political-economic work on public choice.

The first body of research, public policy analysis, is more frequently practiced by economists teaching in economics departments and policy schools than by economically-oriented legal scholars. The theoretical tools are those of welfare economics, with its emphasis on externalities and market failures, and work on imperfect competition that studies the inefficiencies of monopoly power, imperfect information and monopolistic competition. The level of analysis is the market or, in cost-benefit analyses, the public program. The political agenda is one that advocates government regulatory and spending programs to help correct market failures, and the underlying philosophy is utilitarianism or wealth maximization with a side concern for promoting egalitarianism. Therefore, the main differences between the Chicago school and public policy economics are methodological and political-philosophical. The former studies transactions, emphasizes the efficiency of the private sector, and stresses the value of free choice. The latter studies markets, points to the inefficiency of some private arrangements, and frequently has an egalitarian bent. Both approaches, however, are directed toward the achievement of efficient resource allocation.

Intermediate between Chicago school work on the common law and market-oriented public policy analysis is what one might call "reformist-common law" research. This work accepts the Chicagoan's emphasis on torts, contract, and property, but lacks the conservative, status quo, antistatist point of view of that research. Nevertheless, this work has largely accepted the Chicagoans' emphasis on transactions as opposed to markets and, while willing to accept state intervention, has, in fact, mostly analyzed court-generated rules. However, there are important differences between those who fall into this intermediate category and Chicago purists, and I will try to note them as I proceed.

So far, I have emphasized the substantive policy analysis characteristic of reformist work. But there is a second strand of relevant research based on the public choice school of analysis. This research applies economic modeling to the political system [10]. Political actors are viewed as economic actors trying to further their self-interest. One strand emphasizes bargaining and game theory, and is therefore close to the transactions approach of the Chicago school. A second dimension stresses voting and other collective choice mechanisms and is closer to the study of economic markets. However, since strategic behavior is almost always individually rational in politics, the two approaches overlap.

The politics and philosophy of many students in the field of public choice is, like the Chicago school scholars, antistate and pro-individual freedom. Instead of praising the market, however, they criticize the state, but the end result, in policy terms, is much the same. Some public choice work, however, provides a framework for criticizing the Chicago school's sanguine view of common law courts as the preservers and promulgators of efficient legal doctrines. This work demonstrates that the Chicago school has provided no convincing explanation of how efficient rules arise from case-by-case adjudication [11].

In calling for more sophisticated attempts to merge public choice with public policy analysis, I claim that there is nothing inherently conservative about research in public choice. Analysis of political, collective choice institutions does not necessarily lead one to prefer the unfettered market or to support the existing distribution of property rights. Thus a sophisticated political economy of law should attempt to unite these two traditions of research in a way that will enlighten the study of legal institutions and substantive law.

I turn first to an explication and critique of the Chicago school and then go on to sketch the alternative reformist school of political-economic legal scholarship. Since the emphasis in the main body of the chapter is on civil law and economic regulation, I add a short assessment of criminal law before concluding with some observations on fruitful directions for future research.

2. The Chicago School

2.1. Static Analysis

To some, the work of the Chicago school is synonymous with law and economics [12]. In fact, however, it is a rather specialized endeavor based on a particular view of the world and the normative justifications for state action. The basic building blocks of this work are clearly defined property relations, competitive markets, and private bargains [13]. The state's essential function is to establish a system of legally enforceable property rights and to enforce private deals. Since private economic activity is hindered by uncertainty about ownership, the state must behave like a conservative dictator with respect to the definition of property rights. In order to facilitate private economic decisionmaking, democratic political decisionmaking must be constrained. Free market choice takes precedence over free democratic political choice. Therefore, implicit in this work is an authoritarian system for defining property rights that can credibly promise not to redefine rights on which expectations have been based. The dictatorial powers of the state are, however, limited to establishing property rights and perhaps also enforcing laws against monopoly [14]. All other resource allocation choices are made by private individuals acting to maximize their wealth. Democratic choice has little role to play in determining economic policy or in redistributing wealth.

However, in the interest of facilitating private economic activity, the state must recognize certain limitations on the ability of individuals to come together in markets or over a bargaining table. Thus tort law is needed to deter accidents in situations where potential victims would find it very costly either to negotiate with injurers ex ante or to purchase their caretaking in a market [15]. Liability should be placed on the individual best able to prevent the harm [16]. For example, if one firm's actions impose costs on many uninformed customers, liability should be placed on the firm, not because the firm is "at fault," but because such a rule will minimize the costs of negotiating a solution to the externality problem. Similarly, since bargaining is costly, contract law should provide a set of fallback provisions that the state will enforce unless the parties have agreed to alternative contractual language. The expectation measure of damages has been justified as a way to induce the breaching party to take account of the costs of his action [17]. Finally, property rights themselves should be designed to reduce the costs of market and negotiated transactions. Thus, if one firm creates air pollution that harms many nearby landowners, the landowners' property entitlements should include the right to clean air since this solution minimizes transaction costs [18].

These policy prescriptions, however, move the scholars in the Chicago school tradition beyond a simple requirement that the state establish *some* set of property rights to an argument that it should establish a particular set, supplemented by tort and contract law that takes a particular form. But what if the existing legal doctrines are well-established rules that bear only a very rough relationship to those that would best further efficient private economic behavior? The Chicago school scholars are then caught in a contradiction [19].[3] In order to encourage investment, the state should be conservative and reluctant to change the rules. However, if the rules encourage inefficient actions, they need to be changed. Even more troubling, how should these scholars enter the policy debate, given their belief that one cannot expect a democratically elected legislature to view economic efficiency as self-evidently the most basic value?

The solution is to deny that a contradiction exists in Anglo-American jurisprudence. The first step in this analysis is to assume risk neutrality.[4] If only expected values are important to economic actors, then uncertainty per se is costless. It has no independent impact on behavior. This assumption does not, however, undercut a general presumption in favor of private property if the possibility of government regulatory activity reduces expected values. It does, however, make the maximization of expected wealth a more plausible policy goal, and it removes a utilitarian argument for redistribution [20].

The assumption of risk neutrality, while pervasive in the work of Richard Posner and William Landes [21], is not strictly necessary for many Chicago school results and is not universally employed. The second step in the analysis, however, is of central importance. Scholars in the Chicago tradition argue that very little needs to be done to fine-tune the law. They attempt to demonstrate that existing doctrines and property relationships turn out by and large to further efficiency [22]. These doctrines have not been promulgated by democratic legislative bodies but by common law courts whose judges are not directly responsible to the electorate. Legislative meddling would both disrupt private expectations and override efficient legal rules. Doctrines change over time in response to changes in the economic system, but the change is gradual so that current expectations are not seriously eroded. Thus, the property rights "autocrat" turns out to be history whose rules are interpreted and updated by hundreds of decentralized, professional judges with a powerful respect for precedent.

The factual validity of the claim that common law rules are efficient has been questioned by many scholars both in and out of the law and economics field, and I do not propose to dwell on that ongoing debate except to note that the Chicago school scholars have by no means proved their case [23]. More important, however, than the current state of Anglo-American common law is the general observation that even if the case could be proved, such a proof would not resolve the fundamental contradiction in the Chicago school approach. Any finding that the common law is efficient is contingent on the validity of the assumption of risk neutrality and on the particular historical past and current institutions existing in the United States and Great Britain. Chicago school scholars need to ask how contradictions between settled expectations and the creation of efficient substantive rules should be resolved in more general contexts. They also need to consider more fully the role of political institutions other than common law courts [24].⁵ Fruitful comparative work will not be possible until these general problems of substantive policy and institutional competence are, at least, acknowledged.

2.2. Evolutionary Theory

Evolutionary-institutional work provides one way to resolve the tensions in Chicago school law and economics, but it does so by expounding an overly simple historical theory. One strand of this theory takes an economic determinist view of the law that is even stronger than that espoused by scholars who focus on common law courts. The argument is that changes in legal regimes, whether imposed by courts or legislatures, will track changes in the underlying economic situation [25]. Changes in technology play an especially central role. Thus the invention of barbed wire permitted ranchers and farmers in the American West to define and enforce property rights in land more effectively [26]. Differences in resource availability also affect the legal rules that result. Thus water law in the Western United States which has a scarcity of water differs from that in the East [27]. The law adjusts to promote efficient resource use as supply-and-demand conditions change. No special emphasis, however, is placed on judgemade law. Statutes passed by legislatures are also said to reflect underlying economic conditions and to evolve with changes in fundamental economic variables [28]. Evolutionary work, however, generally lacks a theory of politics. It assumes that if something is functional, then it will be produced by the state [29].[6]

Some authors also recognize that the causal link might run the other way so that the legal regime itself affects the way an economy develops. Research opportunities might not be exploited in a world without patent laws. Legal prohibitions against paying interest can restrict investment opportunities [30].

Much evolutionary work, however, focuses on private arrangements rather than law and cannot be neatly cabined within the Chicago tradition [31]. Private individuals and firms develop functional ways of dealing with economic problems in spite of the formal nature of the law. The law acts as a constraint within which individuals act, and over time the body of legal doctrine will be influenced by those private arrangements that have become so pervasive as almost to replace the existing legal structure [32]. Prime examples here are large private corporations that organize production through informal internal rules rather than formal contracts. The nature of contract law itself is then affected by the fact that many contractual parties are large organizations. Another example is the changing nature of patent and copyright law in a world dominated by computers and rapidly changing electronic technology.

2.3. Transactions Versus Markets

Beyond the historically contingent nature of the conclusions reached by the Chicago school of law and economics a second difficulty exists that has the same contradictory nature as the first. Scholars in the Chicago tradition praise the market, but they do not spend much time studying it. They have focused instead on bargained transactions where small numbers of people are involved or on torts where the parties have no contact with each other before the accident. Economic efficiency is the standard used to judge outcomes, but, aside from work on antitrust and securities markets, the analysis is not directed toward perfecting markets. Even work on the way property relationships operate to internalize externalities has been cast in terms of small numbers bargains. This focus seems narrow given the overwhelming importance of markets in our economy and the critical role of private property as a precondition for the existing economic system. Of course, the basic reason for this neglect of markets is the belief that the law need not be concerned with them so long as property relationships are clear and complete. By making this assumption, however, these scholars miss much of crucial importance in the relationship between law and economics.

Indeed, in focusing on individual transactions, the Chicago school sometimes implicitly assumes that imperfect competition is pervasive. This assumption shows up most clearly in contract law, the branch of law and economics most closely associated with market transactions. In discussing alternative remedies for breach, the emphasis has been on distinguishing between the various methods of calculating damages. In practice, the importance of these different damage rules depends upon the existence of good substitutes in the market. The more competitive the market, the less important the distinctions. They all more or less imply the same level of payment. While the issue of substitute performance has, of course, been recognized, there have been few attempts to perform an industrial organization analysis of contract law that considers the competitive consequences of contract doctrine on an industry-by-industry basis. Conversely, there has been little work that seeks to find out how the behavioral consequences of contract rules are affected by the organization of the markets in which the parties operate [33].

Two important exceptions to this generalization are work on self-enforcing contracts and models of asymmetric information in contract law [34]. Research on self-enforcing contracts recognizes that firms facing strong competitive pressures may have an incentive to live up to their promises even when resort to the legal system is costly. This result is especially likely if they face repeat buyers or buyers who communicate with each other. The structure of the market, the nature of the product and the existence of firm-specific capital are keys to analyzing the incentives facing the firm. Work on asymmetric information has used game theoretic models to characterize the relationship between the parties and is beginning to develop models that mimic actual situations in which renegotiation is possible and the courts affect the behavior of the parties on an ongoing basis.

3. The Reformist School

A reformist law and economics begins by denying the primacy of the existing distribution of property rights. This school, however, retains the assumption of methodological individualism that is central to the economic approach. The theory takes individuals seriously and refuses to give godlike stature to precepts beyond human reason. In placing human beings at the center of the discussion, this approach nevertheless refuses to idealize them or to assume more agreement than, in fact, exists. From this base the political economy of law looks in two directions: toward policies that improve the efficient operation of the economy and toward the specification of procedures that can resolve distributive issues fairly. Economics, at least as practiced in the late twentieth century, cannot by itself answer fundamental questions of distributive justice, but work in public choice can analyze the formal properties of alternative methods of collective decision. At present, the two faces of this research have been largely independent of each other. This separation is artificial and should be overcome to produce a genuinely reformist body of scholarship that draws on both traditions and enriches the study of public law. I begin, however, by outlining the basic features of each approach taken by itself.

3.1. The Public Policy Framework

Work on public policy is basically optimistic about the nature of government. This approach views government as a system that designs policies to promote the goals of efficiency and equity. Policy-oriented economists are seen as central to the development of public policy [35]. They produce cost-benefit analyses and other analytic exercises of use to actual policymakers. Economists in this tradition are, however, similar to devotees of the Chicago school in recognizing both the value of markets in promoting efficiency and the importance of economic incentives in all areas of life, both private and public. They are trying to get the economic incentives right, not eliminate them.

A fundamental methodological difference between the Chicago school and reformist work in public policy derives from the public policy analyst's view of the economic system. Instead of studying transactions and letting markets fend for themselves, these analysts study markets and virtually ignore individual bargains. The basic problem is to get markets working well so that the individual transactions will further efficiency. This difference in perspective is linked to the different political institutions that are the focus of analysis. The Chicago school concentrates on courts that generally only consider problems raised by individual transactions. Of course, the decision in one case may affect behavior in future similar situations, but outside of their writings on antitrust, the emphasis is on affecting individual behavior, not reforming market structures. In contrast, students of market failure and welfare economics look to the legislature and the executive as the political institutions where policy change originates. Such institutions can concentrate on policies that affect the overall behavior of markets through laws and regulations that have a comprehensive impact.

Public policy analysis does not, however, go beyond the study of individual sectors of the economy. Problems are analyzed in partial equilibrium terms. The problem of the second best is in the background of all work in this area. Also lacking is a realistic view of the workings of the political process. The work represents the best advice an economist can give to a policymaker, ignoring political feasibility or, rather, leaving it to the politician or top bureaucrat to link the economic prescriptions with political reality.

3.2. Public Choice

Public choice theory attempts both to provide realistic models of politics and to find methods of making collective choices that have certain desirable characteristics. The positive analysis tries to explain how political and bureaucratic bodies actually behave under the assumption that the political actors are self-interested maximizers of something (votes, agency budgets, profits, utility). This work then evaluates the agency-principal and strategic behavior problems central to representative democratic government and to the performance of bureaucracies. The normative theorizing specifies features of collective choice procedures that are thought by the analyst to have normative force, and the researcher then seeks decision processes that satisfy these conditions. The two approaches have multiple points of overlap since many of the abstract normative problems of collective choice also arise in any decisionmaking body that makes choices by aggregating individual preferences.

Normative work on collective choice began with Kenneth Arrow's Impossibility Theorem [36]. Arrow, rather like a medieval alchemist, was searching for a way to transform individual utility functions into a social welfare function without having to assume cardinality or interpersonal comparability. Thus his is a radically individualistic position that seeks to generate a ranking of social alternatives without appeal to any higher power even if that higher power is merely an impersonal utilitarian god seeking to maximize human happiness. Arrow, following the conventional wisdom in economics, recognized that individual utilities could not be added up without specifying a common measuring unit and that any unit that was chosen depended upon some external standard of value. Arrow, nevertheless, hoped to find a way of aggregating individual ordinal preferences that would produce a social welfare function that had the same rationality properties that he was willing to attribute to individuals. Thus the function would order social states in a way that was transitive, complete, and reflexive. Arrow was looking for an aggregation procedure that would accommodate all possible individual perference orderings, was not dictatorial, and that satisfied a unanimity rule. Finally, the procedure should rank any two alternatives solely on the basis of preferences for those alternatives. The presence or absence of other alternatives should not be relevant to the social choice over any pair of alternatives. Given these conditions, Arrow proved that no such process existed. The proof can be seen as the beginning of the recognition by economists that theirs is not a universal science of political-economic life that can resolve ancient questions of political philosophy through formal proofs [37].

However, this line of research did produce major results of more limited scope. Scholars with technical training in economics and mathematics began a fuller analysis of the properties of various voting rules than had been attempted in the past. The narrower task of studying the properties of voting rules has proved very useful in understanding the behavior of democratic decisionmaking bodies and in evaluating the strengths and weaknesses of the alternatives from majority rule to weighted voting schemes to demand-revealing systems [38].

Political scientists who find the assumption of self-interested behavior congenial are mainly responsible for the positive, more institutionally oriented work that models the behavior of representative assemblies and bureaucracies and analyzes the political behavior of individuals [39]. Nevertheless, the seminal works are by economists: Anthony Downs and Mancur Olson [40]. Their starting point is the claim, common in political science, that groups with common interests naturally work to further these interests. Olson uses some elementary economics to show that this perception is false. Downs elaborates the imperfect links between voters' preferences and party platforms, under the assumption that party ideologies are determined by the parties' desire to win reelection. Thus while Arrovian work starts by positing certain desirable properties and establishes a political choice mechanism, this second body of work starts with the assumption that government takes the form of a representative democracy and challenges some of the normative claims for this form of government.

3.3. The Possibility of Synthesis

Synthetic work that attempts to combine the public policy and public choice frameworks has been made difficult by differences in methodology, politics, and philosophy. Consider methodology first. Cost-benefit analysis is essentially a branch of applied neoclassical price theory using the techniques of the calculus in a world with continuous, differentiable functions. These techniques are often entirely inappropriate for the study of politics. Political decisions often represent large, discontinuous changes where the choice set includes a small number of discrete options. However, when economists such as Samuel Peltzman and Gary Becker [41] ventured into the area of political analysis they simply imported the marginal techniques that worked well elsewhere and, as a consequence, were unable to capture much of the structure of politics. Their approach, while highlighting certain features of the relationship between voters, interest groups, and politicians, cannot form the basis of a general political-economic theory. In contrast, the line of research spawned by Arrow's Impossibility Theorem provided major breakthroughs in the analysis of collective choice using the techniques of linear algebra and set theory. Unfortunately, these mathematical techniques were not so broadly familiar to economists as the calculus and were also at such a high level of abstraction that they proved difficult to integrate with applied work on substantive policy. Some scholars point to game theory as providing a unifying set of techniques for political-economic analysis [42], but it seems fair to say that, with its emphasis on strategic interactions, game theory cannot capture all of the essential aspects of either public policy analysis or collective choice. In particular, game theory is an inadequate guide for the normative evaluation of substantive policy and political structure.

Second, sharp differences in politics and philosophy hamper the development of a unified approach. Public policy economists tend to be reformist and utilitarian. They seek policies that will place the economy on the Pareto frontier whether or not the end result is Pareto superior to the status quo. To cost-benefit analysts the status quo has no special sanctity, although the existing distribution of wealth can affect outcomes through its impact on people's potential willingness-to-pay for policy initiatives. Analysts in this area, with a strong commitment to the norm of economic efficiency, are frequently impatient with the reality of the political process and the highly abstract nature of much work in public choice.

In contrast, many well-known practitioners of public choice are very conservative politically. They believe that the problem of government failure is more serious than the problem of market failure and support only minimal government intervention in the economy. The most extreme in this regard in probably James Buchanan [43], who models government as a "Leviathan" maximizing its own revenue, but many other public choice scholars are also highly skeptical of activist government. Because, for some, this skepticism arises from a belief in the sanctity of the existing distribution of private property, much of the work in this area seems basically inhospitable to the more reform-minded policy establishment.

Nevertheless, not all public choice scholars are conservative, and there is nothing inherent in the approach that generates political beliefs favoring the existing distribution of property rights and income or giving priority to market outcomes. In contrast both to "Virginia school" followers of James Buchanan and to Chicago school lawyers and economists, contributors to formal public choice theory in the tradition of Arrow are not, in general, politically conservative and status-quo-oriented [44]. In fact, many of the leading results in this area explicitly deal with models in which the status quo has no special status at all [45]. Public choice scholars are not, however, so likely to share the kneejerk utilitarianism of many public policy analysts. Instead, they are more concerned with finding fair procedures by which distributive choices can be made.

While the abstract, normatively oriented work exemplified by such scholars as Arrow and A. K. Sen does not give any special status either to the existing distribution of resources or to the allocations generated by imperfect markets, the positive work that seeks to explain legislative and bureaucratic behavior is skeptical about the normative claims for democratic government. Even scholars who place no strong normative weight on the distribution of property produced by history and the market, are pessimistic about the degree of rationality that can be expected from representative legislatures [46]. Self-interested, vote-maximizing behavior does not seem broadly compatible with the promulgation of policies that promote efficiency [47]. Those who seek to influence policy must then decide whether their own policy proposals should be influenced by a concern for what is politically feasible. Should some reform proposals be suppressed because of the fear that they will be converted by the political process into something that reduces efficiency? Conversely, should research focus on finding more effective means of making public choices rather than on developing substantive policy proposals that will be transmogrified by the existing system?

Recent empirical work suggests that extreme pessimism is unjustified. A number of authors have found that concern with the substance of policy, independent of the narrow economic interests of constituents and interest groups, does influence Congressional behavior [48]. Nevertheless, this work does not contradict the finding that members of Congress underemphasize the tasks of legislative drafting and coalition building [49]. The design of cost-minimizing solutions to social problems seems not to be very high on anyone's agenda, especially in regulatory areas where the costs will not show up in the federal budget.

3.4. Links to Legal Scholarship

The creation of a reformist school combining public policy and public choice would have much to teach those who study law. Indeed, the individual fields, taken alone, already have had an impact. Work in public policy is, at present, closely linked to the study of most public law fields even if the economic approach is only accepted by a subset of legal scholars. Public choice has had a more selective influence, but even here the scholarly literature is growing, and the level of sophistication is improving.

Public policy analysis has had a relatively easy time establishing a foothold in legal fields where the economic content of policy is obvious. Thus economists first came into law schools to teach antitrust and that field, at least, is still part of the self-definition of law and economics. In fact, this work is sometimes called the "old" law and economics to contrast it with the "new" law and economics of the common law [50]. Notice, however, that in the United States, antitrust, like torts and contracts, is a court-centered field. The enabling statutes in the United States are quite general and most have been interpreted over time by court decisions. The executive branch concentrates on its role as prosecutor, not regulator. Thus the study of antitrust is not fundamentally different from the study of contracts, except insofar as legal challenges seek to reform the structures of entire industries. The judicial opinion remains at the center of the law and economic analysis.

Far from being old in the sense of old-fashioned or out-of-date, the reformist brand of law and economics can be of widespread contemporary significance if it can move beyond policy areas, like antitrust, where courts make substantive policy. The development of the modern welfare state is central to an understanding of American law and central to an understanding of the welfare state are both an appreciation of the economic justifications for regulation and work in public choice that seeks to explain the behavior of bureaucracies and legislatures.

The obvious point of intersection between public policy and public choice, on the one hand, and legal studies, on the other, is in administrative law and in other related statutory fields, such as environmental law and health and safety regulation. A number of scholars have made that connection in recent years in a way that has enriched the field of administrative law [51]. American administrative law is, however, a court-centered field. The typical course emphasizes leading Supreme Court cases that interpret statutes or apply constitutional principles. So long as this field remains court-centered, with judges avoiding substantive policy arguments, commentators can manage to ignore issues related to economic efficiency. Thus, there is an awkward fit between the substantive work of public policy economists and the traditional concerns of administrative law. The economists are not well informed about institutional, bureaucratic realities and are especially ignorant of the courts. The lawyers are used to focusing on procedural issues and the role of lawsuits in producing change but have little understanding of the underlying economic issues.

Even given administrative law's narrow concerns, it would seem that public choice scholars can provide analyses of bureaucratic and legislative institutions that should be directly relevant to judges concerned with procedural fairness. In practice, however, these links have seldom been made. Judges have been reluctant to evaluate the structure of the legislative process and have too often used courtlike models to assess the behavior of the bureaucracy. Scholarly attempts at synthesis have been limited to a few efforts by Chicago school authors. Public choice theory buttresses the court-centered nature of the Chicago approach by emphasizing both the impossibility of consistent public choice and difficulties with representative assemblies and bureaucracies [52]. The criticism of courts as undemocratic institutions is less important if even nominally democratic institutions do not consistently translate individual voters' preferences into public policies. But that criticism slides over the fact that even an assembly that had no difficulty representing voters and producing a consistent majority choice could well violate the wealth-maximizing principles of the Chicago school. A majority may choose a policy that benefits them while imposing a greater total harm on the minority. A majority has no incentive to maximize net benefits. If it acts in an entirely self-interested manner, it will only try to maximize the net benefits flowing to the members of the majority coalition. The fundamental issue is thus the resolution of the tension between free market choice and free political choice. This issue has been successfully blurred by emphasizing the failures of legislatures and bureaucracies, and underemphasizing the failures of markets and courts. But work in public choice need not be part of an apologia for the common law. Instead, it can be a means for understanding the operation of democratic government through a realistic appreciation of the interactions between self-interest and organizational structure [53].

Thus, those who import economic thinking into public law must at the same time reorient the fields in which they study and teach. Of course, similar tensions exist both in antitrust and in the common law areas that have been the focus of the Chicago school. The required shift in orientation is less extreme in these fields, however, because law and economics work has made few attempts to redirect those fields away from a concern with leading cases [54]. Under the influence of economic work on market failure and public choice, in contrast, administrative law becomes more concerned with the way substantive policy is made and with reviewing the paradoxes and inconsistencies of collective choice processes. The focus should be less on whether all the affected interests have been heard or on whether the state is harming individuals, and more on the structural characteristics of the political and policy process and on whether existing procedures produce economically efficient outcomes.

4. A Note on Criminal Law and Procedure

The central argument of this article has avoided any mention of the criminal law. Yet one of the earliest areas where economics was applied to law was in theoretical and empirical work on the deterrence of criminal activity [55], and scholarly interest in this field has continued to the present [56]. Law and economics work on crime recognizes that criminal activity is affected by demographic and social factors, by employment opportunities in the legitimate sector, and by the probability of apprehension and punishment. Thus, on the one hand, this research is a branch of labor economics that derives directly from research on job choice; on the other, it is little different from research on torts that seeks the optimal negligence standard by balancing costs and benefits.

In contrast to Anglo-American tort law, however, criminal law is fundamentally statutory and is tied to massive bureaucratic edifices—the police force and the prison system. Major policy issues are raised by attempts to distinguish crimes from civil offenses, by the question of how to organize and fund police work, by the organization of the system of punishment, by the practice of plea bargaining, and by the procedural protections of the criminal law. Yet when Chicago school lawyers and economists turn to the study of criminal law, they miss much of what distinguishes this field from common law disputes. Although they concentrate on "ordinary" crimes, i.e., acts such as burglary that are uncontroversially in the criminal category, the only formal distinctions between crimes and torts in their models are a probability of detection that is less than one for crimes and the nature of the penalty imposed. Instead of damages paid to the injured party, the state collects fines or places people in prison.

I will argue, however, that the Chicago school's focus on ordinary crime is inconsistent with their basically utilitarian philosophy. Instead, the utilitarian grounding of the Chicago approach is most easily applied to regulatory crimes, i.e., to regulatory violations that are treated as crimes by the legal system [57]. But such a focus would be uncongenial on other grounds because it would force a consideration of the underlying statutory grounds for the criminal sanction. The focus of analysis would shift from courts to legislatures and bureaucracies, a set of institutions that have no claim to legitimacy in the Chicago school view.

Theory in this area is in an awkward state because the utilitarian approach favored by the Chicago school counts the benefits to the person who violates the law as well as the costs to the victim and to society as a whole. The optimal level of crime, just like the optimal level of torts, depends upon the balancing of benefits and costs. But the assumption that the perpetrator's gains should be given weight seems most plausible when the existence of a criminal sanction is part of an overall regulatory strategy designed to curb, but not eliminate, the offending activity. Law violators are not evil, only inefficient. Ordinary crime, however, does not fit this description. Most people are not such thoroughgoing utilitarians as to believe that society should give weight to the benefits obtained by murderers, rapists, and thieves. In fact, one might propose as a working definition of crime the statement that those who commit crimes have no right to have the benefits they obtain count in the social calculus. Society must then decide which actions should be given this stigma. Criminal sanctions would not be available as one among many tools for regulating economic activity. Their use would imply a belief that the level of activity ought to be zero.

But, one might argue, the level of crime is not zero, and this seems to be a conscious social choice. The reason for this obvious truth, however, is not an attempt to balance the gains to criminals against the losses to society but reflects the cost of catching and prosecuting violators and the desire to avoid punishing innocent people. Thus, the social decision as to the level of deterrence involves tradeoffs that permit an economic analysis of the relationship between marginal costs and marginal benefits, but, for all but a died-in-the-wool Chicagoan, this caculus ought to ignore the criminals' benefits.

One implication of this view of the criminal law is to suggest the importance of integrating work on criminal sanctions into the reformist framework outlined above. Outside of a few people in labor economics, the economics profession has not had much to say about the criminal law as a regulatory sanction. It is, however, used frequently to regulate behavior in such areas as the security markets, environmental protection, and health and safety. Very little law and economics work has attempted to view criminal and civil penalties as altenatives and to explore the consequences of the balance between them.[7]

5. Future Directions

Law and economics has been too facilely associated with those scholars who are identified with the Chicago school. While these scholars have laid claim to a wide range of legal subjects, their analysis has a narrow focus that is not representative of the contribution that sophisticated economic thinking can make to the study of the law. The scholars in this group have, of course, encouraged the intellectual synecdoche which makes them emblematic of the field, and in this they have been supported by their rivals in the critical legal studies movement who appreciate having a convenient set of strawmen to excoriate [58].[8] The result is a serious distortion, leading to a persistent tendency to underestimate the promise of the reformist approach. A broader definition implies not only a wider variety of subject matter but also a more diverse group of both analytic techniques and philosophical and policy positions. Both Chicagoans and reformers are concerned with the economist's core interest in Pareto efficiency and the operation of economic incentives, but in combination they provide a more balanced view of modern work in political economy that bears on the evaluation and reform of legal doctrines and institutions.

Nevertheless, some gaps remain. To my mind there are four neglected areas: 1) reformist work on property rights, liability rules, and contract doctrine that studies market processes; 2) work linking evolutionary-institution theory and public choice with welfare economics and the analysis of market failures; 3) work linking public choice with an activist politics and an egalitarian political philosophy; and 4) general equilibrium law and economics of capitalist economies.

To be sure, a good deal of law and economics work on the common law does not take a hard-line Chicago approach. In fact, as I noted above, one can usefully define a category of reformist-common law scholarship that considers the behavior of risk-averse individuals [59] and that sees common law rules as only one among many ways of controlling private behavior [60]. Statutes and common law doctrines are viewed as substitutes. Yet even this work has not had much to say about industrial organization issues. By starting with court cases that pose economic issues in the context of particularized relationships, such research generally avoids dealing with markets per se. The few exceptions have not been central to the development of the field [61]. The core analytic work is concerned with individual transactions. Research that asks whether the impact of legal doctrines is affected by the market positions of the parties could, I believe, have substantial payoffs. Such work would raise the question of whether the rules of tort and contract should be modified to take account of the competitiveness of the market in which the legally challenged transaction took place.

Research on substantive regulatory policy has proceeded largely separate from positive work that attempts to explain the evolution of legal rules and the behavior of political institutions. An attempt to merge these strands of thought would produce a new administrative law that is stronger both in analyzing substantive policy and in evaluating governmental procedures. Once again, some work has taken this approach but its influence has been hampered by the lack of a common vocabulary across fields. Each article starts from the beginning and explains the most basic ideas before moving to constructive theory building [62]. While there are weaknesses in each piece of work taken alone, their integration is a promising area for research.

Political and legal philosophy has not really confronted the challenge posed by public choice theory. While the view of some public choice scholars that government is a budget maximizer is obviously too simplistic [63], and while real legislatures have found ways to avoid voting cycles, the pessimistic implications of public choice have not been adequately refuted by apologists for representative democracy. This work needs to be taken seriously by liberal philosophers and legal activists and not dismissed because of the uncongenial philosophical positions of many of its leading practitioners.

Finally, lawyer-economists need to incorporate a general equilibrium perspective into more of their work. At present, the only area where general systemwide consequences are even considered is the field of taxation where communication between tax lawyers and public finance economists produces estimates of the general equilibrium impacts of tax law changes [64]. The models used in these efforts do not have enough institutional richness to accommodate changes in common law doctrines. They are similarly inadequate for estimating the impact of regulatory statutes. Nevertheless, without a general equilibrium perspective law and economic scholars risk overlooking important side effects of the legal doctrines they analyze.

The existing patterns of research represent only a subset of the fruitful combinations of methodology, philosophy, and politics that could be studied. We need to do more than resist the facile association of law and economics with the common law, with the support of laissez-faire, and with political conservatism. We must construct a genuinely reformist law and economics that can address the problems of the modern welfare, regulatory state.

Notes

1. Minda identifies a "New Haven" school that "has attracted liberal practitioners who adopt the common methodology of the Chicago school but believe that there is a larger need for state intervention in order to cure problems of market failure." My reformist school, while incorporating portions of the work of some of my colleagues, is not pervasive enough at Yale Law School to warrant using my hometown as a label.

2. Kornhauser divides the field three ways into the analysis of legal duties, the analysis of property rights, and the public choice perspective. Each side of my dichotomy contains elements of all three of Kornhauser's categories, but the Chicago school places more emphasis on individual responses to legal duties and to property rights, and the reformist school incorporates work in public choice as a subfield.

3. Calabresi's work does not fall into this contradiction because it is less concerned with the preservation of the status quo and less respectful of private arrangements than the work of Chicago school scholars. His work and much of the work of such scholars as A. M. Polinsky and Steven Shavell belong to what I call the reformist-common law tradition.

4. An individual is risk-neutral if he or she is indifferent between a sure thing and a gamble with the same expected value. The expected value of a gamble is the sum of the probability of each outcome times the value of that outcome. Thus, a risk-neutral person is indifferent between $100 with certainty and a 50 percent chance of receiving $200 and a 50 percent chance of nothing. A risk-neutral person only cares about expected values and is indifferent to the variance or any other characteristics of the distribution of outcomes.

5. Such work as exists by Posner and Easterbrook treats legislative enactments as contracts that should be narrowly construed. Some statutes may serve a broad public interest, but these are basically laws that set up the rules of the game necessary to facilitate private economic activity.

6. Some property rights scholars, such as DeAlessi and Staaf, do, of course, recognize that property rules and institutions do not necessarily take efficient forms.

7. Since in the United States many regulatory defendants are organizations which cannot be jailed, instead of individuals who can, perhaps the choice between criminal and civil status is less important in regulatory areas where the government is in any case a party in the suit. The main differences may be the government agency which brings the action and procedural guarantees available to the accused.

8. Minda, however, argues that the opposition of law and economics and CLS is overdrawn. Both law and economics and CLS "can be seen to be practicing merely a different form of legal criticism-forms of critique which draw upon the legacy of legal realism-in opposing mainstream legal thought" (p. 100). Each approach has "attempted to develop a new theoretical approach to analyzing American law 'across the board'" (p. 102).

References

1. Cf. Minda, Gary, "The Law and Economics and Critical Legal Studies Movements in American Law," in Mercuro, Nicholas (ed.), *Law and Economics* (Boston: Kluwer Nijhoff, 1988), pp. 87–122; and Rowley, Charles, "Public Choice, Law and Economics:," in Mercuro, *Ibid.*, pp. 123–174.
2. Minda, *supra* note 1, p. 111, note 3.
3. Kornhauser, Lewis, "Legal Rules as Incentives," in Mercuro, *supra* note 1, pp. 27–56.
4. Posner, Richard, *Economic Analysis of Law*, 3rd ed. (Boston: Little, Brown and Company, 1986).
5. DeAlessi, Louis, and Staaf, Robert J., "Property Rights and Choice," in Mercuro, *supra* note 1, pp. 175–200.
6. See Rowley, *supra* note 1, for a discussion of the tensions in Richard Posner's work between these not-always-consistent principles.
7. Coase, Ronald, "The Problem of Social Cost," *Journal of Law and Economics*, Vol. 3 (1960), pp. 1–44.
8. DeAlessi and Staaf, *supra* note 5.
9. DeAlessi and Staaf, *supra* note 5, and Schmid, A. Allen, "Law and Economics: An Institutional Perspective," in Mercuro, *supra* note 1, pp. 57–86.
10. Much of this work is reviewed in Rowley, *supra* note 1.
11. Cf. Rowley, *supra* note 1, pp. 137–141, and Cooter, Robert, and Kornhauser, Lewis, "Can Litigation Improve the Law Without the Help of Judges?" *Journal of Legal Studies*, Vol. 9 (January 1982), pp. 139–163.
12. The most comprehensive presentation of this approach is in Posner, *supra* note 4, Part II. The seminal article was by Coase, *supra* note 7. Also important was Calabresi's work on torts which began with Calabresi, G., "Some Thoughts on Risk Distribution and the Law of Torts," *Yale Law Journal*, Vol. 70 (1961), pp. 499–553. Calabresi's work has, however, never had the laissez-faire orientation of the Chicago school work and should not be grouped together with that work except insofar as it has emphasized the common law field of torts.
13. Cf. DeAlessi and Staaf, *supra* note 5.
14. See Posner, *supra* note 4, Part III, whch discusses antitrust policy and the regulation of public utilities.
15. For an overview of work in this area by two leading representatives of the Chicago school, see Landes, W., and Posner, R., *The Economic Structure of Tort Law* (Cambridge: Harvard University Press, 1987).
16. In this respect Calabresi and the Chicago school scholars agree on the principle although they disagree on the best legal rule. See Calabresi, G., *The Cost of Accidents* (New Haven: Yale University Press, 1970).
17. Polinsky, A. M., *An Introduction to Law and Economics* (Boston: Little, Brown and Company, 1983) pp. 25–32.
18. Calabresi, G., and Melamed, A. D., "Property Rules, Liability Rules and

Inalienability: One View of the Cathedral," *Harvard Law Review*, Vol. 85 (1972), pp. 1089–1128.

19. The reformist-common law approach is well represented by Calabresi *supra* note 16, Polinsky, *supra* note 17, and Shavell, Steven, *Economic Analysis of Accident Law* (Cambridge: Harvard University Press, 1987).

20. The last point is emphasized in Balkin, J. M., "Too Good To Be True: The Positive Economic Theory of Law," *Columbia Law Review*, Vol. 87 (1987), pp. 1447–1489.

21. See Landes and Posner, *supra* note 15.

22. See Landes and Posner, *supra* note 15, and Posner, *supra* note 4.

23. See Rowley, *supra* note 1, pp. 137–141; Cooter and Kornhauser, *supra* note 11; Rose-Ackerman, S., "Review of W. Landes and R. Posner, *The Economic Structure of Tort Law* in *Journal of Policy Analysis and Management*, forthcoming (1988); Rose-Ackerman, S., "Dikes, Dams and Vicious Hogs: Conflicts Between Equity and Efficiency in Tort Law," *Journal of Legal Studies*, (forthcoming, 1989), Rubin, Paul, *Business Firms and the Common Law: The Evolution of Efficient Rules* (New York: Praeger, 1983); Priest, G., "Selective Characteristics of Litigation," *Journal of Legal Studies*, Vol. 9 (1980), pp. 399–421; Priest, G., and Klein, B., "The Selection of Disputes for Litigation," *Journal of Legal Studies*, Vol. 9 (Jan. 1984), pp. 1–20; Shavell, S., "The Social Versus the Private Incentive to Bring Suit in a Costly Legal System," *Journal of Legal Studies*, Vol. 9 (June 1982), pp. 333–339; Geistfeld, M., and Rose-Ackerman, S., "The Divergence Between Social and Private Incentives to Sue," *Journal of Legal Studies* Vol. 16 (1987), pp. 483–491;

24. Easterbrook, F., "Statutes' Domains," *University of Chicago Law Review*, Vol. 50 (1983), pp. 533–552; Easterbrook, F., "The Supreme Court 1983 Term: Foreword: The Court and the Economic System," *Harvard Law Review*, Vol. 98 (1984), pp. 4–60, and Posner, R., "Economics, Politics, and the Reading of Statutes and the Constitution," *University of Chicago Law Review* Vol. 49 (1982), pp. 262–291.

25. Demsetz, H., "The Exchange and Enforcement of Property Rights," *Journal of Law and Economics*, Vol. 7 (1964), pp. 11–26 and Demsetz, H., "Toward a Theory of Property Rights," *American Economic Review*, Vol. 57 (May 1967), pp. 347–359. Much of this work is reviewed in Schmid, supra note 9, pp. xx–xx.

26. Anderson, T., and Hill, P.J., "The Evolution of Property Rights: A Study of the American West," *Journal of Law and Economics*, Vol. 8 (1975), pp. 163–179.

27. Gaffney, M., "Economic Aspects of Water Resource Policy," *American Journal of Economics and Sociology*, Vol. 28 (1969), pp. 131–144.

28. Davis, L., and North, Douglas, *Institutional Change and American Economic Growth*, (London: Cambridge University Press, 1971); and North, D., and Thomas, R., *The Rise of the Western World* (New York: Cambridge University Press, 1973).

29. DeAlessi and Staaf, *supra* note 5; p. 180
30. For further examples see Schmid, *supra* note 9, pp. 73–78.
31. See especially the work of Oliver Williamson collected in Williamson, Oliver, *The Economic Institutions of Capitalism* (New York: Free Press, 1985).
32. Macaulay, S., "Non-Contractual Relations in Business," *American Sociological Review*, Vol. 28 (1963), pp. 55–69.
33. Exceptions by scholars who have frequently been critical of the Chicago school are Goetz, C.J., and Scott, R.E., "Enforcing Promises: An Examination of the Basis of Contract, *Yale Law Journal*, Vol. 87 (1980), pp. 1315–1319; and Goetz, C.J., and Scott, R.E., The Mitigation Principle: Toward a General Theory of Contractural Obligation, *Virginia Law Review*, Vol. 69 (1983), pp. 967–1024; Kornhauser, L., "Unconscionability in Standard Forms," *California Law Review*, Vol. 65 (1976), pp. 1151–1183; and Schwartz, A. "A Reexamination of Nonsubstantive Unconscionability, *Virginia Law Review*, Vol. 63 (1977), pp. 1053–1083. See also Kornhauser, *supra* note 3.
34. See DeAlessi and Staaf, *supra* note 5, pp. 190–191 Kornhauser, *supra* note 3, pp. 41–42; Schwartz, A., and Wilde, L., "Intervening in Markets on the Basis of Imperfect Information: A Legal and Economic Analysis," *University of Pennsylvania Law Review*, Vol. 127 (January 1979), pp. 630–682; and Schwartz, A., and Wilde, L., "Imperfect Information in Markets for Contract Terms: The Examples of Warrenties and Security Interests," *Virginia Law Review*, Vol. 69 (November 1983), pp. 1387–1485.
35. Standard works are Musgrave, R., and Musgrave, P., *Public Finance*, (New York: McGraw Hill, 1984); Okun, A., *Equality and Efficiency: The Big Tradeoff* (Washington: The Brookings Institution, 1975); and Jaskow, P., and Noll, R., "Regulation in Theory and Practice: An Overview," in Fromm, G. ed.), *Studies in Public Regulation* (Cambridge: MIT Press, 1981), pp. 1–65.
36. Arrow, K., *Social Choice and Individual Values*, 2nd ed. (New Haven: Yale University Press, 1963).
37. Rowley, *supra* note 1, pp. 151–154, gives more prominence to the normative work of the "Virginia school" exemplified by the work of James Buchanan, e.g., Buchanan, James, *The Limits of Liberty: Between Anarchy and Leviathan* (Chicago: University of Chicago Press, 1975).
38. For review of current work inspired by Arrow's contribution see Mueller, D., *Public Choice* (Cambridge: Cambridge University Press, 1979); Ordeshook, Peter, *Game Theory and Political Theory* (Cambridge: Cambridge University Press, 1986); and Sen, A.K., *Collective Choice and Social Welfare* (San Francisco: Holden-Day, 1970).
39. Mayhew, D., *Congress: The Electoral Connection* (New Haven: Yale University Press, 1974); Fiorina, M., *Congress: Keystone of the Washington Establishment* (New Haven: Yale University Press, 1977); Ferejohn, John, *Pork Barrel Politics* (Stanford: Stanford University Press, 1974); and Shepsle, K., "The Positive Theory of Legislative Institutions: An Enrich-

ment of Social Choice and Spatial Models," *Public Choice*, Vol. 50 (1978), pp. 135–178.

40. Downs, A., *An Economic Theory of Democracy* (New York: Harper and Row, 1957); Olson, M., *The Logic of Collective Action* (Cambridge: Harvard University Press, 1965); Baumol, W., *Welfare Economics and the Theory of the State*, 2nd ed. (Cambridge: Harvard University Press, 1967); Buchanan J., and Tullock, G., *The Calculus of Consent* (Ann Arbor: University of Michigan Press, 1962). See Rowley, *supra* note 1, pp. xx–xx.

41. Peltzman, S., "Toward a More General Theory of Regulation," *Journal of Law and Economics*, Vol. 19 (1983), pp. 211–240; and Becker, Gary, "A Theory of Competition Among Pressure Groups for Political Influence," *Quarterly Journal of Economics*, Vol. 98 (1983), pp. 371–400.

42. Ordeshook, *supra* note 38, and Shubik, Martin, *A Game-theoretic Approach to Political Economy* (Cambridge: MIT Press, 1984).

43. Buchanan, *supra* note 37; and Brennen G., and Buchanan, J., *The Power To Tax* (New York: Cambridge University Press, 1980).

44. See especially Sen, *supra* note 38; and Sen, A. K., *On Economic Inequality* (Oxford: Clarendon Press, 1972).

45. See, for example, May, K. O., "A Set of Independent, Necessary and Sufficient Conditions for Simple Majority Rule," *Econometrica*, Vol. 20 (1952), pp. 680–684. May imposes a condition called neutrality which guarantees that no alternative has a preferred status under the procedures used.

46. Farber, Daniel, and Frickey, Philip, "The Jurisprudence of Public Choice," *Texas Law Review*, Vol. 65 (1987), pp. 873–927.

47. See, for example, Stigler, G., "The Theory of Economic Regulation," *Bell Journal of Economics*, Vol. 2 (1971), pp. 3–21; and Rose-Ackerman, S., "Inefficiency and Reelection," *Kyklos*, Vol. 33 (1980), pp. 287–307.

48. See, for example, Kalt, J., and Zupan, A.M., "Capture and Ideology in the Economic Theory of Politics," *American Economic Review*, Vol. 74 (1984), pp. 301–322, and M. Levine, "Revisionism Revised? Airline Deregulation and the Public Interest," *Law and Contemporary Problems*, Vol. 44 (January 1981), pp. 179–195.

49. See Fiorina, *supra* note 39, and Mayhew, *supra* note 39.

50. Rowley, *supra* note 1, p. 125, and Veljanovski, C., "The Role of Economics in the Common Law," *Research in Law and Economics*, Vol. 7 (1985), pp. 41–64.

51. See especially Breyer, S., *Regulation and Its Reform* (Cambridge.: Harvard University Press, 1982); Stewart, R., "The Reformation of American Administrative Law," *Harvard Law Review*, Vol. 88 (1975), pp. 1667–1813, and Ackerman, B., and Hassler, W., *Clean Coal/Dirty Air* (New Haven: Yale University Press, 1981).

52. See, for example, Easterbrook, *supra* note 24, Posner, *supra* note 24, and Macey, J., "Promoting Public-Regarding Legislation Through Statutory In-

terpretation: An Interest Group Model," *Columbia Law Review*, Vol. 86 (1986), pp. 223–268.

53. See Farber and Frickey, *supra* note 46; Shepsle, Kenneth, "Institutional Arrangements and Equilibrium in Multidimensional Voting Models," in McCubbins, Mathew, and Sullivan, Terry (eds.), *Congress: Structure and Policy* (Cambridge: Cambridge University Press, 1976), pp. 346–375; and Krehbiel, Keith, "Sophisticated Committees and Structure-Induced Equilibria in Congress," pp. 376–402 in *Ibid.*

54. They will, of course, be likely to disagree about what constitutes a leading case. There are some exceptions here in the work of Williamson, *supra* note 31, and Shavell, Steven, "Liability for Harm v. Regulation of Safety," *Journal of Legal Studies*, Vol. 13 (1984), pp. 357–374.

55. The basic sources are Becker, G., "Crime and Punishment: An Economic Approach," *Journal of Political Economy*, Vol. 76 (1968), pp. 169–217; and Stigler, G., "The Optimum Enforcement of Laws," *Journal of Political Economy*, Vol. 78 (1970), pp. 526–536.

56. For a literature review see, Pyle, D., *The Economics of Crime and Law Enforcement* (New York: St. Martins, 1983).

57. Thus, when Polinsky discusses crime, the example he uses is double parking—a crime we have all probably committed in the interest of saving time. See Polinsky, *supra* note 17, pp. 73–84.

58. Kennedy, D., "Cost-Benefit Analysis of Entitlement Programs," *Stanford Law Review*, Vol. 33 (1981), pp. 387–445, and Kelman, M., "Comment," *Columbia Law Review*, Vol. 85 (1985), pp. 1037–1047. But see Minda, *supra* note 1, for an attempt to emphasize the points of commonality between CLS and law and economics.

59. See Polinsky, *supra* note 17, pp. 51–72, for an overview of the impact of risk aversion on the design of efficient legal rules.

60. Calabresi's work has always stressed this broader focus. See *supra* note 16.

61. See Calabresi, *supra* note 12, on torts, and Goetz and Scott *supra* note 33, and Kornhauser, *supra* note 33, on contracts.

62. See, for example, Farber and Frickey, *supra* note 46, and Macey, *supra* note 52.

63. See Brennan and Buchanan, *supra* note 43. For a critical review see Rose-Ackerman, S., "A New Political Economy?" *Michigan Law Review*, Vol. 80 (March 1982), pp. 872–884.

64. See Strand, J., "Taxation of Income from Capital: A Theoretical Reappraisal," *Stanford Law Review*, Vol. 37 (1985), pp. 1023–1107; Kaplow, L., and Warren, A., "An Income Tax by any Other Name: A Comment on Strnad," *Stanford Law Review*, Vol. 38 (1986), pp. 399–421; and Strnad, J., "The Bankruptcy of Correct Tax Timing Wisdom is Deeper Than Semantics. A Rejoinder," *Stanford Law Review*, Vol. 39 (1987), pp. 389–417.

INDEX